Hands On
Visual Basic® 5

How to Order:

For information on quantity discounts contact the publisher: Prima Publishing, P.O. Box 1260BK, Rocklin, CA 95677-1260; (916) 632-4400. On your letterhead include information concerning the intended use of the books and the number of books you wish to purchase. For individual orders, turn to the back of this book for more information.

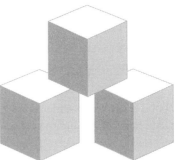

Hands On
Visual Basic® 5

Sharon J. Podlin

with Pamela Palmer

PRIMA PUBLISHING

Acquisitions Manager: Alan L. Harris
Managing Editor: Tad Ringo
Product Marketing Specialist: Julie Barton
Acquisitions Editor: Deborah F. Abshier
Assistant Acquisitions Editor: Christy Clinton
Series Development Editor: Angelique Brittingham
Project Editor: Chris Haidri
Editorial Coordinator: Stacie Drudge
Technical Reviewer: Dick Cravens
Indexer: Sherry Massey

ISBN: 0-7615-1046-X
Library of Congress Catalog Card Number: 97-66157
Printed in the United States of America
99 98 97 AA 6 5 4 3 2

This book is dedicated to my husband, Mark, who supports me in everything I do, and my son, Hunter, who is the joy of my life.

—*SJP*

Acknowledgments

I would like to thank Debbie Abshier for giving me the chance to write this book. It was an opportunity that I had been looking forward to for a long time. I would also like to acknowledge Angelique Brittingham, whose enthusiasm for this project knows no bounds. I would also like to thank Brian Gill for his thoughtful comments and enthusiasm for this book. Many thanks to Chris Haidri and Dick Cravens for making my writing and coding consistent. This author is well aware that a book is only as good as the editors who review it. Thanks also to the production team for making the book and CD look great.

— SJP

About the Authors

Sharon J. Podlin is a graduate of the University of Texas who is president of PTSI, a consulting firm specializing in the development and presentation of computer training courses. Sharon has over 15 years in the industry and has worked primarily with Fortune 100 companies, including JCPenney, Hyatt International Hotels, and United Airlines. She actively participates in the Microsoft Certified Professional program and is a Microsoft Certified Trainer for a wide range of products, including MS SQL Server, Excel, Visual Basic for Applications, and Windows NT. She can be reached via e-mail at **podlin@compuserve.com**.

Pamela Palmer is an independent consultant. She has been a contributing author on several books about Visual Basic, VBA, Word, Excel, and Outlook. She has spent 14 years working with computers and currently spends a majority of her time developing Microsoft applications using Visual Basic and VBA. The remainder of her time is divided between writing training documentation and books and providing training to users and developers. She can be reached via e-mail at **PPalmer@compuserve.com**.

Contents at a Glance

Contents

Introduction

There are dozens of books about Visual Basic, so why publish another one? The answer may surprise you. Most of the books about VB on the market today take the approach of a reference manual. They're designed to be referred to, and aren't necessarily designed to teach you anything other than syntax and structure. This book breaks that mold. It's designed to teach you not only the rudiments of the VB language, but also how to develop truly useful VB applications.

Goals of this Book

This book provides you with experience creating applications from start to finish with the VB development environment. Through hands-on interaction with VB, you experience the language as a developer, not merely a student.

Each project in this book is designed to build on your existing knowledge of programming. You start with some of the basics, move to topics for intermediate users, and end with an advanced project. Notice the use of the word "project" — you're going to create three complete VB projects in the course of the book. You'll add all the necessary forms and modules, design appropriate interfaces, and write all the required code. This book does not allow you to be a passive reader; it expects you to be an interactive learner.

How To Use this Book

This book consists of five main parts. The first part is background information, which is presented in a rather concise manner. This book is designed to teach intermediate-to-advanced VB development techniques, so if you already have some experience developing applications in another language, this is definitely the book for you. If this is your first time developing in VB (or in any Windows environment), you'll get off to a running start with the first two chapters. Even if you've tried your hand at VB before, these chapters will serve as a convenient reference for basic VB development concepts.

The next three parts are the sample projects. By completing these projects, you'll get a sense of how to design and create effective applications using VB. You'll be taken through the full development process: analyzing requirements, building interfaces, creating the code needed to add functionality to the applications, testing, debugging, and even preparing the applications for distribution.

The first project is a quick one that allows you to employ basic VB skills such as control usage, form manipulation, and programming logic. In this project you create a system that tracks the time spent on certain tasks and generates printed invoices.

The second project is an upgrade of the first project; it greatly expands the capabilities of the invoice system. You add several features to the simple user interface created in the first project, including a status bar, a toolbar, and a menu system. You also make the application an MDI application. What's MDI? Don't worry—the second project makes it crystal clear. The second project also heavily emphasizes Automation, which is a way for your VB application to control the functionality of other applications (in this case, Microsoft Excel and Microsoft Word). Excel 97 is recommended (though the sample project will work with Excel 95) and Word 97 is required. You get hands-on experience creating an application that saves its data to an Excel workbook and uses both Excel and Word as report generators. You also learn to write an error handler, which is a necessity for all sophisticated applications. When the second project is complete, you use the Setup Wizard to create an installation program for your application.

The final project provides volumes of useful information. In this project, you create a client management application. The most frequently asked questions in any VB teaching situation always have to do with data access and manipulation. The third project takes you through the entire process of developing an application that can add records to a database, query a database, and modify existing data—all within the VB environment. This project also gives you the opportunity to work with Crystal Reports.

After the projects, there are three chapters that contain additional exercises you might find useful. Chapter 18, "Connecting to the Internet," gives you experience working with some of the Internet controls and objects available to VB. Chapter 19, "Creating a Help System," lets you experiment with setting up a help system for an application. Chapter 20, "ActiveX Controls," teaches you how to use VB's ActiveX Control Interface Wizard to create an ActiveX user control.

There are also four appendixes in this book. Appendix A, "Recommended Naming and Programming Conventions," offers a list of programming standards that will make your applications more consistent and easier to maintain. Appendix B, "Visual Basic 5 Quick Reference," offers rapid access to information you might need during VB application development, such as the VB data types, comparison operators, and message box return values. You can find descriptions of the CD contents in Appendix C, "What's on the CD?" Finally, you can turn to Appendix D, "Glossary," for definitions of important terms.

Conventions Used in this Book

To make it easier for you to use this book, Prima uses some conventions for consistently presenting different kinds of information. You should review these conventions before moving on in the book:

- **Menu names, commands, and dialog box options**—In virtually all Windows programs, each menu name, command name, and dialog box option name contains an underlined letter called a *selection letter*. The selection letter is used to make that particular selection via the keyboard, usually in conjunction with the Ctrl or Alt key. In this book, selection letters are indicated as underlined letters, as in <u>V</u>iew.

- **Code and items that appear on-screen**—Any VB code discussed in this book is presented in a special typeface, to make it easy to distinguish. When reference is made to an error message or other information that appears on-screen, it's also in the special typeface.

- **Text you type**—When you need to type some text to complete a procedure, or when we provide an example of text you can enter, the text you need to type appears in bold, as in the following instruction:

  Type **frmClientInfo** as the name for the new form.

Special Elements

Margin notes are used to provide definitions of new terms.

At times, you'll be provided with information that supplements the discussion at hand. This special information is set off in easy-to-identify sidebars, so you can review or skip these extras as you see fit. You'll find the following types of special elements in this book:

Tip

Tips provide shortcuts to make your job easier, or better ways to accomplish certain tasks.

Note

Notes provide supplemental information that might be of interest to you, but is not essential to performing the task at hand.

Caution

Cautions alert you to potential pitfalls, or warn you when a particular operation is risky and might cause you to lose some of your work.

EXERCISE

Exercises give you a chance to practice using a particular skill just introduced in the regular text. Each exercise is identified by a special bar running alongside all the instructions.

ANALYSIS

After certain code examples, an *Analysis* section walks you through the code line-by-line and explains particular statements in greater detail. After reading the analysis, you'll have an understanding of the specific logic of that code example and you'll know the exact purpose of all the keywords and expressions used in the code.

This icon is used to refer you to items found on the CD that accompanies this book.

This icon informs you that it is time to save your work before continuing.

Necessary Software

This book's sample projects are designed for the Professional and Enterprise Editions of Visual Basic. Many steps you're instructed to take will not work with the Control Creation and Learning Editions.

You need Microsoft Excel and Microsoft Word to complete Project 2. Excel 97 is highly recommended, but Excel 95 will work. Word 97 is required (Word 95 will not work).

For Chapter 19, "Connecting to the Internet," you need an Internet connection and either Microsoft Internet Explorer 3.0 (or above) or a browser that's IE-compatible, such as CompuServe's CIS 3.0 software.

Contacting Us

Prima Publishing welcomes your feedback, and would like to hear more about the kinds of help you need, other computing topics you'd like to read about, or any other questions you have.

For a catalog, call 1-800-632-8676 or visit the Prima Publishing Web site at **http://www.primapublishing.com**.

CHAPTER 1

Features of Visual Basic 5

Visual Basic 5 is a remarkable product. It is one of the first development environments to free programmers from mundane tasks and allow them to concentrate on application development. Because Visual Basic is a *visual development environment (VDE)*, you do not have to write code (or make calls) to use standard interface elements such as command buttons or list boxes. In fact, you can totally design the look of your application and all its windows without writing a single line of code. If you've ever used a drawing program such as Paint, you already have most of the skills necessary to create an effective user interface in VB 5. If you wish to include a control in your application's interface, simply draw it in much the same manner as you would draw a shape using the Paintbrush applet. If you don't like the location of a control, you don't need to write code to relocate it — just drag it to the preferred location. This type of development gives you the ability to quickly design an interface and then spend the bulk of your programming time on functionality.

The features of VB 5 are numerous, to say the least. Some features discussed in this chapter have been part of the language from day one; others are new to this release. Knowing the features and functionality of a language gives you an idea of its capabilities and how you can best use it to your benefit.

Visual Basic's Foundation: Basic

In high school or college you probably were introduced to Basic (Beginner's All-purpose Symbolic Instruction Code) as your first programming language. You probably remember creating programs with lines like A = B + 1 and GoTo 300. You may even have used the form of Basic known as GW Basic that shipped with many early PCs. When you were using Basic back then, you probably never thought it would be a language you would use in the Nineties to develop sophisticated, strategic, corporate graphical applications! But you are!

Because of this common knowledge of Basic among professional and amateur programmers, Microsoft selected Basic as the foundation for the Visual Basic language. Don't think that the structure and abilities of Visual Basic are identical to those of Basic—that would be like saying that you're exactly like your great-grandfather. Even if you look like him, you're very different in your knowledge, abilities, and experiences. It's the same with Visual Basic. It looks a little like its ancestor, Basic, but has grown far beyond what Basic could do as a development tool. Visual Basic 5 contains several hundred statements, functions, and keywords not found in the original Basic language. Many of these additions have to do with the Windows graphical interface.

Visual Basic as a Shared Language

Once upon a time, there was a separate and individual macro language for every application. If you wanted to automate Microsoft Word, you had to learn WordBasic. To automate Microsoft Excel, you had to learn the Excel macro language. For Microsoft Access development, you had to learn Access Basic. And to develop stand-alone applications, you had to learn Visual Basic.

That deplorable era has passed. Now Excel, Access, Word, PowerPoint, Project, and Outlook use Visual Basic, Application Edition (known as *VBA*) as their automation language. Visual Basic shares its language structure with Visual Basic, Application Edition. This is a major boon to the developer. If he knows how to program in one of these environments, he can quickly transfer his knowledge to another environment, thus greatly reducing his learning curve.

The other advantage of having a shared language among these applications comes into play when you wish to control one application from another application.

Because they all share the same foundation language, the process of application automation is greatly simplified.

The Visual Basic Interface

The Visual Basic 5 interface is a *multiple document interface (MDI)*. Several windows open, but only within a main *parent window*. This gives Visual Basic a look similar to that of Word or Excel. In these applications you can have multiple windows open, but they all reside in the main application window.

Other key features of the VB 5 interface include the following:

- **New Project dialog box**—When you start a new project you can choose from the following options, available by clicking the New tab in the Project dialog box:
    - Standard EXE
    - ActiveX EXE
    - ActiveX DLL
    - ActiveX Control
    - VB Application Wizard
    - ActiveX Document DLL
    - Add In
    - ActiveX Document EXE

    You also have the option of selecting a project from the Existing or Recent tab in this dialog box.

- **Properties window**—Using the Properties window you can view properties by category or alphabetically.

- **Project Explorer**—This window has an Explorer-style view and includes View Code, View Object, and Toggle Folders buttons.

- **Form Layout window**—The Form Layout window lets you visually position your forms at design time.

- **Code window**—The Code window is the area you use to write the code needed by your application. The Code window includes Auto Statement Builder, which displays a drop-down list of properties available for the control you're working with. The Code window also provides Auto Quick Info, which displays the syntax for statements and functions.

- **Debugging windows**—There are multiple debugging windows, each with a specific role.

- **Debug toolbar**—The Debug toolbar contains buttons that are shortcuts to some commonly used debugging tools.

- **Object Browser**—The Object Browser is a great tool for navigating your project; it lets you move to modules and procedures. The Object Browser includes a description pane that reminds you of the purpose of particular objects and lets you go to an element's library or object.

- **Edit toolbar**—The Edit toolbar contains toolbar buttons that are shortcuts to some commonly used menu items for editing.

- **Form Editor toolbar**—The Form Editor toolbar has toolbar buttons that are shortcuts to some commonly used menu items used for working with forms.

- **Palettes**—Palettes are used to apply colors and other formatting to your interface.

Note

See Chapter 6, "Building the Time Tracking System," for a detailed discussion on the use of the Code window.

See Chapter 7, "Testing the Time Tracking System," for more information on the debugging windows.

Database File Storage, Retrieval, and Manipulation

The native database for Visual Basic 5 is the *Jet engine*. This means that you can have stand-alone applications that have a file structure based on the one used by Microsoft Access. You can manipulate these files using Visual Basic without having any connection to Access. All the structures native to an Access database—including tables, views and indexes—are available to your Visual Basic applications. To work with these items, you use *Data Access Objects (DAO)*. Several data access features have to do with extensions to the DAO and RDO (Remote Data Objects) object models.

Visual Basic is not limited to the Access database model. You can use Visual Basic to design a front-end client/server application for a heterogeneous data environment. Visual Basic can access most popular database file formats, including Microsoft Visual FoxPro, Microsoft SQL Server, Borland Paradox, and Oracle. Visual Basic provides full *Open Database Connectivity (ODBC)* capabilities with Microsoft SQL Server and Oracle.

Native Code

You can compile a Visual Basic project to *native code* rather than *interpreted code.* This allows for faster execution of the VB applications you create. You also can profile native code using new native code compiler options, and, if you wish, debug native code using the Visual C++ environment.

 See Chapter 17, "Testing the Client Management System," for more information on native code.

OLE Support

Visual Basic has extensive OLE support, including the following:

- Capability to act as an OLE server
- Support for OLE drag-and-drop between applications (you can, for example, drag the contents of a VB text box to a Word document)
- DCOM (Distributed Components Object Model) support; the Remote Automation tools support direct remoting through COM on the 32-bit Windows platforms (95 and NT 4.0), but not on 16-bit Windows
- Out-of-process OLE component creation
- In-process OLE DLL component creation
- Automatic OLE component versioning support

Create Your Own ActiveX Controls

ActiveX controls allow you to extend the Visual Basic environment by adding new functionality. For example, if you want to add a spelling checker to an application you're developing, you can write one from scratch or simply buy an ActiveX control that allows you to incorporate the desired functionality into your application.

Visual Basic allows you to make your own custom ActiveX controls by creating one from scratch or by combining existing controls. The ActiveX controls you create have events and properties, as well as data-binding capabilities and even Internet features.

Wide Range of Add-In Controls Supported

You are not limited to ActiveX controls as a way to extend the Visual Basic environment. You can also use VBX controls (VBXs), OLE controls (OCXs), and dynamic link libraries (DLLs).

ActiveX Documents

Another ActiveX feature is the ability to create *ActiveX documents*. An ActiveX document is an ActiveX object that can be placed and activated within *ActiveX document containers*. Microsoft Internet Explorer is an example of an ActiveX document container. ActiveX documents allow your Visual Basic application to provide Internet and intranet browser windows. ActiveX document features include hyperlink navigation and menu negotiation.

Wizards

Several wizards in VB 5 make application development easier. Some of the available wizards are listed below:

- **Application Wizard**—Application Wizard lets you create a new, fully-functional application using a predefined interface. The application created contains a toolbar with standard toolbar buttons such as New, Open, Save, Cut, Copy, and Paste. It also includes a status bar with information about the state of the application and the current time and date. You can use this application to create a more sophisticated application.

- **Setup Wizard**—Setup Wizard allows you to create a setup program for your application, similar to those you have used to install commercial applications. It facilitates the use of multiple floppy disks for large applications and ensures that the appropriate ActiveX controls, DLL files, and so on are included with your application. Setup Wizard has been enhanced in this release to include the ability to distribute your application across the Internet using automatic code download from version 3.0 of Microsoft Internet Explorer.

- **Data Form Wizard**—Data Form Wizard lets you automatically generate VB forms containing individual bound controls and procedures used to manage information from database tables and queries.

- **ActiveX Control Interface Wizard**—We've already discussed the fact that you can create ActiveX controls using VB. ActiveX Control Interface Wizard assists you in the creation of a public interface for ActiveX controls you create. With ActiveX Control Interface Wizard you can add new custom property, method, and event names for your control, and can define attributes for the public property, method, and event names.
- **Property Page Wizard**—Property Page Wizard helps you build property pages for your ActiveX user controls.
- **ActiveX Document Migration Wizard**—ActiveX Document Migration Wizard helps you transition your existing forms into ActiveX documents.
- **Wizard Manager**—Wizard Manager provides the framework for custom wizard creation. You can create wizards that look and act like the wizards that ship with VB 5.

Visual SourceSafe

Visual SourceSafe is a version-control tool available as part of the Enterprise Edition of VB 5. Visual SourceSafe is integrated with the VB environment and monitors a variety of project-related items, including visual differences and project history.

Visual Basic Editions

Visual Basic 5 is available in four editions, each designed to meet specific development requirements. The following sections discuss these editions.

Learning Edition

The Learning Edition is designed to allow programmers to easily create powerful applications for Windows 95 and NT. This edition includes all intrinsic controls, such as command buttons, list boxes, and option buttons. It also has grid, tab, and data-bound controls.

Learn VB Now, a multimedia CD, is provided with this edition. Other documentation supplied with this edition includes the online Help system and Visual Basic Books Online.

Professional Edition

The Professional Edition gives developers a full-featured set of tools for application development. It includes all features of the Learning Edition and has several additional ActiveX controls. Most notable among these additional controls are some Internet controls and Crystal Report Writer. *Programmer's Guide*, online Help, *Component Tools Guide*, and *Crystal Reports for Visual Basic User's Manual* are provided with this edition.

Enterprise Edition

The Enterprise Edition is geared at developers who need to create distributed applications in a team environment. It includes all features of the Professional Edition as well as advanced tools: Automation Manager, Component Manager, database management tools, and the Microsoft Visual SourceSafe project-oriented version control system, among others. Documentation provided with this edition includes all the documentation found in the Professional Edition, plus *Building Client/Server Applications with Visual Basic* and the SourceSafe *User's Guide*.

Control Creation Edition

ON THE

CD

The Control Creation Edition is new to the VB product line. This edition is designed specifically to be used to create ActiveX controls easily and quickly. It differs from the other three editions in that it cannot be purchased at retail outlets. The only way to get it is by downloading it via the Internet. Other than download and connection costs, the Control Creation Edition is free. This edition cannot be used to create stand-alone applications; it can only create ActiveX controls for use in other development environments.

Summary

This chapter has presented an overview of VB's capabilities and features. This should give you an awareness of some ways that you can use VB as a development tool. The next chapter lays the real groundwork for developing robust applications with VB. It provides background information about the components that make up the VB environment, and gives you an understanding of the entire application development process.

CHAPTER 2

The Visual Basic Development Environment

Chapter 1 explained that Visual Basic is a visual development environment (VDE) that provides you with a quick, graphical interface. This interface has several advantages over traditional development tools. The first advantage you'll notice is in interface design. You actually draw the interface as you go. This not only allows for quick development but also allows you to create a prototype for your users to review. Another advantage Visual Basic provides is *rapid application development (RAD)*. The development cycle of Visual Basic is a fraction of that of more traditional languages. You save time not only in development, but also in learning the language itself. Because of the ease of its foundation language, Basic, Visual Basic is easier to learn than other Windows application development languages. Since you draw the application interface rather than developing code for its creation, you are released from needing to know an entire set of statements.

This chapter gives you the foundation you need to work with Visual Basic. As a developer, you need to be aware of the components that make up the VB environment, along with understanding the development process used in creating applications with VB.

Starting Visual Basic

To start Visual Basic, you simply double-click its icon. VB starts and you are ready to begin your first application. VB prompts you to indicate whether you want to start a new project or open an existing one. A *project* is the set of files that combine to create the particular application you are developing. (For example, each window in your application is a separate file.) So, in VB terms, you are working on a project whenever you are creating an application. You can create several types of new project files:

- **Standard EXE**—This is the option you probably will use the most. It allows you to create a standard executable file.

- **ActiveX EXE**—Use this option if you want to develop an ActiveX executable file.

- **ActiveX DLL**—VB allows you to create ActiveX DLL files. Select this option to create one.

- **ActiveX Control**—The creation of ActiveX controls is now supported by VB. Select this option to create an ActiveX control.

- **VB Application Wizard**—Application Wizard helps you create a new application, which can be used as a foundation to develop a more complex application.

- **ADDIN**—Add-ins are tools that you bring into the VB development environment to customize the environment.

- **ActiveX Document DLL**—By using ActiveX documents you can create forms that will appear within Internet browser windows.

- **ActiveX Document EXE**—ActiveX documents are forms that can appear within Internet browser windows in a browser such as Internet Explorer.

To start VB and begin a new standard project, use the following steps:

1. From the Windows desktop in Windows 95, select Start. Select Programs and choose the Visual Basic 5.0 folder. Select the Visual Basic 5.0 program. VB starts and the New Project dialog box is displayed (see Figure 2-1).

2. Since you are creating a standard EXE project, which is the default, select <u>O</u>pen.

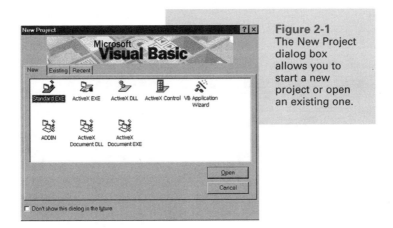

Figure 2-1
The New Project dialog box allows you to start a new project or open an existing one.

At this point the VB development environment is displayed. The next section discusses the environment in detail.

Parts of the VB Environment

The VB development environment provides several tools to aid you in creating your application. Figure 2-2 shows the windows that open by default when you start VB and choose to create a standard EXE project.

If your toolbox is not displayed automatically, select View, Toolbox.

You can have up to seven windows open at once in the VB environment. Each of these windows can be resized, moved, and docked. This allows you to customize the appearance of your work environment to best suit your needs.

Customizing the Windows in the VB Environment

Sometimes you want a particular window to take up more or less space on your screen. Resizing a window in VB is done the same way as resizing a window anywhere in the Windows environment: drag one of the window's borders until the window is the desired size.

Title bar   Project Explorer

Menu bar

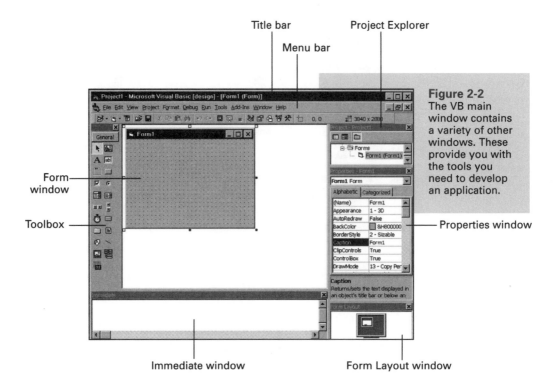

Figure 2-2
The VB main
window contains
a variety of other
windows. These
provide you with
the tools you
need to develop
an application.

Form
window

Toolbox

Properties window

Immediate window   Form Layout window

Moving a window, toolbox, or toolbar is also accomplished in the traditional manner. To move one of these items, click its title bar and drag it to its new location.

VB 5 allows you to *dock* windows, the toolbox, and toolbars. This anchors the item to another dockable item. If an item is dockable, then when you move the item it snaps to the nearest dockable location. If an item is not dockable, you can move it anywhere on-screen and leave it there. Docking an item provides a distinct advantage: docked items always remain visible; they cannot be hidden behind other windows. You can turn the docking feature of an item on and off using the Options dialog box. Follow these steps to change docking options:

1. Select Tools, Options to display the Options dialog box.
2. Select the Docking tab (see Figure 2-3).
3. Deselect the check box of each tool you want to stand on its own.
4. Select the check box of each tool you want to make dockable.
5. Click OK to save the changes.

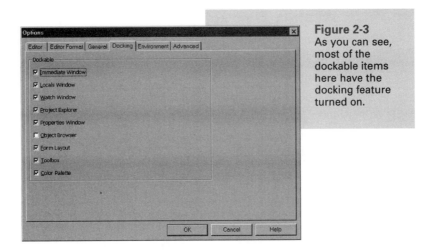

Figure 2-3
As you can see, most of the dockable items here have the docking feature turned on.

VB Programmer Tools

VB provides a rich set of tools for you to use in application development. Here's a list of the tools:

- Menu bar
- Toolbars
- The toolbox
- Form windows
- Form Layout window
- Project Explorer
- Properties window
- Code window
- Object Browser
- Color Palette
- Online help
- Immediate window
- Locals window
- Watch window

These tools are discussed in detail in the following sections.

The Menu Bar

The *menu bar* should be familiar to you from your work with other Windows applications. It gives you access to most of the commands that you use to control VB's environment. Menus you probably have used in other applications include the File, Edit, and Help menus. Figure 2-4 shows VB's full menu bar.

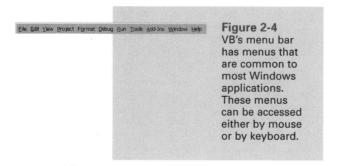

Figure 2-4
VB's menu bar has menus that are common to most Windows applications. These menus can be accessed either by mouse or by keyboard.

Toolbars

Below the menu bar is the *toolbar*. The toolbar provides you with an alternative to the menu bar for executing commonly used commands. VB 5 has four available toolbars:

- **Standard**—The Standard toolbar is the default toolbar for VB. Its buttons represent the most commonly used VB commands (see Figure 2-5).

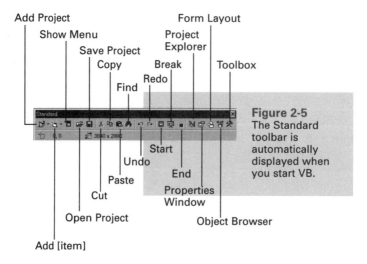

Figure 2-5
The Standard toolbar is automatically displayed when you start VB.

■ **Edit**—The buttons on the Edit toolbar are shortcuts to some of the commands you use when editing code (see Figure 2-6).

List Properties/Methods

Quick Info

Complete Word

Outdent

Comment Block

Toggle Bookmark

Previous Bookmark

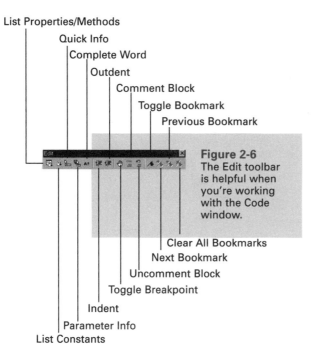

Figure 2-6
The Edit toolbar is helpful when you're working with the Code window.

Clear All Bookmarks

Next Bookmark

Uncomment Block

Toggle Breakpoint

Indent

Parameter Info

List Constants

■ **Debug**—When you are testing an application you've created, you may want to display and use the Debug toolbar (see Figure 2-7).

■ **Form Editor**—The Form Editor toolbar's buttons, shown in Figure 2-8, provide access to commands that are useful when you're working with a form and the controls on that form.

VB does not limit you to these toolbars. You can add buttons to (or remove them from) any existing toolbar, or you can create a new toolbar from scratch. This allows you to further customize the VB environment to meet your needs and preferences.

Adding and removing toolbar buttons is easy. Use the following steps to remove a toolbar button:

1. Right-click a toolbar to display the toolbar shortcut menu.

2. Select Customize to display the Customize dialog box, as shown in Figure 2-9.

Start
End
Step Into
Step Out
Immediate Window
Quick Watch

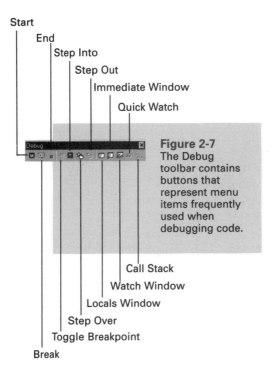

Figure 2-7
The Debug toolbar contains buttons that represent menu items frequently used when debugging code.

Call Stack
Watch Window
Locals Window
Step Over
Toggle Breakpoint
Break

Send to Back
Center
Lock Controls Toggle

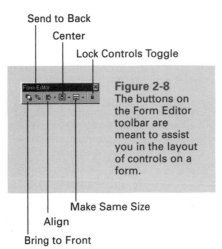

Figure 2-8
The buttons on the Form Editor toolbar are meant to assist you in the layout of controls on a form.

Make Same Size
Align
Bring to Front

3. Drag the unwanted button off the toolbar.

4. Click Close to close the Customize dialog box.

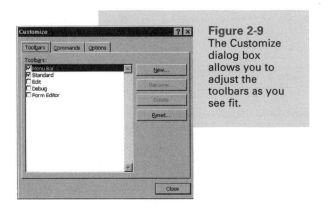

Figure 2-9
The Customize dialog box allows you to adjust the toolbars as you see fit.

Adding a toolbar button to a toolbar is done through the Commands tab of the Customize dialog box. On this tab, toolbar buttons are organized into groups that match VB's menu system. Use the following steps to add a toolbar button to a toolbar:

1. Right-click a toolbar to display the toolbar shortcut menu.
2. Select Customize to display the Customize dialog box.
3. Select the Commands tab to display the available toolbar buttons as shown in Figure 2-10.

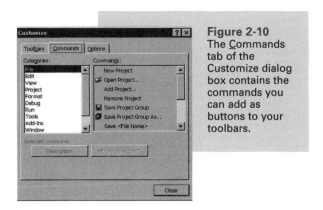

Figure 2-10
The Commands tab of the Customize dialog box contains the commands you can add as buttons to your toolbars.

4. Select the menu category you want from the Categories list box.
5. Select the command you want from the Commands list box. The icons to the left of the listed commands represent the corresponding button images.

6. Drag the desired command onto a toolbar. A vertical bar appears on the toolbar representing the location of the new button. When you reach the desired location, drop the command. This adds the new button.

If you add or remove toolbar buttons and then want to return to the default set of buttons for a particular toolbar, select the toolbar's name from the Toolbars tab of the Customize dialog box. Click Reset to return the toolbar to the way it was immediately after installation. This only applies to the built-in toolbars.

Rather than modifying the built-in toolbars, you may want to create one from scratch. You can use the Customize dialog box to create new toolbars. Just follow these steps:

1. Right-click a toolbar to display the toolbar shortcut menu.

2. Select Customize to display the Customize dialog box.

3. Select the Toolbars tab.

4. Click New to display the New Toolbar dialog box (see Figure 2-11).

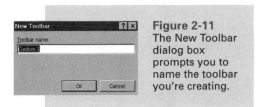

Figure 2-11
The New Toolbar dialog box prompts you to name the toolbar you're creating.

5. Type a name for the toolbar in the Toolbar name text box. The name may contain spaces.

6. Click OK. As Figure 2-12 shows, the new toolbar looks like a small gray square.

7. Add the desired buttons to the new toolbar using the steps given earlier in this section.

Figure 2-12
Your new toolbar begins as an empty container waiting to receive toolbar buttons.

Tip

To delete a toolbar, select the toolbar's name from the Toolbars tab of the Customize dialog box. Click Delete to delete the toolbar.

The Toolbox

In traditional development environments such as C or COBOL, your tool set was limited to the keyboard. This is not true in VB. The tool set in VB has been extended to include a whole palette of tools called the *toolbox* (see Figure 2-13). Using the controls found in the toolbox, you create your user interface. These controls and their uses are discussed in detail in Chapter 5, "Designing the Time Tracking System." By using toolbox controls, you can add the following elements to the user interface:

- Pictures and images
- Labels
- Command buttons
- Check boxes and option buttons
- List and combo boxes
- Scroll bars
- File system controls
- Timers
- Shapes
- Data controls
- OLE controls

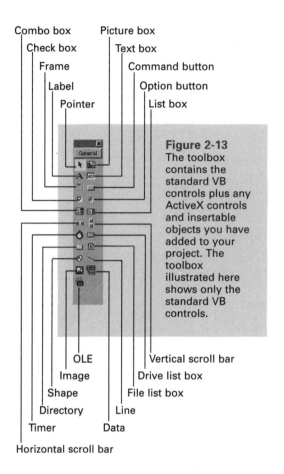

Combo box
Check box
Frame
Label
Pointer

Picture box
Text box
Command button
Option button
List box

Figure 2-13
The toolbox contains the standard VB controls plus any ActiveX controls and insertable objects you have added to your project. The toolbox illustrated here shows only the standard VB controls.

OLE
Image
Shape
Directory
Timer
Horizontal scroll bar

Vertical scroll bar
Drive list box
File list box
Line
Data

Form Windows

When you start VB using a standard EXE project, a default *form window* (see Figure 2-14) appears in the middle of the screen. The *form* contained in this window is named Form1 and has a grid on it. The grid is there to help you position controls on the form. You can add as many forms to a project as you need; each form is displayed in its own form window.

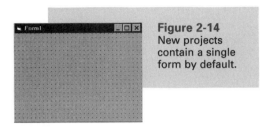

Figure 2-14
New projects contain a single form by default.

The Form Layout Window

New to this release of VB is the Form Layout window (see Figure 2-15). This window is used to control the placement of forms as they are displayed by your application. This is a great tool to use when several windows will be displayed in a layered fashion by your application.

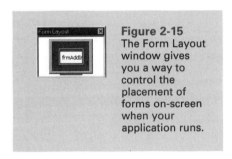

Figure 2-15
The Form Layout window gives you a way to control the placement of forms on-screen when your application runs.

The Properties Window

When working with forms and controls, you'll often want to change the way they look and behave. This is done with *properties*. When you design your interface, you'll use the Properties window (see Figure 2-16) to change the characteristics (properties) of the forms and controls. For example, the *Height* and *Width* properties control the size of an object. The Properties window has the following parts:

- **A drop-down list box**—This list displays the properties available at design time for the currently selected control.
- **A sheet with two tabs**—This sheet lists the property settings that can be changed for each object. You can list them alphabetically or by category, depending on which tab you've selected.

Figure 2-16
The Properties window allows you to change characteristics of an object without using code.

Tip   **You can quickly enlarge the Properties window by double-clicking its title bar.**

Project Explorer

Earlier in this chapter we defined a *project* as a collection of files required for the creation of your application. The Project Explorer gives you a quick way to navigate back and forth between these files. The files associated with your project are stored in a project file with the VBP extension. Figure 2-17 shows the Project Explorer.

View Object

View Code

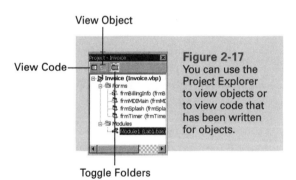

Figure 2-17
You can use the Project Explorer to view objects or to view code that has been written for objects.

Toggle Folders

The Code Window

A lot of the work associated with creating the interface of your application is done by placing objects on forms and then setting properties for objects through the Properties window. At some point, however, you need to write code for various operations your application needs to perform. You enter program statements in the Code window (see Figure 2-18). The Code window acts as the text editor for VB. You can access the Code window either by clicking the View Code button in the Project Explorer or by choosing View, Code from the menu. You also can access the Code window by double-clicking an object while in design mode.

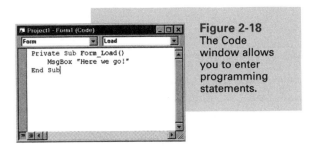

Figure 2-18
The Code window allows you to enter programming statements.

The Object Browser

You might have used an Object Browser before if you've worked with an application that supports VBA (such as Microsoft Excel). The Object Browser (see Figure 2-19) displays classes, properties, methods, events, and constants available from object libraries and from procedures in your project. It is useful for finding objects available for you to use, and is also useful as a way to access online help through its Help button.

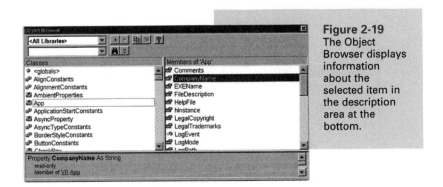

Figure 2-19
The Object Browser displays information about the selected item in the description area at the bottom.

Color Palette

The Color Palette (see Figure 2-20) is used to change the colors of a form or control. It also is used to set up a custom color scheme. Using the Color Palette you can change the foreground and background colors for forms, controls, and text.

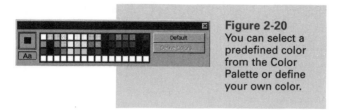

Figure 2-20
You can select a predefined color from the Color Palette or define your own color.

Online Help System

VB offers an outstanding online help system. The available help ranges from tutorial information to a language reference. You can get context-sensitive help basically anywhere within the VB environment by pressing F1.

Other help features are available through the Help menu. If you wish to get detailed information on a topic, select Help, Books Online. Visual Basic Books Online has all the VB documentation in one online location.

 Tip

If you're unable to access the Books Online feature, you need to install it from your Visual Basic CD.

Another useful help feature is Microsoft on the Web. If you have access to the Internet, you can select this option from the Help menu, and then connect to one of the Microsoft-provided VB Web sites listed on the submenu.

The Immediate Window

One of the VB debugging tools is the Immediate window, shown in Figure 2-21. This window allows you to enter programming statements, execute them, and view the results immediately in the same window. This gives you a way to quickly test statements and see if the expected result occurs. You also can use this window to test the values of variables while you're running your application.

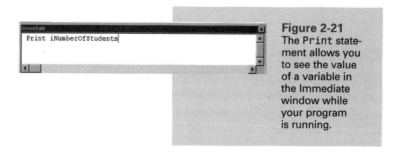

Figure 2-21
The Print statement allows you to see the value of a variable in the Immediate window while your program is running.

The Locals Window

The Locals window displays all the declared variables in the current procedure and their current values (see Figure 2-22). This window is automatically updated every time there is a change from Run to Break mode (for example, when the program hits a breakpoint). It is also updated when you navigate through the stack display. To display the Locals window, select View, Locals Window.

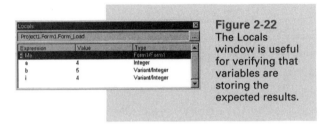

Figure 2-22
The Locals window is useful for verifying that variables are storing the expected results.

The Watch Window

Another tool to assist you in the debugging process is the *watch expression*. This is a variable or expression whose value you want to monitor as your application progresses. The Watch window (see Figure 2-23) is automatically displayed when you have watch expressions defined in your project.

Figure 2-23
The Watch window displays the current value of any defined watch expressions.

Basic Steps for Building a VB Project

Before tackling the steps for building a VB project, you need to understand what a project is. A *project* is a set of procedures, functions, and forms. Once you finish designing and creating a project, you compile it into an *application*. You've probably worked with dozens of applications, including word processors, spreadsheet applications, and even Solitaire! Your goal is to create a great application by designing an attractive interface, and by building the logic and purpose of your application using VB statements.

The steps for creating an application using VB are fairly straightforward:

1. Analyze and document the purpose of the application.
2. Build the interface.
3. Build the logic and functionality of the application.
4. Save your work as a project.
5. Test and debug the application.
6. Compile and distribute the application.

Analyzing and Documenting the Purpose of the Application

This step hopefully is obvious to you. If you don't know what the application is supposed to do, how can you design and code it? Analyzing the purpose of the application can be done in a variety of ways. You can ask the person or group for whom you're creating the application to provide you with a description of what is needed. If the people who will use the application aren't the ones for whom you're developing it, you might also want to interview the users. Finally, you can analyze the current process that your application will replace.

Once you determine the purpose of the application, you need to document the purpose. Write down everything you know about the application requirements. Include the goal of the application, lists of data that will need to be tracked and stored by the application, and any other requirements. This is one of the steps most likely to be skipped by a programmer, but documenting the purpose and requirements of an application up-front and then reviewing this information with your client can save you many headaches. Typical questions you need to have answers for include the following:

- **What is the purpose of the application I am writing?**

  As was pointed out earlier, you cannot write an application if you don't know what it's supposed to do.

- **Is the application replacing a current process?**

  For example, is it replacing a paper-based system? Understanding the current process helps you design the new system.

- **Are there any paper forms that I am automating?**

  Paper forms can be used easily as a foundation for screen and report design.

- **Who will use the application?**

  Are they novice or experienced Windows users? Are they touch-typists or do they prefer to use a mouse? Factors like these can greatly impact the approach of your interface.

- **What type of data will the user enter while using the application?**

  Knowing this early in the project helps you in interface design as well as in the design of the database files used by the application.

- **What will the data be used for?**

  Collecting data is one thing, but using data is another. Unless you understand how the data will be used, you cannot design an effective, efficient application.

- **What types of output will the application produce?**

  Should the output be displayed on-screen or as a printed report, or both? This knowledge helps you in several areas: interface design, database creation and usage, and report creation.

It is highly recommended that you place this information in a formal document (often referred to as a *requirements document* or *application specifications*). When you create such a document, you and your client both know the exact goals for this application. Any subsequent modifications to the scope or approach of the application should be added to the requirements document.

Building the Interface

After you have documented the requirements of the application, you are ready to begin designing the application's interface. The *interface* is the set of screens and the objects contained within those screens that the user uses to interact with your application. The application's interface includes command buttons, list boxes, option buttons, toolbars, message boxes, menus, and so on. Several of the questions discussed in the previous section help with this process. At this point you should know what fields the screens in your application should have and what audience you are designing for. Do not underestimate the importance of knowing your audience! If you are designing for a user who strongly prefers using a mouse, your application should have lots of buttons, icons, and lists. If you are designing for a user who is a fast touch-typist, your application should have more text boxes and keyboard shortcuts, allowing the user to keep both hands on the keyboard as much as possible.

When you start a new project, VB automatically places a blank *form* in the project. You'll place a variety of controls on this form. You'll add a new form to the project for each screen you plan to have in your application. After you place the desired controls on the form, you set appropriate values for the properties of the controls and of the form itself. *Properties* are settings that control the appearance and behavior of an object. Properties can be set either as you design your application (at design time) or through code that changes them when the application executes (at runtime). You change properties at design time by using the Properties window. Properties are discussed in detail in Chapter 5, "Designing the Time Tracking System."

After designing the screens, show your client your work to this point so that she can get an idea of the approach you are using for the application. If your client doesn't agree with your approach, you can redesign the interface before you invest any time in programming.

Building the Logic and Functionality of the Application

After designing the interface and verifying that it meets the client's needs, you're ready to write the necessary programming code for the application. This is the process of attaching code to the different functions associated with the objects found in your interface. For example, what will happen with the user clicks the OK button on a particular screen? What will happen if they access a certain menu item? The code you write will perform a variety of tasks. Some of these tasks include the following:

- Test and respond to user responses
- Query a database
- Save user input
- Display requested information
- Perform calculations based on data received from the user
- Analyze data through the use of charts, formulas, views, and so on
- Modify existing information

You use the Code window to write VB code. The Code window is a text editor especially designed to support the VB language; it provides automatic syntax checking and debugging tools. The VB language has hundreds of statements and functions, but don't be intimidated by the large number of language constructs. You'll use a core collection of statements and functions frequently, and there will be many language elements that you rarely use. The VB help system makes it easy to work with the latter by providing correct syntax, usage information, and even code examples.

Saving the Program as a Project

One of the oldest adages in the computer world is that you cannot save too often. This can be especially true in the VB environment. Whenever you get to a point where you are happy with the state of your program, save it. That way if you make changes that you aren't happy with, you have something to revert to.

To save a project, you select File, Save Project. A typical Save File As dialog box is displayed. For more information on saving files, see Chapter 7, "Testing the Time Tracking System." When you first save your project, a file with the extension VBP is created. Each form is saved into a file with the extension FRM, and some other files are also saved. These are all discussed in Chapter 7.

Okay, let's say that you've created your application's interface and have written the code for it. What now? Well, you're ready for testing and debugging. *Testing* a program is the process of checking it in a variety of real-life operating conditions to determine if it works as expected. If it doesn't work as expected, it's said to have a defect known as a *bug*.

Obviously you want to test any application as thoroughly as possible before releasing it. You want to anticipate anything a user could do to your application, so the best candidate for testing your application is *not* you. Have several other people test it for you. They'll probably do things to your program that you would never have thought of! As the testers find problems with your program, they need to document exactly what they did before each error occurred. Then it is your job to correct the error. This is called *debugging*. The testing and debugging stage of application development is every bit as important as interface design or coding. Without it, your application will have numerous flaws, which are known sarcastically as "undocumented features!"

Compiling and Distributing the Program

After you have completed the testing and debugging stage, you are ready to release the program to your client. You need to compile it into an executable (EXE) program using the File menu. Once it's compiled, you may want to test it one more time before you distribute it.

VB provides a tool to create a setup program (similar to those you've used to install commercial applications) to facilitate distribution of your application. This tool is called Setup Wizard and it walks you through the necessary steps to generate a setup program. All needed files are copied to disk during this process. You create copies of these disks and give them to your users, who then run the setup program to install your application.

Summary

This chapter has given you the foundation you need to create your first VB application. You are familiar with the components of its development environment, and you have an understanding of the steps required to develop applications using VB.

You are ready now to tackle developing your first application. The first project (Chapters 3 through 7) will take you through the basics of creating an application.

HANDS ON PROJECT 1

THE TIME TRACKING SYSTEM

- ■ **Analyzing and documenting the purpose of your application**
- ■ **Working with forms**
- ■ **Adding a splash screen to your application**
- ■ **Using controls correctly**
- ■ **Setting properties at design time and runtime**
- ■ **Using variables and constants**
- ■ **Using message boxes and input boxes for user input**
- ■ **Employing conditional logic to control the flow of your application**
- ■ **Creating animated images**
- ■ **Using simple print operations**
- ■ **Testing your application**
- ■ **Using debug techniques to locate problems**
- ■ **Writing error-handling routines**
- ■ **Saving your project and making it an EXE File**

Project Overview

The time tracking application is designed to allow you to build on the basic knowledge you already have of Visual Basic. When you are finished with this project, you will know how to design an application interface. Using this interface you will receive input from a user and apply that input to other parts of the application.

Once the project itself is completely built, you will learn and apply application testing and debugging techniques. You also will learn to write an error-handling routine as part of this project so that your application can tolerate mishaps at runtime.

CHAPTER 3

What is the Time Tracking System?

To this point in the book, you've been working with Visual Basic in a general manner so that you can become familiar with its environment. Now it's time to get specific and start your first project. This chapter begins the process by describing the project you're going to create and by giving you an overview of the key topics presented in the remaining chapters in this section.

System Requirements of the Time Tracking System

The first project you're going to create is a time tracking system. This system allows users (attorneys in this example) to track their time and how that time is allocated. Attorneys need to track the following details about how they spend their time:

- The date
- The time period (amount of time spent on a task)
- The task performed during that time period

- Whether that work is billed by the task or by the hour
- The client associated with the time spent
- The billing rate
- Who spent the time on the task

This list is comprised of the basic system requirements of the application. Some other user requirements need to be considered before you begin developing the application:

- **Users should be able to select task categories and client names from a list.**

  By having users select particular input items from a list, you eliminate the possibility of incorrect input in these fields.

- **Users should be allowed to either enter the amount of time spent on a task or use a timer to determine the amount of time.**

  This gives users flexibility. If they're not at the computer, they can write down the amount of time spent on a client task and input it later. If they're at the computer, they can let the application do the work of measuring the time period.

- **Users should be able to preview the billing before printing it.**

  This allows users to review the information before committing it to hard copy.

Goals of the Time Tracking System

What should you hope to accomplish in terms of learning Visual Basic while creating the time tracking system? This project is designed to be suitable for a beginning VB programmer, and therefore is going to introduce basic key concepts. The following sections describe these key concepts.

Working with Forms

Forms translate into the windows of your application, and therefore are the foundation of your project. Most, if not all, of your applications will have more than one form. This means that you need to know how to handle forms so that your application flows well from one window to another. After completing this project, you'll have an understanding of form-management techniques, including how to load and unload a form from memory and how to show and hide forms as your application runs. You'll also be introduced to the concept of properties by setting a variety of properties for forms.

Using Controls Correctly

Controls provide the tools your application's users need in order to interact with your program. VB provides several controls you can use as part of your application's interface. The time tracking system project shows you how to work with most of the standard controls. You'll learn how to place controls on forms, resize and move controls, and set controls' properties at design time.

You should notice in the exercises associated with this topic how specific controls are used and that their use is consistent. Consistency is one of the most important concepts in interface design. Think about other Windows-based applications you've used. Have you noticed that all the windows can be opened, maximized, resized, minimized, and closed using the same method—no matter what application you're using? The title bar is always at the top of the screen and the menu bar is always below the title bar. You don't spend time learning to use the basic application interface, and this frees you to learn the features particular to that application.

Command buttons are a great example of the consistency associated with controls. The OK and Cancel buttons are typically placed at the right side of a window or in the lower-right corner of a window. If you saw OK and Cancel buttons in the upper-left corner of a window, you'd probably think they looked weird. When you design the forms for the time tracking system, look closely at how they're designed—where buttons are located, how they are grouped, and so on. The easiest way to learn interface design is by studying other applications.

Using Variables and Constants

After you have created your application's user interface, you're ready to start writing code. Before you can write any code, you have to understand the key concepts of using variables and constants. *Variables* are places for holding data that can change each time your application runs, and even within one running of the application. For example, if you ask a user to type in her name, you need a variable to hold the name that she enters. *Constants* add readability and maintainability to your application. In a given code line, you might use either an actual value like .05 or a constant like SALESTAX. When you see SALESTAX in code you have an immediate idea of its purpose, which doesn't happen when you see .05 in code. Also, if you ever need to update a value that's important to your program (such as the sales tax rate if it changes), you have to find and change each occurrence of that value throughout the code—unless you've used a named constant to represent the value, in which case you just change the constant in one place and the whole program is updated.

The concept of *scope* is also introduced in this project. In VB, the location and way in which you define your variables, constants, and procedures will determine where you can use them.

Using Message Boxes and Input Boxes for User Input

Variables are used in conjunction with the MsgBox and InputBox functions (which create message boxes and input boxes, respectively) to receive user input. Once that input is received, it can be used to set properties, serve as database input, or facilitate calculations.

Conditional Logic and Controlling the Flow of Your Application

Another key programming concept relates to the flow of your application. You may want to do one action if a user types, let's say, Georgia, but another action if the user types Florida. You can handle this routing in your code through conditional logic.

You'll also learn how simple it is to add animation to your application by setting a couple of properties and using a control mechanism called the For...Next statement.

Using Simple Print Operations

You can create simple output from your applications using the Print and PrintForm statements.

Testing Your Application

Once you complete your application, you need to test it to make sure that it does what you expect it to! Through this project you'll learn how to test an application and what tools to use to find various types of errors.

Saving and Distributing the Project

Once you've written and tested your application, you face the exciting task of finishing it! You'll be taken through the steps of saving your application and creating an EXE file. As part of this lab, you'll learn about files that need to be included with your EXE file to make it work.

Programming Windows Applications

If you have worked with other programming languages such as Basic or COBOL, you have done *top-down programming*. With these languages you essentially have point A (the starting point of the program) and point B (the ending point of the program) and you connect them with code. You drive the user very carefully through the application. This is not true in the VB environment; here, the user drives the direction of the application. At any given time, the user may select an option button, click a command button, choose a toolbar button, use a menu item, or whatever action he wants. Rather than programming in a linear fashion, you have to program specific reactions for all the potential actions a user can perform. This is called *event-driven programming* and requires a new way of thinking for many programmers, but you can become used to it in no time.

VB is very different from other Windows development languages such as Microsoft C++. In a language like C++, the programmer directly interacts with something called the Windows API (Application Programming Interface). This is a set of routines that Windows programmers use to create applications. These routines are why all windows look the same, why all menus look the same, why all applications use the same controls, and so on. The API controls how the Windows environment looks and responds to the user, and also controls operations such as file saving and printing. VB also interacts with the Windows API, but does so in a very different way from C++. VB can be thought of as a shield between the programmer and the API (which can be extremely tricky to use). VB lets the programmer avoid most of the calls being made to the API; the calls are still made, but they're hidden. VB's interpreter does this. You as the application developer do not need any detailed knowledge of the operating system. This is further proof of VB being easy to use and allowing rapid application development.

Summary

There are a few things to keep in mind as you start the first project in this book. Visual Basic is based on the Basic language. If you have programmed using Basic, you'll see some familiar things in the next few chapters—as well as plenty of new things. Even if you've had some experience programming in VB, you should benefit from the application development approach of this project, which allows you to create a complete application in a hurry. Remember that the best way to learn VB is to use VB. Reading an introductory book on VB may have given you a good foundation, but you won't fully appreciate that knowledge until you use it.

Gathering for the Time Tracking System

The previous chapter explained the requirements of the application you're going to work with in the first project. Using that information you're now going to analyze the user input needed by the system, and then organize that input.

The first thing you'll do in this chapter is create a list of data you need to get from the user. You'll not only create a list of data fields but will analyze the specifics of that data. "Should the data be numeric or text?" and "Should there be a list from which the user can pick values for this field?" are just a couple of the questions you'll answer as part of your analysis.

The second major goal of this chapter is organizing the data fields once they're determined. This process breaks the information into groups, and the groups lead you to determine the screens needed by the application.

What Type of Information Do You Plan to Track?

Because of VB's graphical nature, the first thing you think about in terms of developing an application is the user interface. In fact, you may design every window of your application before you write a single line of code. There are many advantages to this, the most important being an organized approach to the application's design. Before you can design the interface, you need to know what types of input you require of your user. This forces you to decide how you plan to get that information from the user, and therefore what your application needs to look like.

Designing the User Interface

There are two common approaches to designing a user interface. Some programmers prefer to sketch the needed screens before creating them. The main advantage to this approach is that it helps you organize the application before committing yourself to the actual creation of the application. This is especially helpful when several developers are working on the same project; by sketching windows before designing them, the team can agree on standards for a consistent interface. The second approach is to simply start creating the interface using VB. To be honest, this is the more common approach. You just start placing controls on forms, and fine-tune the interface as you go.

Determining Required Input

No matter which approach you use, you need to figure out what input is required from the user. Once you know the required input, you'll know what types of controls you need for your interface.

Let's start this process for our time tracking system. Recall that this is a system to track how attorneys use their time. The last chapter presented a list of the data to be tracked. You know that you need to associate a client with each time entry, because unless you know who the client is, you can't bill the time. When thinking about the input for this field, you might think you need two fields: first name and last name. This isn't necessarily true. If you were designing a system used to track clients, you *would* want to do that. In the case of the time tracking system, however, you're working with existing accounts that may be a company name such as ABC Corporation or an individual name such as John Smith. Because of this you will use only one field for this input. In this project, the client you're developing the system for does not want users to enter client names, but wants them instead to select clients from a list of predefined values.

Predefined values are values, usually presented in a list, from which the user may select a value to serve as user input for a particular purpose. This is a way to force the user to enter valid input. Typically the user must select one of the predefined values, but in certain situations you might allow users the option of either selecting a predefined value or entering one from scratch.

The user needs to assign a *task category* to the time being tracked. Task categories should already be defined for reporting reasons. If you allowed attorneys to type the task name, one attorney might enter `Family Law` while another might type `Child Custody` for the same task. This would make reporting how time was spent within the firm very challenging. Predefined task categories eliminate this issue, and also save the user some typing.

Another thing that needs to be tracked for each time entry is the amount of time spent on the task. You could use a list for this, but because of the large number of acceptable values for time, a list would not really benefit the user. A list with entries of 15 minutes, 30 minutes, 45 minutes, 1 hour, 1 hour 15 minutes, etc. wouldn't add to the usability of your system. You therefore want the user to type a value for this field. Since time has a consistent format of `hh:mm`, you should make this an entry field with a defined format template.

You may want to give the user a choice of not typing in a value for the time entry. Some users avoid typing as much as possible. You can create a timer that, once initiated by the user, measures how long the user spends on a task and then enters the amount of time for them. This adds nice functionality to your system. Any time you can do some work for the user, go for it! The users appreciate it and your system looks well thought out and professional.

The next consideration is whether a particular task is billed at a flat rate or hourly. Some tasks, such as a simple will, are a fixed price. Other tasks, such as a contract negotiation or court appearance, are billed by the hour. You know that there are only two possible values for this piece of input, but you still need to decide exactly how to get this information from the user.

So far, you've dealt with how much time is billable and whether that time is at a fixed or hourly rate. The next piece of information you need from the user is the billing rate for that work. You could use a list for this, but if the range of values is broad, you might want to have the user type in the correct amount.

We also need to know who spent the time on this task so that they can get credit for it. The user will type the value for this field.

The only thing left for you to find out about the task is the date it was performed. A list of predefined values isn't practical for this input because of the infinite range of possible values. This is another field you need to have the user type. One design possibility is that this field can have a format template: `mm/dd/yy`. Another thing to consider is automatically entering the current date into this field for the user. This is easily done with code and saves the user the chore of entering the date if the task was performed today (but gives them the flexibility of entering another date if necessary).

Reviewing Business Rules and Requirements

You've dealt with the data issues. Now you need to review any business rules and requirements. Some of these were addressed during the data analysis. The person for whom you're developing this system wants users to be able to select task categories and client names from lists to eliminate the possibility of incorrect input in these fields. Whenever possible, in fact, you want to present a list from which the user selects input data. This not only avoids misspellings, but eliminates having to code for various casing (for example, different users might type Smith, smith, or SMITH, leaving your program with the task of handling all possible casing). Having the users select Smith from a list of names avoids this issue.

Another requirement the client has for this system is that users be able to preview the billing before printing it. This allows users to review the information before committing it to hard copy.

Now that you've determined what input you need from the user, you're ready to organize that input. The next step, deciding how to group the input fields, leads to the process of designing the windows for your application.

Organizing the User Input

Chapter 2, "The Visual Basic Development Environment," provided a list of questions as a tool for documenting the purpose of an application. At this point, you can use those questions to coordinate the analysis process.

- **What is the purpose of the application I am writing?**

  The application needs to allow a user to enter task and time information for billing purposes.

- **Is this application replacing a current process?**

  You can assume that this project is replacing a paper-based tracking system.

- **Are there paper forms that I am automating?**

  Yes, you are automating two existing paper forms: the current tracking form and invoice.

- **Who will use the application?**

  The users of this application are attorneys who must track their billable hours.

- **What type of data will the user enter in the application?**

  This is a complicated question that will be examined in detail throughout the remainder of this chapter.

- **What will the data be used for?**

  The collected data is used for client billing.

- **What types of output will the application produce?**

  The output of this application is a preview of a client invoice for each task performed.

Determining the Number of Forms for Your Application

Examining the answers to the questions in the preceding section, you'll find that this application needs a minimum of two windows (which we call forms from this point forward). You need one form for the user input and one form to display the preview of the invoice information.

You may want to consider a couple of additional forms for this system. Think about most applications that you use. When you launch the application, are you immediately taken to an input screen for that application? Your first reaction may be yes, but think again—you usually are shown a *splash screen* bearing the name and logo of the application as well as some copyright information. This is displayed briefly before the main form is displayed. Many users expect to see a splash screen, so using one might make your application look more professional.

Another addition to the application you may want to consider is a form that prompts the user for her name. There are a couple of reasons for doing this. One is the obvious reason of security. If the user types an invalid name, she is not allowed to continue. A second reason is to give the user a definite beginning point; when she is prompted for her name, she knows that the application has started and will soon present her with the forms she needs.

In the earlier description of desired functionality for this application, a timer feature was mentioned. This allows the user to click a button to start a timer and click another button to end the timer, with the amount of time spent then automatically entered. You can accomplish this by adding another form to your application.

Two of the questions in the preceding section relate to specific user input: "What type of data will the user enter in the application?" and "What will the data be used for?" These two questions should make you pinpoint exactly what you need from the user. With this in mind, you are ready to organize your user input. You know by now that you're going to have the following five forms in your application:

- Startup splash screen
- Form prompting the user for his/her name
- Form to obtain the remainder of required user input

- Form for timer feature
- Form to display preview of invoice

Once you have identified the forms you need, it's a good idea to name them. A standard for naming forms is to prefix them with `frm`. Using this convention, you would name the first form, for example, `frmStartUp`. The second form would be named something like `frmUserName`. The third and fourth forms would be `frmBillingInfo` and `frmInvoice`, respectively.

Defining the Fields for User Input

The next thing you want to do is list the fields you want to place on each form. You may want to use a table like Table 4-1 to determine the fields, as well as necessary information associated with the fields.

As you can see, each row starts with the name of a field. List all the required fields first. Don't worry about which forms they need to reside on at this point—you'll figure that out eventually.

Table 4-1 Table for Tracking Field Information							
Field Name	Description	Predefined Values?	If So, Many or Few?	Numeric or Text Data?	Standard Format?	Control Type	Name of of Form

After naming the fields, describe the data contained in each field. The remaining columns in each row are important for determining what type of control to use as the input mechanism for that field.

Table 4-2 Fields Needed for the Time Tracking System

Field Name	Description	Predefined Values?	If So, Many or Few?	Numeric or Text Data?	Standard Format?	Control Type	Name of Form
Client	The client associated with the time spent	Yes	Many	Text	No		frmBillingInfo
Task	The task performed during the time period	Yes	Many	Text	No		frmBillingInfo
Time	The amount of time spent on the task	No		Numeric	Yes		frmBillingInfo
HourOrTask	Whether this is to be billed by task or by hour	Yes	Few	Text	No		frmBillingInfo
BillingRate	The billing rate associated with this task	No		Numeric	Yes		frmBillingInfo
BilledBy	The person who spent this time	No		Text	No		frmUserName
Date	The date on which the task was performed	No		Numeric	Yes		frmBillingInfo
StartTime	The starting time for the timer	No		Numeric	Yes		frmTimer
EndTime	The ending time for the timer	No		Numeric	Yes		frmTimer

If you used such a table to organize the user input for this application, it would look like Table 4-2. Because you haven't learned about controls yet, the Control Type column is blank; you'll fill it in during Chapter 5, "Designing the Time Tracking System."

You can see from this table that most of your work will be on the `frmBillingInfo` form. As you fill out the Control Type column in Chapter 5, you'll modify the name of each field to reflect the type of control, and add a descriptive prefix similar to the one used for forms.

Also notice that of the five forms you plan to have in your application, only three are listed in this table. The other two forms, `frmStartUp` and `frmInvoice`, are used to present information to the user, but never to prompt the user for input.

Remember that this table is a rough draft—just a tool to help you get started with your application. You most likely will make changes to this table as you start designing the actual application.

Summary

This chapter solidified the analysis needed for the time tracking system. You used two tools in this analysis. You used the questionnaire from Chapter 2 to determine the goal of the application, decide the number of forms the application needs, and initiate the process for ascertaining the required user input fields. You then built upon that analysis by using the table provided in this chapter to document detailed information about those fields.

With the analysis stage complete, you're ready to start designing the interface for the application. The next chapter gives you the skills you need to complete that step of the VB development process.

CHAPTER 5

Designing the Time Tracking System

In Chapter 4 you completed the necessary planning for the time tracking system for a hypothetical law firm. In this chapter you are going to work on designing and creating an interface for the application.

Your First Form

In previous chapters you learned that the windows in your application are referred to in the VB environment as *forms*. Form modules are the files that represent the windows in your application and contain the controls you use to build your interface. These files have the FRM file extension.

When you start a new project, it automatically contains one form named Form1. Start a new project using these steps:

1. Launch Visual Basic 5 to display the New Project dialog box (see Figure 5-1).

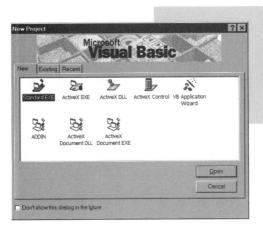

Figure 5-1
When you launch VB, it asks you whether or not to start a new project.

Tip   If you do not want to see the New Project dialog box every time you start VB, select Don't show this dialog in the future.

2. Select Standard EXE and click <u>O</u>pen to start a new project. Form1 displays in the middle of the screen (see Figure 5-2).

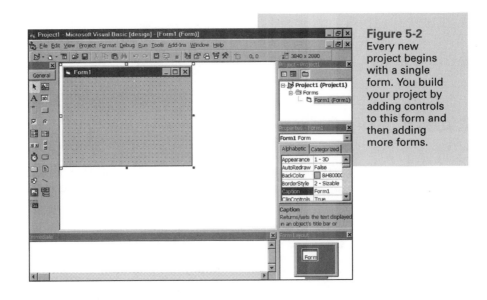

Figure 5-2
Every new project begins with a single form. You build your project by adding controls to this form and then adding more forms.

Notice the main VB title bar. It starts with the project's name, which is currently Project1. Then it says Microsoft Visual Basic. After that it says [design]. This means you are in *design mode*, the mode in which you build the application. This is the mode in which you'll add forms to your application and place controls on those forms.

Examining Built-In Form Functionality

New users of VB are often surprised to find out how much functionality is native to forms. The following exercise demonstrates these built-in functions.

To get an idea of what you can do with a form, complete these steps:

1. Select <u>R</u>un, <u>S</u>tart or press F5 to run the project as it is. At this point you have done nothing to the project, so your screen will look like the one shown in Figure 5-3.

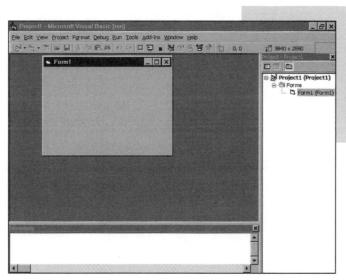

Figure 5-3
When you are running a project in the VB environment, the title of the main window says [run] instead of [design].

2. Resize the window (which has Form1 as its title) using its border.

3. Maximize the window.

4. Restore the window.

5. Click the upper-left corner of the window to display its navigation menu. Notice that the standard navigation menu items are here: <u>R</u>estore, <u>M</u>ove, <u>S</u>ize, Mi<u>n</u>imize, Ma<u>x</u>imize, and <u>C</u>lose.

6. Close the window to end the program.

This demonstrates getting all the standard window functions without writing a single line of code. This is one of the reasons why VB is so popular. Functionality that in other languages would have to be coded is native to the VB environment. The VB development team had the attitude that since you need these features for every form, they should handle them for you! This should give you a hint of how rapidly applications can be developed using VB.

During this exercise you were in *run mode*. In run mode you interact with the application as a user. This is the opposite of *design mode*, where you interact with the application as a developer.

What are Objects?

Before you go further you need to understand the concept of *objects*. All the components you work with in the Windows environment are objects. Forms are objects, command buttons are objects, and so are the following: option buttons, check boxes, list boxes, and menus. As far as Windows is concerned, your printer is also an object (named, aptly enough, `Printer`). If you can point to something, it's an object. One way to think of objects is that they are the nouns of the VB environment. They are everything you control and interact with through your application.

Setting Form Properties at Design Time

At this point you have an application with a single form that has the title `Form1`. This is hardly an exciting application! One of the ways you can build your application's appearance is by using *properties*. Properties control the appearance and behavior of objects. Since a form is an object, it has a particular set of properties. In a way, the properties act as the adjectives of the VB environment.

Some things you can control through properties are the text in the form's title bar, the color of the form's background, the size of the form, and the position of the form on-screen. Some properties can be set only through programming statements; these are referred to as *runtime properties*. Other properties can be set at either runtime or design time; these are listed in the *Properties window*. This window lists all the available design-time properties (and all the available settings for certain properties), making it easy for you to work with the properties of a given object.

The best way to learn what you can do with properties is to actually set a few.

Complete the following steps to set several properties using the Properties window:

1. The Properties window (see Figure 5-4) should be displayed at the right side of your screen. If it is not displayed, select <u>V</u>iew, Properties <u>W</u>indow (or press F4).

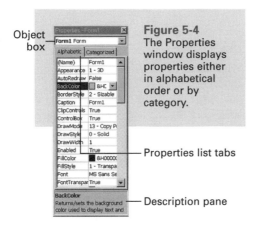

Object box

Figure 5-4
The Properties window displays properties either in alphabetical order or by category.

Properties list tabs

Description pane

2. If the Alphabetic tab is not already selected in the Properties window, click it. This displays the selected object's properties in alphabetical order. In your case, the only object in your project is Form1, so it is automatically selected. You can verify this by looking at the Properties window's *Object box*, which is at the top of the window. The Object box should have Form1 in it; notice that the full item in the Object box is Form1 Form. The word Form represents the type of object that is currently active.

3. Using the Properties window's scroll bar, locate the *Caption* property. This property currently is set to Form1. Select this property. At the bottom of the Properties window is an area called the *Description pane*, which gives a brief description of the selected property.

Tip

If you do not want to see the Description pane, you can turn it off. Right-click the Properties window to display its shortcut menu, and then select <u>D</u>escription—this is a toggle menu command.

4. Type **My Form**. Notice that as you type new text for this property, the text in the form's title bar immediately changes.

52

5. Locate and select the *BackColor* property. This is an example of a property that modifies the appearance of an object. When this property is selected, a down-arrow button is displayed. Click this button to display a drop-down tab box. Select the Palette tab to see a palette of available colors, as shown in Figure 5-5.

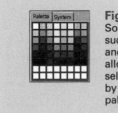

Figure 5-5
Some properties, such as *BackColor* and *ForeColor*, allow you to select a value by using a color palette.

6. Select the desired color by clicking it.

7. Locate and select the *WindowState* property. This is an example of a property that controls the behavior of an object. When you select this property, you see a selection button like the one for the *BackColor* property. Click this button, and you're offered a list of acceptable values for this property. Select 2 - Maximize.

8. Run the application by pressing F5. The form window is automatically displayed in a maximized state.

9. Close the form to return to design mode.

Using the *BorderStyle* Property

In the last exercise, you ran the new project without making any changes to it. One of the things demonstrated in that exercise was the fact that you can resize the window. Using the *BorderStyle* property, you can control whether or not users may resize a window at runtime. Even if you allow users to resize a window, you can use the *BorderStyle* property to control how they can resize it.

Complete the following steps to use some of the settings available for this property and see the impact of these settings on a form:

1. Locate and select the *BorderStyle* property.

2. Click the selection button and select 1 - Fixed Single.

3. Run the application by pressing F5. Notice the border of the window. When you move the pointer over the form's border, it does not change to a resizing pointer. Setting *BorderStyle* to Fixed Single means that the only

way a user can resize this window is by using the Maximize and Minimize buttons. You can use this setting whenever you do not mind if users want a larger, maximized window but you definitely do not want them to resize the window to a smaller size (for instance, because you need them to see all the fields in that window at once).

4. Close the form to return to design mode. Set the *BorderStyle* property to 3 - Fixed Dialog.

5. Press F5 to run the project. Notice that there is no Maximize or Minimize button on the form now—this window is not resizable. Close the form to return to design mode. The Fixed Dialog setting is useful when you're creating specialized dialog or message boxes.

6. Set the *BorderStyle* property back to its default by selecting 2 - Sizable.

Using the *WindowState* Property

What would you do if you wanted a form to automatically display in a maximized state? Or if you wanted your application to start in a minimized state in the same way that many utilities do? You would use the *WindowState* property! This property is used to set the visual state of a form window, as demonstrated in the following exercise.

Complete the following steps to see how the *WindowState* property works:

1. Locate and select the *WindowState* property.

2. Click the *WindowState* property's selection button and select 2 - Maximized.

3. Run the application by pressing F5. Notice that the form is displayed full-screen.

4. Close the form to return to design mode.

5. Select the *WindowState* property again.

6. Click the selection button and select 1 - Minimized.

7. Run the application by pressing F5. The form is not shown on-screen. If you look on your taskbar, though, you'll find the project listed there as Form1. Restore the project using the taskbar, and then close the form to return to design mode.

8. Select the *WindowState* property again. Click the selection button and select 0 - Normal.

Using the Form Layout Window

The Form Layout window (see Figure 5-6) is located in the lower-right corner of VB's design area. The Form Layout window is a tool that you use to visually position your forms at design time. Positioning a window is done with a simple drag operation, as the following exercise shows.

Reposition a form by completing the following steps:

EXERCISE

1. Scroll to the *Top* property in the Properties window.
2. Drag the object representing the form in the Form Layout window to a lower position. Notice that when you release your mouse, the value of the *Top* property changes to reflect the new location.
3. Scroll to the *Left* property in the Properties window.
4. Drag the object representing the form in the Form Layout window to a different horizontal position. Notice that when you release your mouse, the value of the *Left* property changes to reflect the new location.

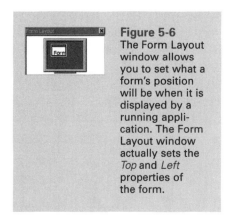

Figure 5-6
The Form Layout window allows you to set what a form's position will be when it is displayed by a running application. The Form Layout window actually sets the *Top* and *Left* properties of the form.

A twip is 1/20 of a point. 1,440 twips equal one inch.

You could accomplish the same thing by entering values directly into the *Top* and *Left* properties. It is much easier to use the Form Layout window, however, than to figure out the right number of twips!

Setting Up the First Form for the Time Tracking System

You are going to set several properties for the form you currently have in your project. This form is going to be used for the majority of user input in your application. Complete these steps to prepare this form by setting its properties:

1. Within the Properties window, locate and select the *Caption* property.
2. Type **Billing Information** for this property's value.
3. Select the *Name* property and set it to **frmBillingInfo**.

> **The Name property is placed in parenthesis in the Properties window so that it will appear at the top of the list of each object's properties.**

4. Select the *Height* property and set it to **4000**.
5. Select the *Width* property and set it to **5500**.

> **Another way to resize a form is to use its resizing handles.**

6. Using the Form Layout window, position the form in the middle of the screen. When you have completed these steps, your screen will look similar to the one shown in Figure 5-7.

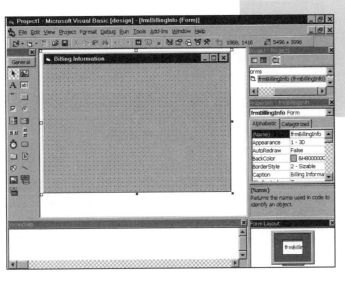

Figure 5-7
The main user input form of the time tracking system is ready for the addition of controls.

Placing Controls on Forms

If you can draw a rectangle using the Paint applet that ships with Windows, you have all the skills you need to place controls on a form. In the previous section you set properties for the Billing Information form. The goal of this form, which is shown in its completed state in Figure 5-8, is to accept input from a user concerning how that user spent their billable time.

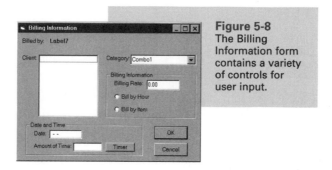

Figure 5-8
The Billing Information form contains a variety of controls for user input.

When you draw a control, you can see its current size by stopping the drag action. Don't let the mouse go—just stop moving the mouse and a pop-up, ToolTip-style yellow box is displayed with the current dimensions of the control displayed in *width × height* format.

You are ready to start working with the controls you need for your interface. The following steps have you place controls on a form and work with properties:

1. Select the Label tool from the toolbox.

2. Position the mouse pointer in the upper-left corner of the form. Press and hold down the mouse button, draw a 732×252 rectangle, and release the mouse button.

 The sizes given in these steps are guidelines. If you do not match them exactly, it will not affect the functionality and capabilities of the application you are creating.

3. You have created a label with the caption Label1. At this point, the control's name is also Label1. Using the technique you used in step 2, create another label to the right of the first label. The new label should have a size of 2652×252.

4. Create another label below `Label1` with a size of 532×252. This is going to be used as a label for a list box.

5. Select the ListBox tool from the toolbox. Draw a list box to the right of `Label3` with a size of 1812×1812.

6. To the right of the list box—at the same height as `Label3`—draw a label that has a size of 732×252.

7. Next to the newest label, draw a combo box with a size of 1572×288.

8. Below `Label4`, draw a frame with a size of 2292×1332. Inside the frame, draw a label with a size of 852×252.

9. Next to the newest label, draw a text box with a size of 972×252. The text box automatically adjusts its height to 288 due to a required minimum.

10. Below `Label5`, draw two option buttons, each with a size of 1692×252. In the lower-left corner of the form, draw another frame with a size of 3492×972.

11. Inside the new frame, draw a label with a size of 492×252. To the right of the newest label, draw a text box with a size of 972×252.

12. Below the newest label, draw a 1212×252 label. Next to the newest label (`Label7`), draw a text box with a size of 852×252.

13. Next to the `Text2` text box, draw a command button that is 852×252.

14. Double-click the command button tool in the toolbox. Drag the newly created command button as far down as possible in the lower-right corner of the form.

15. Double-click the command button tool again. Position the new command button directly above the command button you moved in the previous step. When you're finished, your form should look similar to the one shown in Figure 5-9.

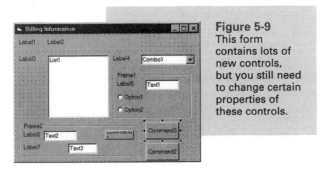

Figure 5-9
This form contains lots of new controls, but you still need to change certain properties of these controls.

Saving the Project

At this point you have invested significant time in the creation of this form. Your main thought probably is, "How do I save this work so that I don't lose it?" You actually need to save two things, the project and the form. To save both in one step, select File, Save Project from the menu. Here are the steps in more detail:

1. Select File, Save Project to display the Save File As dialog box (see Figure 5-10). Each form is saved into a separate file. VB knows that the form has not been saved yet, so it prompts you to do so.

Tip

You may want to create a new directory for this project, because projects are easier to manage if each one has its own directory. In this case it makes sense to create a directory named something like T_Track.

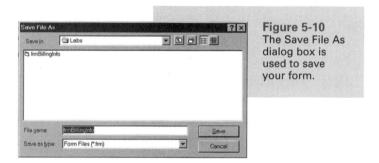

Figure 5-10
The Save File As dialog box is used to save your form.

2. In the File name text box is the file name frmBillingInfo. VB automatically assumes that you want to use the name of the form from the *Name* property for the file name. Form files are saved with the extension FRM. Click Save to save the form.

Note

You can use frmBillingInfo for the file name on Windows 95 or NT operating systems. If you are using a 16-bit version of Windows, you must shorten the name to eight characters. You could, for example, name the file frmBill.

3. The Save Project As dialog box is displayed (see Figure 5-11). A project file keeps track of all the files associated with the project. For example, the project file knows that frmBillingInfo is part of this project. In the File name text box, type **Lawtrack** and then click Save to save the project.

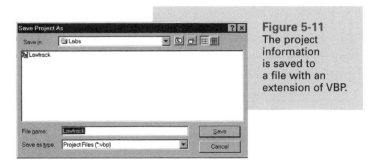

Figure 5-11
The project information is saved to a file with an extension of VBP.

Moving Controls

After creating the controls, you may need to move them to improve the look of your interface. You can drag controls to new locations or you can use the Format menu to align controls. These techniques are demonstrated in the following steps:

1. You need to relocate the Command1 command button, which is located in Frame2. Drag it so that it's next to the Text3 text box.

2. If Label1 and Label3 are lined up, move Label1 to the right slightly. You do this in order to see how the Format menu works in a later step.

3. Select Label1 by clicking it. Hold down the Shift key and click Label3. The Shift key allows you to select multiple controls.

4. Select Format, Align, Lefts. Label1 and Label3 are now aligned based on their left side. These controls align to the control that is furthest right. This changes the *Left* property of any control that is moved by this operation.

5. Continue the process of aligning controls. Label1, Label3, and Frame2 should be aligned left. Label4 and Frame1 should also be aligned left. Within Frame1, the option buttons should be aligned left. Within Frame2, Label3 and Label7 should be aligned left. Finally, the Command2 and Command3 command buttons should be aligned left.

6. This technique can be used to align left, center, right, top, middle, or bottom. Label1 and Label2 should be aligned top. Label3, List1, Label4, and Combo1 should also be aligned top.

Resizing Controls

When you are working with controls on a form, you frequently have to resize them. You may have made them too large or too small for the data they are to receive. To resize a control, you first select it by clicking it. This displays the control's resizing handles. You then resize the control by clicking and dragging one of these handles to a new location.

What if you want to make several controls the same size? You can resize them individually, but you also can resize them as a group by using the F̲ormat menu. Here's how to do that with some controls on the billing form:

1. Select the Command3 command button by clicking it.
2. Resize Command3 so that it's shorter (it should be 972×372).
3. Hold down the Shift key and click Command2.
4. Select F̲ormat, M̲ake Same Size, H̲eight. This handles the resizing automatically.

Setting Control Properties

Most programmers prefer to draw one control, set its properties, and then draw the next control. For this lab, you've already drawn all the controls, so now you're going to set all their properties. Each type of control has its own set of properties. Just as you saw with form properties, control properties are used to determine both appearance and behavior.

Some properties—such as *Name, Height, Width, Top,* and *Left*—are used by most controls. Other properties—such as *Text*—are used by fewer controls.

The steps for setting control properties are identical to those for setting form properties. What you want to concentrate on in the upcoming steps are the properties themselves. The properties you set are the ones typically set at design time for these controls. For example, in the design phase you set the *Name* property for all controls. When the intrinsic controls were discussed earlier in this chapter, naming convention prefixes were introduced. These prefixes are used in the following sections.

Setting Properties for Labels

The first type of control you're going to work with is the *label*. During the design phase, you typically set only two properties for a label control. First the *Name* property needs to be set. (As a reminder, the recommended prefix for label

In most dialog boxes, certain control captions have one letter underscored—this is a keyboard access character. Pressing the Alt key and the keyboard access character is an alternative to clicking the control.

names is lbl). The other property you need to set is the *Caption* property. The *Caption* property controls the text that is to be displayed by the label. When setting the *Caption* property of controls, you might want to add a keyboard access character.

This is done by preceding the character you want as the keyboard access character with an ampersand (&). For example, if you have a control with the caption Address and you want to make A the keyboard access character, you simply type **&Address** for the caption.

The following steps help you set the *Name* and *Caption* properties for the billing form's labels:

1. Select Label1.
2. Select and locate the *Name* property in the Properties window.
3. Type **lblBilledBy** as the value.

> **Note** An object's *Name* property must start with a letter and can be a maximum of 40 characters. It can include numbers and the underscore (_) character, but it cannot include spaces, punctuation marks, or other special characters.

4. Select and locate the *Caption* property. Type **&Billed by:** as the value.
5. Continue setting the *Name* and *Caption* properties for the labels on this form. Table 5-1 contains the correct settings. If there is no entry for the control in the Caption column, don't enter anything in the *Caption* property. The *Caption* property for certain controls will be modified using code in Chapter 6, "Building the Time Tracking System."

Table 5-1 *Name* and *Caption* Property Settings for the Labels

Original Name	New Name	Caption
Label2	lblBillingName	
Label3	lblClient	&Client:
Label4	lblCategory	Cate&gory:
Label5	lblBillingRate	Billing &Rate:
Label6	lblDate	&Date:
Label7	lblAmountOfTime	&Amount of Time:

Note Some programmers do not bother giving meaningful names to controls that are not referred to in code. (The majority of the labels you're working with here will not be referred to or modified by code.) The primary advantage to naming all controls—whether or not they are referred to in code—is that they are grouped together in the Properties window's control list box because of their naming prefix.

Working with Text Box Properties

The next type of control to work with is the *text box*. At design time you typically set the values of two properties for text box controls: *Name* and *Text*. The *Text* property, like the Label's *Caption* property, controls the text displayed by the control. Often you simply remove all text from the *Text* property, as in the following steps:

1. Select the Text1 text box.
2. Locate and select the *Name* property in the Properties window.
3. Type **txtBillingRate**.
4. Locate and select the *Text* property. Delete the default value for this property and leave the setting blank.
5. Continue setting the *Name* and *Text* properties for the text boxes on this form. Table 5-2 shows the necessary *Name* settings. Make the value of the *Text* property blank for each text box.

Table 5-2 *Name* Property Settings for the Text Boxes	
Original Name	**New Name**
Text2	txtDate
Text3	txtAmountOfTime

Naming the List Box

On the Billing Information form is a *list box* to display the law firm's clients. Depending on the type of list box, you might want to set only the *Name* property and no other property. That is the case with this list box, so follow these steps to set the *Name* property:

1. Select the List1 list box.
2. Locate and select the *Name* property in the Properties window.
3. Type **lstClient** for the value of this property.

Depending on the application, you may set several other properties for list box controls. One is the *Sorted* property. The *Sorted* property is set by default to True. This means that the items listed in the list box are automatically sorted in alphabetical order. If you want to display the items in a list box in a specific order other than alphabetical, you need to set *Sorted* to False.

Typically list boxes allow a user to select only one item; however, there are exceptions to this rule. An example of a list box that allows you to select more than one item is a file list box—many times you can select multiple files from a list. If you want to provide users the ability to select multiple items from a list, set the *MultiSelect* property to Simple or Extended. Setting the value to Simple means that the user can use either the mouse or the spacebar along with the Shift or Ctrl key to select multiple items. Setting the value to Extended gives the user additional ways to select multiple items from the list box. The user can press Shift and click the mouse or press an arrow key to select a range of items, or can similarly use the Ctrl key to select discontinuous multiple items.

If you need a multiselect list box, you may also want to set the *Style* property. List boxes support two values for this property. The default value is Standard, and a nicer value to use for multiselect list boxes is Checkboxes. The latter value sets a style that readily lets users know that they can choose multiple items from the list.

During the design phase you typically do not place any items in a list box. This can be done during the design phase using the *List* property, but usually is done with code using the AddItem method.

Setting Combo Box Properties

A cousin to the list box is the *combo box*. On this form is one combo box that you'll use to display a list of billing categories. The properties of the combo box are similar to those of the list box. For example, the combo box supports the *Sorted* property and the *Style* property. The values for the *Style* property for a combo box differ from those for a list box. With a combo box, the default value for *Style* is Dropdown Combo. This style includes a drop-down list and a text box— the user can either select from the list or type in the text box. Another available value for this property is Simple Combo. This style includes a text box and a list— the user can either select from the list or type in the text box. The size of a simple combo box includes both the edit and list portions, but by default its list area is sized so that none of the list is displayed. The last available value for this property is Dropdown List, which means that the user only can select from the drop-down list.

For this project's interface you only need to set the *Name* property for the combo box control at design time:

1. Select the Combo1 combo box.
2. Locate and select the *Name* property in the Properties window.
3. Type **cboCategory**.

Setting Frame Captions

There are two *frames* on this form. One is used to group the date and time controls and the other is used to group the billing information controls. You need to set two properties for each frame:

1. Select Frame1.
2. Set its *Name* property to **fraBillingInfo**.
3. Set its *Caption* property to **Billing Information**.

A shortcut for moving through the properties list is to press Ctrl+Shift plus the first character of the name of the property you're looking for. For example, Ctrl+Shift+C takes you to the *Caption* property.

4. Select Frame2.
5. Set its *Caption* property to **Date and Time**.
6. Set its *Name* property to **fraDateAndTime**.

A quick way to return to the *Name* property is to press the Home key, which takes you to the first property in the list.

Working with the Option Button Properties

Like list boxes and combo boxes, *option buttons* are a way that the user can select from several choices. On this form option buttons are used to select whether an activity is to be billed by the hour or as a flat rate. An option button control has two properties you've already worked with, *Name* and *Caption*. You might also want to set the *Value* property at design time. When an option button is selected, *Value* is set to True, and the other option buttons in that group have *Value* set to False.

> **Option buttons should be grouped within frames. If you do not place option buttons in frames, all option buttons on the form are considered one group.**

> **If you create option buttons and later need to place them in frames, you must cut the option buttons from the form, create (if necessary) and select the frame, and then paste the option buttons in the frame. Drawing a frame around existing option buttons does not place them in the frame.**

Use the following steps to set the necessary values for this project:

1. Select the Option1 option button.
2. Set its *Name* property to **optByHour**.
3. Set its *Caption* property to **Bill by &Hour**.
4. Set its *Value* property to **True**. (For any group of option buttons, you should decide which option button is most likely to be selected—place it first and set its *Value* property to True.)
5. Select the Option2 option button.
6. Set its *Name* property to **optBillByItem**.
7. Set its *Caption* property to **Bill by &Item**.

Setting Command Button Properties

The final controls you need to set properties for on this form are the *command buttons*. You obviously need to name each of them, and you should set their *Caption* properties. Moreover, command buttons have two properties, *Default* and *Cancel*, that other controls do not have. Setting the *Default* property to True means that the button executes if a user simply presses the Enter key; only one button on a form can have *Default* set to True. Setting the *Cancel* property to True means that the button executes if a user presses the Esc key; only one button on a form can have *Cancel* set to True.

> **Tip**
>
> The same button can have both the *Default* and *Cancel* properties set to True. Typically both properties are set to True if there's only one button on the form.

To set the necessary property values for command buttons on this form, follow these steps:

1. Select the Command1 command button.
2. Set its *Name* property to **cmdTimer**.
3. Set its *Caption* property to **&Timer**.
4. Select the Command3 command button.
5. Set its *Name* property to **cmdOK**.
6. Set its *Caption* property to **OK**.
7. Set its *Default* property to **True**. (The OK button on a form is typically the default button.)
8. Select the Command2 command button.
9. Set its *Name* property to **cmdCancel**.
10. Set its *Caption* property to **Cancel**.
11. Set its *Cancel* property to **True**. (The Cancel button on a form should always have this property set to True.)

Your form now should look like the one shown in Figure 5-12.

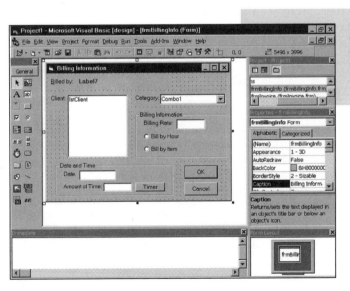

Figure 5-12
The completed form is ready for you to automate it using VB code.

Saving the Form

After you have completed working on a form, you definitely should save it. This is done through the File menu:

1. Select the File menu.

2. Select Save frmBillingInfo.frm (the Save *form* menu item always reflects the name of the current form).

Adding Controls to the Toolbox

Now that you have completed the Billing Information form, you might notice that something does not seem right. In the analysis phase of this project it was determined that certain fields should have a fixed format—the date should have the format *mm-dd-yy* and the billing rate should show two decimal places. As you were setting properties for these controls, you did not see a place to specify a format. That's because there isn't a property to do this with text boxes. You need a different control called a *masked edit control.*

This is not one of the default controls in the toolbox. You need to add it to the toolbox before you can use it. Do so as follows:

1. Right-click the toolbox to display its pop-up menu.

2. Select Components to display the Components dialog box (see Figure 5-13).

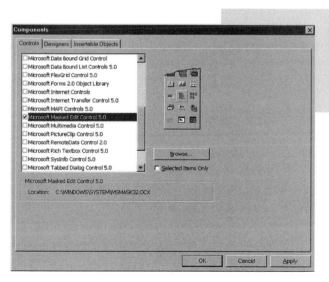

Figure 5-13
The Components dialog box lists all the installed controls found on your system.

3. Locate and select `Microsoft Masked Edit Control 5.0`.

4. Click OK to add this control to the toolbox. The masked edit control is now available for you to use (see Figure 5-14).

Figure 5-14
A tool representing the masked edit control has been added to the toolbox.

— Masked Edit Control

Using the Masked Edit Control

Think of the masked edit control as a text box with added functionality. It allows you to define a format for acceptable input. This restricts input and formats output. This formatting is accomplished by setting a value for the *Mask* property. If the value of the *Mask* property is an empty string, a masked edit control acts like a standard text box.

If you enter a value for the *Mask* property, each character position in the masked edit control maps to either a placeholder or a literal character (often just called a *literal*). The literals give visual cues to your user about the type of data that belongs in that box. For example, the dashes in `###-##-####` tell the user that a Social Security number is expected.

If a user enters a character that is not acceptable based on the *Mask* property value, the masked edit control generates a `ValidationError` event. With a Social Security number, for example, if a user enters a letter of the alphabet, the `ValidationError` event occurs.

Note **You as the programmer have to write code to generate error messages or to do whatever else is required when `ValidationError` occurs. This is covered in Chapter 6, "Building the Time Tracking System."**

The value entered in the *Mask* property is usually a combination of placeholders and literals. If the mask contains literals, they are automatically skipped when the user enters text in the control. With a Social Security number, for example, the user just needs to type nine numbers without any dashes.

> **Tip**
>
> The *Mask* property's value can be specified at design time or runtime, but typically it's done at design time.

The input mask can consist of any of the characters listed in Table 5-3.

Table 5-3   Mask Characters

Mask Character	Type	Description
#	Placeholder	Numeric with entry required
.	Literal	Decimal point
,	Literal	Thousands separator
:	Literal	Time separator
/	Literal	Date separator
&	Placeholder	Precedes an ANSI character value; acceptable values are 32–126 and 128–255
>	Special Character	Converts all characters that follow to uppercase
<	Special Character	Converts all characters that follow to lowercase
A	Placeholder	Alphanumeric with entry required; acceptable values are a–z, A–Z, and 0–9
a	Placeholder	Alphanumeric with entry optional; acceptable values are a–z, A–Z, and 0–9
9	Placeholder	Numeric with entry optional; acceptable values are 0–9
C	Placeholder	Character placeholder; this is exactly like the & placeholder, and is supported to ensure compatibility with Microsoft Access
?	Placeholder	Letter with entry required; acceptable values are a–z and A–Z
\	Special Character	Indicates that the next character in the mask is a literal; this allows you to include C, 9, <, >, #, &, A, or ? in a mask
	Literal	Any other specific symbol or alphanumeric character; for example, $, (,), %, -, ^, *, b, D, or 2

For example, if you want to create a mask for a product number that always begins with the letter "T" and has 4 digits, the best mask to use is T####. If the product number must begin with "T" but can be either three or four digits, use T###9.

Table 5-4 lists some masks that have special meanings to the masked edit control. When the value of the *Mask* property is an empty string (""), the control acts like a text box control.

Table 5-4	Special Case Masks	
Mask	**Description**	**Example**
##-???-##	Medium date (US)	14-Feb-98
##-##-##	Short date (US)	02-14-98
##:##	Short time	14:02
##:## ??	Medium time	02:02 PM

> **Note**
>
> Using a mask for a long date or time is possible but not practical. You could, for example, create a mask of CCCCCCCCC #9, ####. However, the user would end up using the space-bar or arrow keys to move to the required characters in the mask, thus slowing down their input.

When a value other that an empty string has been entered for the *Mask* property, underscores are displayed in the masked edit control beneath each placeholder at runtime. If an invalid character is entered, the masked edit control rejects the character and initiates a ValidationError event.

The frmBillingInfo form needs one masked edit control. The txtDate text box should actually be a masked edit control, so you need to delete the current control and create a new masked edit control:

1. Select the txtDate control.
2. Press the Delete key to remove the control from the form.
3. Select the Masked Edit Control tool from the toolbox.
4. Draw a masked edit control in the location where txtDate used to be.
5. Set the properties for the new control using the values shown in Table 5-5.

 6. Select File, Save frmBillingInfo.frm to save the changes.

Table 5-5 mskDate Property Settings	
Property	**Value**
Name	mskDate
Height	252
Mask	##-##-##
Width	972

Adding Forms to the Application

At this point frmBillingInfo has a complete interface. You are now ready to add additional forms. Adding a form to a project can be done through the Project menu or by using the New Form toolbar button to display the Add Form dialog box. When you add a new form, it is displayed on-screen and is added to the Project Explorer.

There are several form templates that you can use as a foundation for form creation. The form template you will use the most is called Standard, and is just a blank form. VB 5 provides other templates, which are listed below:

- About Dialog
- VB Data Form Wizard
- Log In Dialog
- Options Dialog
- Splash Dialog
- Tip of the Day
- Addin
- ODBC Log In
- Browser
- DataGrid
- Querys

Creating the Timer Form

You've determined that the project you're working on needs four forms. Add another form to the project using the following steps:

1. Select Project, Add Form to display the Add Form dialog box (see Figure 5-15).

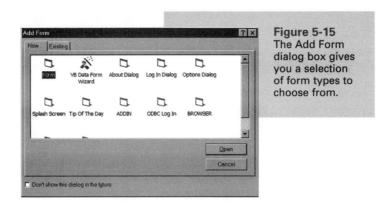

Figure 5-15
The Add Form dialog box gives you a selection of form types to choose from.

2. Select Form from the New tab.

3. Click <u>O</u>pen to add the form to the project. The new blank form is displayed.

When it's complete, the form will look like the one shown in Figure 5-16.

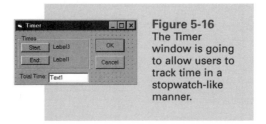

Figure 5-16
The Timer window is going to allow users to track time in a stopwatch-like manner.

Using the following steps, add controls to this form just as you did for frmBillingInfo:

1. Resize the form to set its *Height* property to **1900** and its *Width* property to **3700**.

2. Name the form **frmTimer**.

3. Set the form's *Caption* property to **Timer**.

4. Create a frame and place it in the upper-right corner of the form.

5. Use the values from Table 5-6 to set property settings for the frame.

6. Create a command button within the frame (in the frame's upper-left corner).

Table 5-6 fraTimes Property Settings	
Property	**Setting**
Caption	Times
Height	972
Left	50
Name	fraTimes
Top	120
Width	2182

7. Use the values from Table 5-7 to set property settings for the command button.

Table 5-7 cmdStart Property Settings	
Property	**Setting**
Caption	Start:
Default	True
Height	252
Left	120
Name	cmdStart
Top	240
Width	852

8. Create another command button within the frame (below the previous command button).

9. Use the values from Table 5-8 to set property settings for this command button.

Table 5-8 cmdEnd Property Settings	
Property	**Setting**
Caption	End:
Height	252
Left	120
Name	cmdEnd
Top	600
Width	852

10. Create a label within the frame (next to the first command button).

11. Use the values from Table 5-9 to set property settings for the label.

Table 5-9   lblStart Property Settings

Property	Setting
Height	252
Left	1080
Name	lblStart
Top	240
Width	852

12. Create another label within the frame (next to the second command button).

13. Use the values from Table 5-10 to set property settings for this label.

Table 5-10   lblEnd Property Settings

Property	Setting
Height	252
Left	1080
Name	lblEnd
Top	600
Width	852

14. Create another label just below the frame.

15. Use the values from Table 5-11 to set property settings for this label.

Table 5-11   lblTotalTime Property Settings

Property	Setting
Caption	Total Time:
Height	252
Left	120
Name	lblTotalTime
Top	1200
Width	852

16. Create a text box beside the last label you created.

17. Use the values from Table 5-12 to set property settings for this text box.

Table 5-12	`txtTime` Property Settings
Property	**Setting**
Height	288
Left	1000
Name	txtTime
Top	1200
Width	1200

18. Create a command button in the upper-right corner of the form.

19. Use the values from Table 5-13 to set property settings for this command button.

Table 5-13	cmdOK Property Settings
Property	**Setting**
Caption	OK
Height	372
Left	2400
Name	cmdOK
Top	240
Width	852

20. Create a command button below the command button you just created.

21. Use the values from Table 5-14 to set property settings for this command button.

Table 5-14	cmdCancel Property Settings
Property	**Setting**
Cancel	True
Caption	Cancel
Height	372
Left	2400
Name	cmdCancel
Top	720
Width	852

22. The form now should look like the one shown in Figure 5-17. Select File, Save Project.

23. Press Enter in response to the Save File As dialog box. This saves the new form with the name `frmTimer` and saves all your changes to the project.

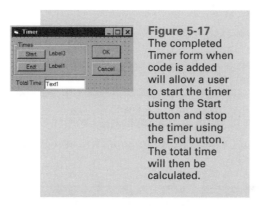

Figure 5-17
The completed Timer form when code is added will allow a user to start the timer using the Start button and stop the timer using the End button. The total time will then be calculated.

Adding a Splash Screen

Another form you determined the project needed during the analysis phase of project design was a *splash screen* (or *startup screen*). Most professional applications have a splash screen containing the name of the application, a logo, copyright information, version number, and so on. You can create a splash screen from scratch or you can use one of the form templates that ship with VB. Using a form template greatly reduces the time required for this form. In the following steps you'll use the Splash Dialog form template in your project:

1. Select Project, Add Form to display the Add Form dialog box.

2. Select Splash Dialog from the New tab.

3. Click Open to add the new form to the project. The new form is displayed as shown in Figure 5-18.

Figure 5-18
The newly added splash form is ready to be customized for your specific project.

4. Look at the Properties window. You can see that the name of this form is `frmSplash`.

5. Select the graphic on this form. The Properties window shows that this is an image control named `imgLogo`. To change the image to another graphic, locate and select its *Picture* property.

ON THE

CD

6. Select the `Time.pcx` file located in the `\examples\Lab1\` directory on the CD accompanying this book. This changes the logo that will appear on the splash dialog box.

7. Select the label with the caption `License To`. Press the Delete key to remove this label. You do not need it for this project.

8. Select the label with the caption `CompanyProduct`.

9. Locate and select its *Caption* property.

10. Type the name of your company.

11. Select the label with the caption `Platform`.

12. Type **Windows 95** as the new value of its *Caption* property. (You can type another platform—such as **Windows NT**—if you need to.)

13. Select the label with the caption `Copyright`.

14. Type **Copyright 1997** as the new value of its *Caption* property.

15. Select the label with the caption `Company`.

16. Type your company name as the new value of this label's *Caption* property.

17. Select the label with the caption `Warning`.

18. Type **Warning: This computer program is protected by copyright law.** as the new value of its *Caption* property. The splash form is now complete and should look like the one shown in Figure 5-19.

Save
Here

19. Select File, Save `frmSplash.frm` to save the form. Click Save.

20. Select File, Save Project to update the project.

Figure 5-19
This splash form has been customized for your project.

Notice that you did not change the captions of the `Version` and `Project` labels. This is because the form contains code to set the *Caption* properties of these two controls at runtime.

Creating the Invoice Form

The next form you're going to create is the Invoice form. This form is going to be used as a print preview of the billing information. This form begins with the standard form template, but when completed will look like the form shown in Figure 5-20.

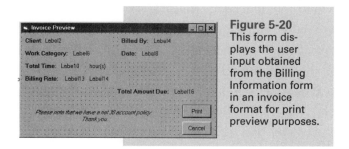

Figure 5-20
This form displays the user input obtained from the Billing Information form in an invoice format for print preview purposes.

1. Select Project, New Form to display the Add Form dialog box.
2. Select Form from the New tab.
3. Click Open to add the form to the project.
4. Use the values from Table 5-15 to set the properties for this form.

Table 5-15	frmInvoice Form Property Settings
Property	**Setting**
Caption	Invoice Preview
Height	3324
Name	frmInvoice
Width	5868

5. Add the controls listed in Table 5-16, using Figure 5-20 as a guide. Set the properties for these controls as indicated in the table.

Table 5-16	Property Settings for Controls on `frmInvoice`	
Control	**Property**	**Setting**
Label1	*Caption*	Client:
	Height	252
	Left	120
	Top	120
	Width	492
Label2	*Height*	252
	Left	720
	Name	lblClient
	Top	120
	Width	1932
Label3	*Caption*	Billed By:
	Height	252
	Left	3000
	Top	120
	Width	852
Label4	*Height*	252
	Left	3960
	Name	lblBilledBy
	Top	120
	Width	1692
Label5	*Caption*	Work Category:
	Height	252
	Left	120
	Top	480
	Width	1332
Label6	*Height*	252
	Left	1560
	Name	lblWorkCategory
	Top	480
	Width	1400
Label7	*Caption*	Date:
	Height	252
	Left	3000
	Top	480
	Width	492
Label8	*Height*	252
	Left	3600
	Name	lblDate
	Top	480
	Width	972

continues

Table 5-16	Continued	
Control	**Property**	**Setting**
Label9	*Caption*	Total Time:
	Height	252
	Left	120
	Top	840
	Width	1092
Label10	*Height*	252
	Left	1200
	Name	lblTotalTime
	Top	840
	Width	612
Label11	*Caption*	hour(s)
	Height	252
	Left	2040
	Top	840
	Width	612
Label12	*Caption*	Billing Rate:
	Height	252
	Left	120
	Top	1200
	Width	900
Label13	*Height*	252
	Left	1150
	Name	lblRate
	Top	1200
	Width	612
Label14	*Height*	252
	Left	2040
	Name	lblHourOrJob
	Top	1200
	Width	1092
Label15	*Caption*	Total Amount Due:
	Height	252
	Left	2880
	Top	1560
	Width	1572
Label16	*Height*	252
	Left	4560
	Name	lblTotalAmount
	Top	1560
	Width	852

Control	Property	Setting
Label17	Alignment	2 - Center
	Caption	Please note that we have a net 30 account policy. Thank you.
	Font	MS Sans Serif Italic 8 point
	Height	492
	Left	360
	Top	2160
	Width	3732
Command1	Caption	&Print
	Default	True
	Height	372
	Left	4800
	Name	cmdPrint
	Top	2040
	Width	852
Command2	Cancel	True
	Caption	Cancel
	Height	372
	Left	4800
	Name	cmdCancel
	Top	2520
	Width	852

6. Select File, Save frmInvoice.frm to save the form. Click Save.

7. Select File, Save Project to update the project.

At this point only one form for this project has not been created. In the analysis phase it was stated that a form should prompt the user for her name. Instead of designing such a form, you're going to create a dialog box using code. This is discussed in Chapter 6.

Final Design Phase Checklist

The checklist below provides a way for you to verify that all steps have been completed for the design phase. If you find yourself using additional controls, you can expand this list to include the properties you need to set for those controls.

✔ Have you named all the forms and controls?

✔ Have you set the *Caption* property for the labels?

✔ Have you set the *Text* property for the text boxes?

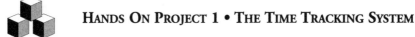
✔ Have you set the following properties for the list boxes:

Sorted (optional)

MultiSelect (optional)

Style (optional)

✔ Have you set the following properties for the combo boxes:

Sorted (optional)

Style (optional)

✔ Have you set the *Caption* property for the frames?

✔ Have you set the following properties for the option buttons:

Caption

Value

✔ Have you set the *Caption* property for the command buttons?

✔ Have you set the *Default* property to True for one command button on the form?

✔ Have you set the *Cancel* property to True for one command button on the form?

✔ If you're using masked edit controls, have you set the *Mask* property for each of them?

✔ Have you created a splash screen for the application?

✔ Have you saved the project and forms?

Summary

In this chapter you got hands-on experience designing several forms. Two forms used the Form template, and one used the Splash Dialog template. You placed a variety of controls on these forms, including frames, command buttons, images, option buttons, labels, and text boxes. You set the appropriate design-time properties for these controls.

The next step in the process is to automate your forms. In the next chapter you will write the code necessary to do this. You will learn how to move from window to window and use information obtained from one window in another window.

CHAPTER 6

Building the Time Tracking System

By designing the interface for your application in the previous chapter, you built a solid foundation for the time tracking system. One of the advantages of developing applications using Visual Basic is the ability to create all the needed forms without having to write any code. You then can use the forms as a prototype for the system to show to your user. All necessary modifications to the interface can be made before any code is written.

Once the interface is accepted, you're ready to code. The first thing you'll want to write code for is movement from one form to another. After that you'll want to write a procedure to automatically populate certain parts of your forms. Finally you'll want to add the complete logic needed for your application.

The goal of this chapter is to give you these skills. You'll learn all the language constructs needed to perform these actions. At the end of this chapter you'll have a working application ready to be tested and debugged.

The Code Window

The *Code window* is used to enter, view, and edit VB code. The following exercise walks you through several techniques to access the Code window.

EXERCISE

Complete the following steps to learn the various methods of accessing the Code window:

1. If you do not have the `frmBillingInfo` form already displayed, open it using the Project Explorer.

2. Double-click the OK button on the form.

3. This displays the Code window. Notice what is listed at the top of the Code window: `cmdOK`. This area is the Object box; it lets you know which object you are currently working with. Next to the Object box is the Event box. The Event box lists the event whose procedure you are currently working with (in this case, it's `Click`). In the Code window text area, these two items are combined into the procedure name: `cmdOK_Click`.

4. Close the Code window.

5. Click to select the form and then select View, Code. This is another way to access the Code window. Notice that the same procedure name is showing.

6. Close the Code window.

7. Select `frmBillingInfo` from the list in Project Explorer. Click the View Code toolbar button located at the top of the Project Explorer. This is yet another way to access the Code window. No matter how you access the Code window, you see the same contents.

8. Close the Code window.

Once you have accessed the Code window (see Figure 6-1), you'll be looking at a text editor environment. This works much like other text editors you've used, such as Microsoft Word or Notepad. The Code window has several parts:

- **The Object box**—The Object box is located under the toolbar on the left side. It displays the name of the selected object. If an object was not selected before opening the Code window, the word `(General)` is displayed in this box. To see a list of objects associated with the current form, click the arrow to the right of the list box. These objects are in alphabetical order and reinforce the advantage of using a standardized prefix when naming your objects.

A procedure is a unit of code that is called from other code elsewhere in the application. This code may be called from another procedure or function, or may be initiated because of an event. An event is an action that occurs at runtime, such as the user selecting a menu or clicking a button.

■ **The Procedure/Event box**—The Procedure/Event box is to the right of the Object box and lists all the events recognized by the object displayed in the Object box. To see a list of the events associated with the selected object, click the arrow to the right of the list box. Any events with procedures created for them are displayed in bold in this list. If (General) is displayed in the Object box, then the Procedure/Event box lists any declarations and all the general procedures that have been created for the form.

■ **Text area**—The text area is used to enter, view, and modify VB code.

■ **The Procedure View icon**—Under the text area in the left corner is the Procedure View icon. There are two views supported in this window, the procedure view and the full module view. When procedure view is selected (using the Procedure View icon), only one procedure at a time is displayed in the text area.

■ **The Full Module View icon**—The Full Module View icon is to the right of the Procedure View icon. When full module view is selected (using the Full Module View icon), the entire code in the module is displayed.

■ **The Immediate window**—The Immediate window is used as a testing and debugging tool. This window is discussed in detail in Chapter 7, "Testing the Time Tracking System."

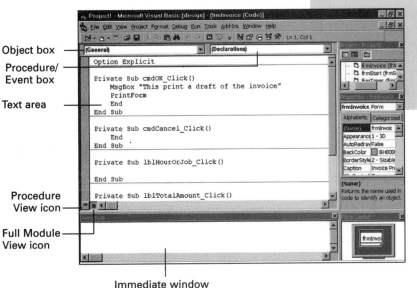

Object box
Procedure/
Event box
Text area
Procedure
View icon
Full Module
View icon
Immediate window

Figure 6-1
The Code window is the window you use to create VB code.

EXERCISE

The Code window is a text editor that allows you to enter text and navigate to other procedures. To become comfortable working with the Code window, complete these steps:

1. If you do not have the frmBillingInfo form already displayed, open it using the Project Explorer.

2. Double-click the form, making sure not to double-click any of the objects on the form. The Code window is displayed. In the Object box, Form is displayed. In the Event box, Load is displayed.

3. The name of the procedure displayed in the text area of the Code window is Form_Load. Enter the following line of code in this procedure:

   MsgBox "Here I am!"

4. Now you are going to enter code for a different event. Select Click from the Event box. The Form_Click procedure is displayed in the text area of the Code window.

5. Enter the following line of code in this procedure:

   MsgBox "I've been clicked!"

6. Press F5 to run the application.

7. When the form loads, a message box displays Here I am!. Click OK to remove this message box.

8. Click the form, making sure not to click any of the objects on the form. A message box displays I've been clicked!. Click OK to remove this message box.

9. End the application by closing the Billing Information window.

10. Double-click the form, making sure not to double-click any of the objects on the form. If Click is not already listed in the Event box, select Click from the list of events. The Form_Click procedure is displayed.

11. Delete the line of code you added in Step 5.

12. Select Load from the Event box. Notice that Load is in bold—this means that code has been entered for this event.

13. Delete the line of code you added in Step 3.

14. Close the Code window.

Now you are going to open the Code window for the frmBillingInfo object and type VB program statements for the time tracking system. Follow these steps:

1. If you do not have the frmBillingInfo form already displayed, open it using the Project Explorer.

2. Double-click the form (the area with the grid behind the controls). This opens the Code window. The procedure currently displayed in this window is `Private Sub Form_Load`, as shown in Figure 6-2.

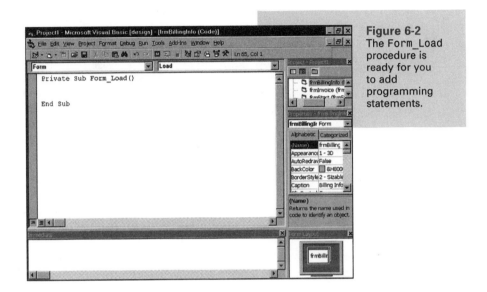

Figure 6-2
The Form_Load procedure is ready for you to add programming statements.

The `Form_Load` procedure is the event procedure that occurs when the form is loaded into memory. An example of the type of statements that might go into a `Form_Load` procedure are statements to populate fields on the form. Notice that three of the words in the text area are blue: `Private`, `Sub`, and `End`. These are *keywords*. The next section tells you how to get information about these and other keywords.

Using Help

There are several ways to get help when writing VB code. One is the way you're already familiar with from using other Windows applications—using the Help menu. VB's Help menu provides several options, including accessing the Microsoft Visual Basic Help topics and searching the Help and Master indexes. Another Help menu option is Microsoft on the Web. When you select this option, a list of Internet sites is displayed; these sites can assist you in your search for VB help and documentation.

The Code window also supports context-sensitive help. If, for example, you're reviewing someone else's code and you see a function or other statement with which you're unfamiliar, you can position your cursor on the unknown word and press F1 to display the help topic for that item. This is also useful if you're typing a statement and need more information on its syntax. Just type the command and press F1. This only works on keywords, which are a different color than the other words in the text area (keywords are blue by default).

> **If you want to make keywords a color other than blue, select Tools, Options and then select the Editor Format tab in the Options dialog box. Select Keyword Text from the Code Colors list box, select a new color for Foreground, and click OK to implement the change.**

To demonstrate this help feature, complete these steps:

1. Position the cursor on the word Private in the text area of the Code window.
2. Press F1. The help topic for the Private keyword is displayed.
3. Click the Sub Statement line to get additional information.
4. Review the information and then close Help to return to the Code window.

VB provides syntax clues called *Quick Info* whenever you type a statement. These clues are provided for variables, functions, procedures, methods, and statements.

To see an example of the Quick Info clues, complete these steps:

1. Position your cursor in the blank line beneath the Private Sub Form_Load() line.
2. Type **lstClient.A** on this line.
3. The Quick Info pops up in a small, yellow box much like a ToolTip. The method you want is AddItem, which is now selected. Press the spacebar to accept this method, and the remainder of the method is typed for you. As you can see, Quick Info not only jogs your memory, but saves typing as well.
4. Complete the statement so that it looks like the following:

   lstClient.AddItem "ABC Corp."

> **If Auto Quick Info is not enabled, select Tools, Options and then select the Editor tab. Click to place a check in the Auto Quick Info check box and then click OK to save the change.**

Form Management

Your application has four forms associated with it. The first phase of automating the application is to manage your forms so that the application switches from one screen to another. To do this you need to learn how to load forms into memory, how to unload them from memory, and how to hide and show them.

Setting Project Properties

Let's run the application as it stands now. You want to see your splash screen displayed first. To run the application, press F5. Is the splash screen displayed? No...the Billing Information window is displayed. Why is that? When you start a new project, VB designates `Form1` as the startup form. You made `Form1` into `frmBillingInfo`, so it's now the startup form. You need to make `frmSplash` the startup form. To do so, complete the following steps:

1. Select Project, `Project1` Properties to display the Project Properties dialog box (see Figure 6-3).

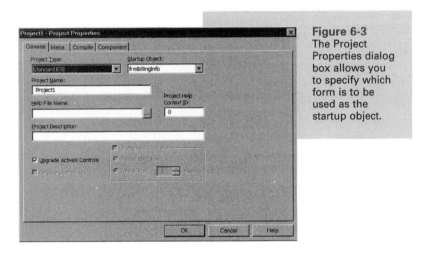

Figure 6-3
The Project Properties dialog box allows you to specify which form is to be used as the startup object.

2. Select `frmSplash` from the Startup Object drop-down list.

3. Click OK to save the change.

4. Press F5 to run your application. The splash screen is now displayed as shown in Figure 6-4.

5. Click the form to end the application.

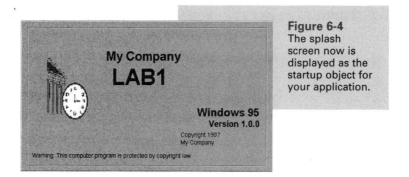

When you created the splash screen in Chapter 5, there were two labels, Version and Product, whose captions you did not change. The values for these two captions are controlled by the project's properties. To set the necessary values, follow these steps:

1. Select Project, Project1 Properties to display the Project Properties dialog box.

2. Select the Make tab (see Figure 6-5).

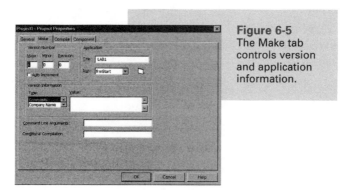

Figure 6-5
The Make tab controls version and application information.

3. To change the version number to 1.0.1, type **1** in the Revision text box.

4. To change the product name, type **Time Tracker** in the Title text box.

5. Click OK to save the changes.

6. Press F5 to run the application and display the splash screen. Notice the changes to the screen.

7. Click the form to end the application.

Loading and Unloading Forms

So far you have an application that displays just a splash screen. While it's an attractive splash screen, you certainly want users to see the rest of the application. To do this you must understand the process of getting a form into memory. One way to do this is using the Load statement, which places a form into memory for use by the application. The syntax for this statement is as follows:

```
Load formname
```

Replace *formname* with the specific name of the form you want to load into memory, as in the following example:

```
Load frmBillingInfo
```

Once a form has been loaded, you can use it from any event procedure in the application. You also can use all of its runtime properties and methods.

If you have a form that you no longer need in memory, you should unload it using the Unload statement. After you unload a form, its runtime values and properties are lost. Any property values you set at runtime are lost, and those properties are returned to the design-time values. Here is the syntax for the Unload statement:

```
Unload formname
```

Replace *formname* with the specific name of the form you want to unload, as in the following example:

```
Unload frmBillingInfo
```

If you want to unload the current form, you can use the reserved word Me:

```
Unload Me
```

Double-click the frame on frmSplash. Notice that the only line of code in Private Sub Frame1_Click is Unload Me. This is why the application stops when you click the form.

Showing and Hiding Forms

You use the Show method to display a form. If the form has not been loaded into memory, the Show method automatically loads it. If you are going to immediately display a form, don't bother loading it—just show it. The syntax for the Show method is as follows:

```
formname.Show [mode]
```

formname is the name of the form. The optional *mode* argument allows you to display the form as either modal or nonmodal. The default is 0 for nonmodal; if this argument is set to 1, the form loads as a modal form. To show `frmBillingInfo`, use the following steps:

1. Position your cursor in the `Private Sub Frame1_Click` procedure at the end of the `Unload Me` line.
2. Press Enter to create a blank line.
3. Type the following:

   `frmBillingInfo.Show`

4. Notice that you did not need to load `frmBillingInfo`. Press F5 to run the application.
5. Click the splash screen. It is removed from the display and the Billing Information window is shown.
6. Close the Billing Information window to end the application.

As the application stands, you cannot click the Cancel button on `frmBillingInfo` to end the application. To enable this feature, complete the following steps:

1. Display `frmBillingInfo`.
2. Double-click the Cancel button to open the Code window. The currently displayed procedure is `Private Sub cmdCancel_Click`.
3. On the blank line of this procedure, type **Unload Me**.
4. Press F5 to run the application.
5. Click the splash screen to display `frmBillingInfo`.
6. Click Cancel to end the application.

If you're designing an application that is graphics-intensive — or that will run on older, slower machines — you might want to preload your application's forms. As part of the `Form_Load` procedure of your splash screen, load all the forms your application is likely to use. This places the forms in memory, and when you eventually use the `Show` method to display them, they appear more quickly than if you hadn't preloaded them. In reality it takes basically the same amount of time to load the forms, but the user thinks the application runs faster because the forms are loaded at the beginning of the application, when the user expects to have to wait a little.

Keep in mind that this approach does consume memory. When a form is loaded, it stays in memory until it is unloaded or until the application ends.

If a form won't be used by an application again during the current run, as is the case with a splash screen, unload it so that the memory its objects and graphics are using is freed. If you think you'll need to use a particular form again during a program run, hide it instead of unloading it. Hiding a form makes it invisible but leaves it in memory. When a form is hidden, it's removed from the screen and its *Visible* property is set to `False`. The syntax for the `Hide` method is as follows:

```
formname.Hide
```

The following line, for example, hides `frmBillingInfo`:

```
frmBillingInfo.Hide
```

Now that you know how to load, unload, show, and hide forms, you're ready to automate this process for the remainder of your project. To do so, complete these steps:

1. If `frmBillingInfo` is not displayed, open it.

2. Double-click the OK button on this form to open the Code window. The `Private Sub cmdOK_Click` procedure is displayed.

3. Enter the following code for this procedure:
   ```
   Me.Hide
   frmInvoice.Show
   ```

You might want to indent these lines by pressing the Tab key at the beginning of each line. This makes the procedure easier to read.

4. Select `cmdTimer` from the Code window's Object box. The `Private Sub cmdTimer_Click` procedure is displayed.

5. Enter the following code for this procedure:
   ```
   frmTimer.Show
   ```

6. Close the Code window.

7. Open `frmInvoice` from the Project Explorer.

8. Double-click the OK button to open the Code window. The `Private Sub cmdPrint_Click` procedure is displayed.

9. Enter the following code for this procedure:
   ```
   Unload Me
   ```

10. You do not show another form in this procedure because it's the last form of the application. From the Code window's Object box, select `cmdCancel` to display `cmdCancel_Click`.

11. Enter the following code for this procedure:

    ```
    Unload Me
    ```

12. At this point you're putting the same code in both the Print and Cancel buttons of this form. You'll expand on this later. For now, close the Code window.

13. Open `frmTimer` from the Project Explorer.

14. Double-click the OK button to open the Code window. The `Private Sub cmdOK_Click` procedure is displayed.

15. Type the following code for this procedure:

    ```
    Unload Me
    ```

    This returns the user to the previous form, which in this case is `frmBillingInfo`. You do not have to load or show `frmBillingInfo` because it was not unloaded or hidden prior to the display of `frmTimer`.

16. From the Code window's Object box, select `cmdCancel` to display `cmdCancel_Click`.

17. Enter the following code for this procedure:

    ```
    Unload Me
    ```

18. At this point you're putting the same code in both the OK and Cancel buttons of this form. You'll expand on this later. For now, close the Code window.

19. Press F5 to run the application.

20. Click the splash screen to go to the Billing Information window.

21. Click the Timer button to display the Timer window.

22. Click OK to return to the Billing Information window.

23. Click OK to go to the Invoice window.

24. Click Cancel to end the application.

Your application now moves from window to window. As you progress through this lab you will build onto the existing code and add more functionality to the application.

Using Message Boxes and Input Boxes To Receive User Input

The first way you are going to use variables is in conjunction with message boxes and input boxes. These are two tools for getting information from your user through a dialog box interface.

Using the MsgBox Function

The message box you probably have seen most often is the one that displays when you try to exit an application without saving your work. Through a message box (a specialized form of a dialog box) you're prompted with a question like Do you want to save your work?—you can click Yes, No, or Cancel. Message boxes are created in VB with the MsgBox function.

At this point in the project, complete the following steps to add a message box to frmInvoice:

1. Open frmBillingInfo from the Project Explorer.
2. Double-click the OK button to open the Code window.
3. Add a blank line after the frmInvoice.Show statement in this procedure.
4. Type the following on the blank line:

   ```
   MsgBox "This prints a draft of the invoice."
   ```

You will add more statements to this procedure later in the chapter.

5. Press F5 to run the application.
6. Click the splash screen to go to the Billing Information window.
7. Click the Timer button to display the Timer window.
8. Click OK to return to the Billing Information window.
9. Click OK to display the message box shown in Figure 6-6.
10. Select Yes to display the Invoice window.
11. Click Cancel to end the application.

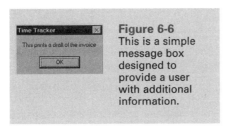

Figure 6-6
This is a simple message box designed to provide a user with additional information.

You could create the same result by adding a form to the project, changing the *Caption* property of the form, adding a label, changing the value of the label's *Caption* property, placing a command button on the form, and displaying the form using the Show method. Why do all that, however, when you can just type one line of code? This is the beauty of the MsgBox function.

Using the InputBox Statement

Another tool for getting a response from a user is the InputBox statement. The InputBox statement creates a dialog box that contains a text box. The user types a response into the text box and clicks OK. This saves the user's response to a variable. The syntax for this statement is as follows:

```
InputBox(prompt[, title] [, default] [, xpos] [, ypos] [, helpfile, context])
```

The *prompt* argument is required; this is a text string to be displayed as a message in the input box.

title is an optional argument; this is the text used in the title bar of the dialog box. If you do not provide a value for *title*, the name of the application is used.

If you want to provide a default value for the user's input, enter a string for the optional *default* argument. To accept the default response, the user just clicks OK or presses Enter.

xpos and *ypos* are optional and control the positioning of the input box. These arguments are numeric expressions that specify, respectively, the horizontal and vertical distance in twips of the left and top edges of the dialog box from the left and top edges of the screen. If *xpos* and *ypos* are omitted, the dialog box is horizontally and vertically centered.

The optional *helpfile* argument is a string that identifies the help file to be used to provide context-sensitive help for this dialog box. The optional *context* argument works in conjunction with *helpfile* by providing a numeric expression that is the help context number assigned to the appropriate help topic by the help author. If you provide a value for *context*, you must also provide a value for *helpfile*.

You need to add one input box to the time tracking application. This input box is displayed after the splash screen to ask for the user's name. While you add this, you'll also practice using a form-level variable:

1. Open frmSplash from the Project Explorer.
2. Double-click the frame to open the Code window. The Frame1_Click procedure is displayed.

3. Enter the following line of code below the `Unload Me` statement:

   `gsMyName = InputBox("Please enter your name: ")`

4. You need to add a module to the project, because you need a public variable to hold the name that's entered in the input box. Select Project, Add Module to display the Add Module dialog box.

5. Select `Module` and click Open to add the module to the project.

6. Type the following statement in the newly created module:

   `Public gsMyName as string`

7. Select File, Save `Module1`. Enter **Lab1** for the file name and click Save.

8. Press F5 to run the program.

9. Click the splash screen to display the input box (see Figure 6-7).

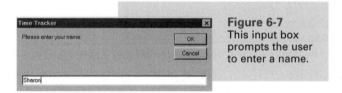

Figure 6-7
This input box prompts the user to enter a name.

10. Type your name and press Enter to go to the Billing Information window. The name you typed in the input box will be used in the next section of this chapter.

11. Click OK to go to the Invoice window.

12. Select Yes in response to the message box.

13. Click Cancel to end the application.

Save Here

Automatically Populating a Form

Before a form is displayed on-screen, its `Form_Load` procedure is executed. Therefore `Form_Load` is the perfect place to include the statements needed to populate control values. Typical operations include the following:

- Setting runtime properties
- Entering or selecting default values for controls
- Populating list and combo boxes
- Displaying current date information

The next sections demonstrate how to do these types of operations. You will work extensively with the Form_Load procedure for frmBillingInfo.

Setting Properties at Runtime

Some properties can only be set at runtime. Suppose that you want to place the date into a label. It won't do you any good to set this at design time, because the date is different every day. You need to do this at runtime. You set properties at runtime using the following syntax:

```
objectname.propertyname = value
```

objectname is the name of the control, form, or other object you're working with. *propertyname* is the name of the property as it appears in the Properties window. *value* is whatever value you want to set for this property. Here are some examples of property statements:

```
lblDate.Caption = "1/1/97"
lblCurrentDate.Caption = Format(Now, "m/d/yy")
gsMyName = InputBox("Please enter your name: ")
lblMyName.Caption = gsMyName
optMale.Value = True
chkPrintAllPages.Value = 1
```

In your application you need to set several properties during the Form_Load event procedure of frmBillingInfo. Complete the following steps to set these properties:

1. Open frmBillingInfo from the Project Explorer.

2. Double-click the form (not on a control) to open the Code window. The Form_Load procedure is displayed.

3. At the top of the procedure, below the Private Sub Form_Load() line, add a blank line. Starting on this blank line, type the following:

```
'gsMyName contains the name entered in the InputBox that
'precedes the display of this form.
lblBilledBy.Caption = gsMyName

'Most of the time the users bill by the hour so we want
'to select this for them.
optByHour.Value = True

'Using the Date function we are placing today's date in
'the Date masked edit control. The Format statement
'formats the result of the Date function.
mskDate.Text = Format(Date, "mm-dd-yy")
'The billing rate also needs to be set to 0.
txtBillingRate = "0.00"
```

To get more information on any of these properties, position your cursor in the property's name and press **F1**.

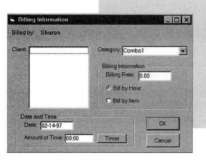

Figure 6-8
Dynamic pieces of information such as the user's name and today's date have been used in this window.

4. Press F5 to run the application.

5. Click the splash screen to display the input box.

6. Type your name and press Enter to go to the Billing Information window. Notice the controls that have runtime properties set (see Figure 6-8).

7. Click OK to go to the Invoice window.

8. Select Yes in response to the message box.

9. Click Cancel to end the application.

Notice the final line in the previous code. It has no property name as part of its syntax, yet it doesn't cause an error when you run the application. This is because each object has a default property. For example, the default property of a text box is *Text* and the default property of a label is *Caption*. If you are setting the object's default property, you can omit the property name from the statement.

It is recommended that you include the default property name anyway, just for readability.

Setting Properties and Using Methods with the With Statement

Sometimes you need to set multiple properties and use several methods on the same control, as in the following lines:

```
lstStates.Sorted = True
lstStates.MultiSelect = False
lstStates.AddItem "Georgia"
lstStates.AddItem "Florida"
lstStates.AddItem "Alabama"
lstStates.AddItem "North Carolina"
```

You see that it can become tedious typing the same object name over and over. VB provides a statement to save you from doing this—the With statement. The With statement precedes a series of property and method statements for an object.

You are now going to further initiate frmBillingInfo using the With statement. You are also going to set properties for frmTimer. Complete these steps:

1. The Code window should already be open and displaying the Form_Load procedure for frmBillingInfo.

2. Delete the following line from the procedure:

   ```
   lstClient.AddItem "ABC Corp."
   ```

3. Add a blank line before the End Sub statement.

4. Starting on this blank line, enter the following code:

   ```
   With lstClient
   'The AddItem method is used to add items to
   'a list box or combo box.
       .AddItem "ABC Corp."
       .AddItem "XYZ Inc."
       .AddItem "KD Dime Stores"
       .AddItem "Bigg Company"
       .AddItem "Bigger Company"
       .AddItem "Simons Widgets"
       .AddItem "Mark's Markers"
       .AddItem "Reginald G. Hunn, Esquire"
       .AddItem "Georgia's Gems"
       .AddItem "KennedyCo"
       .AddItem "Kathy's Moo Cows"
       'The next statement selects the first item in the
       'list. List item numbering begins with 0.
       .Selected(0) = True
   End With

   With cboCategory
       .AddItem "Divorce"
   ```

```
            .AddItem "Will"
            .AddItem "Retail Lease"
            .AddItem "Contract Review"
            .AddItem "Living Trust"
            .AddItem "Residental Lease"
            .AddItem "Employment Contract"
            .AddItem "Litigation"
            .ListIndex = 0
        End With
```

5. Open `frmTimer` from the Project Explorer.

6. Double-click the form (not on a control) to display the Code window. The `Form_Load` procedure is displayed.

7. Enter the following code for this procedure:

```
'The following public variables are used to track the time used. The
'Empty keyword removes any values previously placed in these variables.
gdtmStart = Empty
gdtmEnd = Empty

lblStart.Caption = "0:00"
lblEnd.Caption = "0:00"
txtTime.Text = "0:00"
```

8. Open the `Module1` module from the Project Explorer.

9. Add the following variable declarations:

```
Public gdtmStart As Date
Public gdtmEnd As Date
```

10. Press F5 to run the application.

11. Click the splash screen to display the input box.

12. Type your name and press Enter to go to the Billing Information window. The Billing Information window now has items in its list box and combo box (see Figure 6-9).

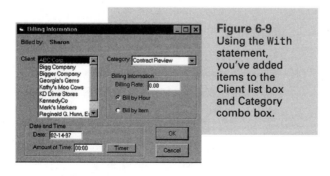

Figure 6-9
Using the With statement, you've added items to the Client list box and Category combo box.

13. Click the Timer button to display the Timer window. Notice the populated fields.

14. Click Cancel to return to the Billing Information window.

15. Click OK to go to the Invoice window.

16. Select Yes in response to the message box.

17. Click Cancel to end the application.

Using Date and Time Functions

In a previous exercise you used a function to populate the *Text* property of the mskDate masked edit control. That function was Date and the code statement looked like this:

```
mskDate.Text = Format(Date, "mm-dd-yy")
```

The Date function returns the current system date and has a very simple syntax:

```
Date
```

Let's reexamine the statement where you populated the *Text* property of the masked edit control. Notice the use of Format. In this application you need to display the date in *mm-dd-yy* format, but the Date function returns the date in *mm/dd/yy* format. To deal with this you use the Format function, which has the following syntax:

```
Format(expression[, format[, firstdayofweek[, firstweekofyear]]])
```

The *expression* argument contains the item to be formatted. *format* defines how the expression is to be formatted. This can be a named format or a user-defined format.

Adding the Timer Function

By selecting the Timer button on the Billing Information window, you can access the Timer window. This window allows the user to click a button and have the system track the amount of time they've spent on a task in stopwatch-like fashion. To add this feature to your application, complete these steps:

1. Open frmTimer from the Project Explorer.

2. Double-click the Start command button to open the Code window. The cmdStart_Click procedure is displayed.

3. Add the following lines to this procedure:

```
dtmStart = Time
lblStart.Caption = Format(dtmStart, "h:mm:ss")
```

4. Select `cmdEnd` from the Object box.

5. Add the following lines to the `cmdEnd_Click` procedure:

```
dtmEnd = Time
lblEnd.Caption = Format(dtmEnd, "h:mm:ss")
dtmTotalTime = dtmEnd - dtmStart
txtTime.Text = Format(dtmTotalTime, "hh:mm")
```

6. Select `(General)` from the Object box.

7. Add the following line to the `General Declarations` section:

```
Dim dtmStart As Date, dtmEnd As Date, dtmTotalTime As Date
```

8. Select `cmdOK` from the Object box.

9. Add the following lines to the `cmdOK_Click` procedure:

```
frmBillingInfo.txtAmountOfTime.Text = txtTime.Text
Unload Me
```

10. Run the application by pressing F5.

11. Click the splash screen to display the input box.

12. Type your name.

13. Select a client from the Client list.

14. Select a billing category from the Category drop-down list.

15. Type **10** in the Billing Rate text box.

16. Click the Timer button to display the Timer window.

17. Click the Start button.

18. Wait at least one minute and then click the End button. Notice that the amount of time has been calculated.

19. Click OK to return to the Billing Information window.

20. Click OK.

21. Select Yes in response to the message box.

22. Click Cancel to end the application.

Conditional Logic

Most of the functionality of a VB application can be attributed to the use of *conditional logic*. This project is going to use both `If` statements and `Select Case` statements to implement conditional logic.

Using the If Statement To Validate User Input

A great use of `If` statements is for *input validation*. This is the process of verifying that a user has entered acceptable values before you save the input data to a file. Typically you use an `If` statement to do this. You test to see if the value of a control's *Value* or *Text* property—depending on the control type—is correct. If it is, the procedure continues to run. If it isn't, you usually notify the user with a message, return the user to the offending control, and end the procedure without further processing. To return to the offending control, you use the `SetFocus` method, which has the following syntax:

```
controlname.SetFocus
```

For example, to return to the `txtBillingRate` text box, you would use the following statement:

```
txtBillingRate.SetFocus
```

The final step is to exit the procedure. This is done with the `Exit Sub` statement.

To add input validation to your time tracking application, complete the following steps:

1. Open `frmBillingInfo` from the Project Explorer.

2. Double-click the OK button to open the Code window. The `cmdOK_Click` procedure is displayed.

3. Modify this procedure so that it looks like the following:

```
Private Sub cmdOK_Click()
    If txtTime.Text = "0:00" Then
        MsgBox "You must enter the time spent."
        txtAmountOfTime.SetFocus
        Exit Sub
    ElseIf txtBillingRate.Text <= 0 Then
        MsgBox "You must enter the billing rate."
        txtBillingRate.SetFocus
        Exit Sub
    ElseIf lblBilledBy.Caption = "" Then
        lblBilledBy.Caption = InputBox("Please enter your name: ")
    End If
    Me.Hide
    frmInvoice.Show
End Sub
```

4. Run the application by pressing F5.

5. Click the splash screen to display the input box.

6. Do not type your name. (You want to check the validation of this item.)

7. Select a client from the Client list.

8. Select a billing category from the Category drop-down list.

9. Click OK.

10. You are reminded that you must enter the time spent. Click OK to return to the Billing Information window. Type **1:16** in the Amount of Time text box and click OK.

11. You are reminded that you need to enter the billing rate. Click OK to return to the Billing Information window. Type **10** in the Billing Rate text box and click OK.

12. You are prompted for your name. Type your name and click OK. The Invoice window is displayed.

13. Select Yes in response to the message box.

14. Click Cancel to end the application.

Using `Select Case` and `If` Statements To Populate a Form

Once you have determined that the user is entering valid values for data, you are ready to write the data to the desired location, either a file or another form. This process often involves the use of `Select Case` and `If` statements, as the following steps demonstrate:

1. Open `frmBillingInfo` from the Project Explorer.

2. Double-click the OK button to open the Code window. The `cmdOK_Click` procedure is displayed.

3. Modify this procedure so that it looks like the following:

```
Private Sub cmdOK_Click()
    Dim sngBilledTime As Single, iMinutes As Integer, iHours As Integer
    Dim iResponse As Integer

    If txtTime.Text = "0:00" Then
        MsgBox "You must enter the time spent."
        txtTime.SetFocus
        Exit Sub
    ElseIf txtBillingRate.Text <= 0 Then
        MsgBox "You must enter the billing rate."
        txtBillingRate.SetFocus
        Exit Sub
    ElseIf lblBilledBy.Caption = "" Then
        lblBilledBy.Caption = InputBox("Please enter your name: ")
    End If
```

```
        iResponse = MsgBox("Do you want to preview the invoice?", vbYesNo,
➥"Invoice")
    If iResponse = vbNo Then
        End
    Else
    Load frmInvoice
    With frmInvoice
        .lblBilledBy.Caption = frmBillingInfo.lblBilledBy
        .lblClient.Caption = frmBillingInfo.lstClient.Text
        .lblDate.Caption = frmBillingInfo.mskDate.Text
        .lblRate.Caption = Format(frmBillingInfo.txtBillingRate.Text,
➥"$####.00")
        .lblTotalTime.Caption = sngBilledTime
        .lblWorkCategory.Caption = frmBillingInfo.cboCategory.Text
        If frmBillingInfo.optByHour.Value = True Then
            .lblHourOrJob.Caption = "an hour"
            iMinutes = Val(Right(Me.txtTime.Text, 2))
            iHours = Left(Me.txtTime.Text, (InStr(1, Me.txtTime.Text,
➥":") - 1))

            Select Case iMinutes
                Case Is < 15
                    If iHours > 0 Then
                        sngBilledTime = iHours
                    Else
                        sngBilledTime = 0.5
                    End If
                Case Is >= 15 And iMinutes <= 30
                    sngBilledTime = iHours + 0.5
                Case Is > 30 And iMinutes <= 59
                    sngBilledTime = iHours + 1
            End Select
        .lblTotalTime.Caption = sngBilledTime
        .lblTotalAmount.Caption = _
Format(frmBillingInfo.txtBillingRate.Text * sngBilledTime, "$####.00")
        Else
            .lblHourOrJob = "for item"
            .lblTotalTime = "N/A"
            .lblTotalAmount = Format(.lblRate.Caption, "$####.00")
        End If
    End With

    Me.Hide

        frmInvoice.Show
    End If
End Sub
```

4. Run the application by pressing F5.

5. Click the splash screen to display the input box.

6. Type your name.

7. Select a client from the Client list.

8. Select a billing category from the Category drop-down list.

9. Type **10** in the Billing Rate text box.

10. Type **1:16** in the Amount of Time text box.

11. Click OK.

12. Select Yes in response to the message box. The Invoice window is displayed, as shown in Figure 6-10.

13. Click Cancel to end the application.

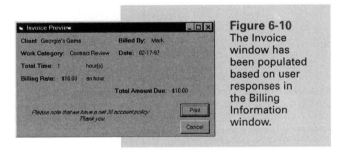

Figure 6-10
The Invoice window has been populated based on user responses in the Billing Information window.

Animating a Control Using the `For...Next` Statement

The `For...Next` statement can be used to animate a control such as an image. Animation is surprisingly easy to do. You are working with only two properties, *Left* and *Top*, of the control you want to animate. You make a control move by changing the values of these properties. For example, if you had an image named `imgHappyFace` that you wanted to move from left to right across a form, you could use the following code:

```
Dim i As Integer

For i = 1 to 100
    imgHappyFace.Left = imgHappyFace.Left + 10
Next
```

The following code would make the image move down and then back up the screen:

```
Dim i As Integer

For i = 1 to 100
    imgHappyFace.Left = imgHappyFace.Left + 10
Next
For I = 100 to 1 Step -1
    imgHappyFace.Left = imgHappyFace.Left - 10
Next
```

This final example would make the control move diagonally across the screen:

```
i As Integer

For i = 1 to 100
    imgHappyFace.Left = imgHappyFace.Left + 10
    imgHappyFace.Top = imgHappyFace.Top + 10
Next
```

For the time tracking application, you want to animate the logo that appears on the splash screen (a little "ooh" and "aah" from the users never hurts). To do so, you're going to use a *timer control* as the trigger that initiates the animation.

The timer control is a control that you place on a form but that remains invisible to the user at runtime. It is a tool for the programmer, not an interface tool. It allows for operations such as background processing and triggering events.

After you add a timer to a form, you need to set the *timer interval* using the *Interval* property. After you set the interval, you activate the timer by setting its *Enabled* property to True. Once a timer is enabled, it runs continuously. The program executes the timer event procedure according to the interval setting and will continue to execute the timer event at the specified interval until the user stops the program or the timer's *Enabled* property is set to False. To add animation to your application using the For...Next statement and a timer control, complete the following steps:

1. Open frmSplash from the Project Explorer.
2. Place a timer control on the form.
3. Set the timer's *Name* property to **tmrAnimate**.
4. Double-click the timer control to open the Code window.
5. Enter the following lines in the tmrAnimate_Timer procedure:

   ```
   Dim i As Integer

   For i = 1 To 40
       imgLogo.Left = imgLogo.Left + 10
       imgLogo.Top = imgLogo.Top + 10
   Next
   ```

```
For i = 40 To 1 Step -1
    imgLogo.Left = imgLogo.Left - 10
    imgLogo.Top = imgLogo.Top - 10
Next
```

6. Select `Form` from the Object box.

7. Add the following lines to the `Form_Load` procedure:

```
tmrAnimate.Interval = 1000
tmrAnimate.Enabled = True
```

8. Select `KeyPress` from the Event box.

9. In this step you want to give the user the ability to press the spacebar to stop and start the animation. Modify the `Form_KeyPress` procedure so that it matches the following:

```
Private Sub Form_KeyPress(KeyAscii As Integer)
    'KeyAscii is passed to this procedure as an argument.
    If KeyAscii = vbKeySpace Then
    'This sets the spacebar up as a toggle. The first time
    'a user presses the spacebar, the animation stops. If he
    'presses it again, it starts again, and so on.
        tmrAnimate.Enabled = Not tmrAnimate.Enabled
    Else
        Unload Me
        gsMyName = InputBox("Please enter your name: ")
        frmBillingInfo.Show
    End If
End Sub
```

10. Press F5 to run the application.

11. Notice the animated logo. Press your spacebar to stop the animation. Press the spacebar again to restart the animation.

12. Click the splash screen to display the input box.

13. Type your name and press Enter.

14. Click Cancel to end the application.

Summary

This chapter concentrated on giving you skills you need to increase the functionality of your application. You now know how to move from one form to another, and when to unload a form as opposed to hiding it. You also know how to populate a form's controls and validate user input.

Using conditional logic you can test user input and perform appropriate actions based on that input. You even know how to add a few bells and whistles to your application by adding animation.

The development of this application is almost finished. You still need to provide a way for users to print the invoice. After that, you'll be ready to test and debug the application. Once the application is working, you'll want to distribute it. You'll learn to do all of that in Chapter 7, "Testing the Time Tracking System."

CHAPTER 7

Testing the Time Tracking System

This chapter helps you complete the time tracking system. The application development is finished except for one feature, printing the invoice. You'll create that feature in this chapter. You'll also go through the process of testing your application. As part of the testing process you typically find things that you didn't expect in your applications. Whether you call them mistakes, bugs, or "undocumented features," you need to use the debugging techniques presented in this chapter to locate and resolve them. After that, you'll be ready to distribute your application. This chapter teaches you how to prepare for distribution by making your application an executable file.

Printing the Invoice Form

Remember that this programming environment is called Visual Basic for a reason —the language has its roots in the Basic language. With that in mind, you're ready for the scary truth about printing with Visual Basic. If you want to print using only the capabilities of VB, without add-ins, you have just two choices: `Print` and `PrintForm`.

The use of `PrintForm` *is sometimes referred to as quick-and-dirty printing because you get a printout of whatever you have on your form. There's no chance for additional formatting.*

`Print` is the same command you may have used in older versions of Basic, such as GW-Basic. With this command you create a printout line by line. As much fun as that can be—yes, that's sarcasm—you're going to instead use `PrintForm` when completing this project. `PrintForm` is a method that was added to the VB language to do exactly what it implies—print a form.

This section walks you through the use of `Print` and `PrintForm`. To support more sophisticated printing capabilities, you'll want to use Crystal Reports, which is discussed in Chapter 17, "Testing the Client Management System."

Using the `PrintForm` Method

If you want to print the majority of the material on a form, you can use the `PrintForm` method. This actually makes a lot of sense, because you should design forms to look like their paper counterparts. Since they mimic paper forms, it stands to reason that you should be able to print online forms from your application and have them be immediately useful.

You can use `PrintForm` to send the entire contents of a form to the printer. When you do so, there are two major issues. First, `PrintForm` prints forms at the current resolution of your display adapter, which in some cases may be quite small. Second, when you tell VB to use `PrintForm`, it takes you literally—it prints everything on the form, including command buttons.

Complete these steps to see the basic results of using the `PrintForm` method:

1. Open `frmInvoice` from the Project Explorer.

2. Double-click the `cmdPrint` command button to open the Code window. The `cmdPrint_Click` procedure is displayed.

3. Modify this procedure so that it looks like the following:

```
Private Sub cmdPrint_Click()
    PrintForm
    Unload Me
End Sub
```

4. Run the application by pressing F5.

5. Click the splash screen to display the input box.

6. Type your name and press Enter to display the Billing Information window.

7. Select a client from the Client list.

8. Select a billing category from the Category drop-down list.

9. Type **50** in the Billing Rate text box.

10. Type **1:16** in the Amount of Time text box.

11. Click OK.

12. Select Yes in response to the message box.

13. Click Print to print the form and end the application.

As you can see from the hard copy version of this form, you are printing a lot of things you don't want. The following section explains how to write code to deal with this.

Hiding Unwanted Objects

When you use `PrintForm`, you want the output to look like a paper form. A paper form typically does not have a command button printed in the corner. To avoid printing unwanted objects, you need to hide them before printing the form. This is done with the *Visible* property for each object. Before executing the `PrintForm` method, set `False` as the value for the *Visible* property of each control you don't want printed.

If you don't unload the form after printing, you need to return these *Visible* property values to `True`. Imagine if users could not read a form after printing it, because the OK button had been hidden! This would not make you very popular! If you do unload the form after printing, though, don't bother setting the controls' *Visible* property values back to `True`—they'll automatically return to the design-time settings.

To give your application the capability to print the Invoice form, complete these steps:

1. Open `frmInvoice` from the Project Explorer.

2. Double-click the `cmdPrint` command button to open the Code window. The `cmdPrint_Click` procedure is displayed.

3. Modify this procedure so that it looks like the following:

```
Private Sub cmdPrint_Click()
    cmdPrint.Visible = False
    cmdCancel.Visible = False
    PrintForm
    Unload Me
End Sub
```

4. Run the application by pressing F5.

5. Click the splash screen to display the input box.

6. Type your name and press Enter to display the Billing Information form.

7. Select a client from the Client list.

8. Select a billing category from the Category drop-down list.

9. Type **10** in the Billing Rate text box.

10. Type **1:16** in the Amount of Time text box.

11. Click OK.

12. Select Yes in response to the message box.

13. Click Print to print the form and end the application.

When you printed this form you probably noticed another problem with the form. If you used a laser jet or ink jet printer, you got an undesirable gray background on your printout.

Using the For Each...Next Statement

To get rid of the gray background on printouts, you need to change the *BackColor* property of the form and all controls on the form. You can do this the hard way or the easy way. The hard way is to change the *BackColor* property of each individual object as follows:

```
' &HFFFFFF is the hexadecimal value for the color white.
lblClient.BackColor = &HFFFFFF
lblBilledBy.BackColor = &HFFFFFF
lblWorkCategory.BackColor = &HFFFFFF
lblDate.BackColor = &HFFFFFF
    .
    .
    .
```

An easier way to do this is with the For Each...Next statement. This statement lets you perform the same operation on multiple objects. You first create an object variable where each control can temporarily reside as the operations are being done to it. Since you want to do this action to each control on the form, you can use the Controls collection, which represents each control on a form. Using this collection with the For Each...Next statement allows you to set the *BackColor* property of each control on the form without even knowing a control's name. Whether you have one control on the form or a hundred, it takes the same amount of code to do this operation. To code this for the time tracking application, complete the following steps:

1. Open frmInvoice from the Project Explorer.

2. Double-click the cmdPrint command button to open the Code window. The cmdPrint_Click procedure is displayed.

3. Modify this procedure so that it looks like the following:

```
Private Sub cmdPrint_Click()
    Dim x As Object
```

```
        cmdPrint.Visible = False
        cmdCancel.Visible = False

        'Change the BackColor of the current form.
        Me.BackColor = &HFFFFFF

        'Change the BackColor of all controls.
        For Each x In frmInvoice.Controls
            x.BackColor = &HFFFFFF
        Next

        PrintForm
        Unload Me
    End Sub
```

Save Here

4. Run the application by pressing F5.

5. Click the splash screen to display the input box.

6. Type your name and press Enter to display the Billing Information form.

7. Select a client from the Client list.

8. Select a billing category from the Category drop-down list.

9. Type **10** in the Billing Rate text box.

10. Type **1:16** in the Amount of Time text box.

11. Click OK.

12. Select Yes in response to the message box.

13. Click Print to print the form and end the application. Figure 7-1 shows how the printout looks.

Client:	Georgia's Gems		Billed By:	Hunter
Work Category:		Retail Lease	Date:	04-13-97
Total Time:	5	hour(s)		
Billing Rate:	$100.00	an hour		
			Total Amount Due:	$500.00

Please note that we have a net 30 account policy.
Thank you.

Figure 7-1
The new printed form doesn't show the Print and Cancel buttons, and doesn't have a gray background.

Ending an Application

Up to this point, you've ended the application by unloading the current form and not loading any other form. Frankly, that's the wrong way to do it. The correct way is to use the End statement. To add this statement to the time tracking application, complete these steps:

1. If frmInvoice is not open already, open it from the Project Explorer and access the Code window. Select cmdCancel from the Object box to display the cmdCancel_Click procedure.

2. Modify this procedure so that it matches the following:
   ```
   Private Sub cmdCancel_Click()
       End
   End Sub
   ```

3. Open frmBillingInfo from the Project Explorer.

4. Double-click the cmdOK button to open the Code window. The cmdOK_Click procedure is displayed.

5. From the Object box of the Code window, select cmdCancel to display the cmdCancel_Click procedure.

6. Modify this procedure so that it matches the following:
   ```
   Private Sub cmdCancel_Click()
       End
   End Sub
   ```

7. Open frmSplash from the Project Explorer.

8. Double-click the frame control to open the Code window. The Frame1_Click procedure is displayed.

9. Modify this procedure so that it matches the following:
   ```
   Private Sub Frame1_Click()
       Dim iResponse As Integer

       Unload Me

   'TryAgain is a line label.
   TryAgain:
       gsMyName = InputBox("Please enter your name: ")
       'Test to see if the user clicked Cancel.
       If gsMyName = "" Then
           iResponse = MsgBox("Do you want to leave the application?",
   ➡vbYesNo)
           If iResponse = vbOK Then
               End
           Else
   ```

```
'Let the user type in their name.
    GoTo TryAgain
End If
frmBillingInfo.Show
    End If


    frmBillingInfo.Show
End Sub
```

10. Save the forms and the project, but do not run the application.

Notice a couple of new things in this `Frame1_Click` procedure. The first is the use of a line label and the `GoTo` statement. `GoTo` allows you to branch unconditionally to a specific statement. `GoTo` is supported in Visual Basic and is used in conjunction with line labels. VB knows that a statement is a line label if a colon (:) terminates the statement.

> You might have used the `GoTo` statement in forms of the original Basic language. Statements such as `GoTo 300` were common in Basic.

A line label is a descriptive term that you use to create a branching point within a procedure. Line labels must be terminated with a colon.

The other thing you haven't done earlier in this project is testing to see if the user has clicked the Cancel button on an input box. When the Cancel button on an input box is clicked, the variable holding the user's response receives an empty string (""). You need to ask the user if they meant to exit the application, because they may have pressed Enter accidentally without entering text—this would result in the variable being set to an empty string.

The last step instructed you not to run the application because you're going to work with this updated procedure during the testing and debugging sections later in this chapter.

> A mistake has been made in this code on purpose so that it can be used for the testing and debugging sections of this chapter.

Testing Your Application

Testing is the process of guessing everything your user can do to your application. During testing you want to verify that, for example, when a user clicks a certain button, the expected result occurs. You are looking for the unexpected, such as incorrect results from a calculation or an inappropriate response to an action—especially things that might result in the premature termination of the application.

There are several ways to minimize these types of mistakes in your application. The first way is to spend time, as you did in earlier chapters, carefully designing the application. Understanding the goals and features of the application gives you a clear picture of the events you need to support in the application, and how to respond to those events.

Consistent *naming conventions* for variables and objects will help you debug, support, and maintain your application. For more information on naming conventions, see Appendix A, "Recommended Naming and Programming Conventions." Another thing that helps you maintain your application is adequate commenting. *Comments* make your approach easier to understand and they act as aids if you need to analyze your code. When deciding where to comment, assume that you will not be the one supporting the application in the future. Add the type of comments you would want to see in an application you were supporting but did not write. In other words, the Golden Rule applies.

To test the changes you've made to the time tracking application, use the following steps:

1. Run the application by pressing F5.
2. Click the splash screen to display the input box.
3. The first thing you want to test is the ability to exit the application from this input box. Press the Cancel key. The `Do you want to leave the application?` message is displayed. Select Yes.
4. Instead of the application ending, the input box was displayed again! This is a problem you'll need to debug.
5. Type your name and press Enter.
6. Click Cancel to end the application.

By testing the modification to the application, you've found a bug. When you click Cancel and select Yes, the application should terminate—but it doesn't. Now is the time to debug.

Debugging Your Application

The only mistakes you've made to this point probably have been typos. These typos, otherwise known as *syntax errors*, were pointed out to you as you typed. (VB checks each statement for syntax errors when you press Enter.) The error you discovered while testing your application in the previous section, however, is a *logic error*. There's nothing wrong with the language of the statement, yet it does not do what you intend it to do. This means that something is wrong with the logic of the statement. You'll find that most of your debugging effort will deal with logic errors, but you should be familiar with all three basic types of programming errors:

- **Syntax errors**—As was already pointed out, a syntax error occurs when you incorrectly use the VB language.

- **Runtime errors**—A runtime error is any error that makes a program stop running. Sometimes this is the fault of the programmer (for example, if you mistype the name of a procedure when calling it from another procedure). Other times it's the result of a user action that you cannot control or even predict (for example, if you have a program that needs to save something to a floppy drive and the user forgets to insert a diskette).

- **Logic errors**—A logic error is the result of a programmer mistake. Logic errors typically have to do with your approach to a situation. More often than not, these errors occur when you set up conditional tests, and a mistake somewhere in the test produces an incorrect result at runtime. Sometimes logic errors result from mistakes in calculations. If unexpected results occur during your application, but the application continues to run, you have a logic error.

Pausing Program Execution

One technique for locating logic errors is to force the application to go to *break mode*. Break mode temporarily suspends the execution of the application. This allows you to examine the values of variables and properties at that point in application execution and apply other debugging techniques. When the application is in break mode, you can do the following actions:

- Change the code of the application
- Examine the values of variables, properties, and statements
- Set the values of variables and properties
- Run VB statements using the Immediate window
- Determine which active procedures have been called

In the time tracking application you know that the error occurs somewhere after the InputBox statement. Therefore a good candidate line to break on is the InputBox statement itself. There are several ways to break program execution:

- Add the Stop statement to your code
- Select a statement to use as a breakpoint and select <u>D</u>ebug, <u>T</u>oggle Breakpoint from the menu
- Select a statement to use as a breakpoint and press F9
- Select a statement to use as a breakpoint and click the margin indicator bar of the Code window

Caution

> Be sure to remove all Stop statements from your procedures before you create an EXE file. If a compiled VB application encounters a Stop statement, it treats it as an End statement and immediately terminates execution.

The last three actions in the previous list create a *breakpoint*, which can only be set on a line of executable code. You can't set a breakpoint on a line containing nonexecutable code—this includes comments, variable and constant declaration statements, and blank lines.

Tip

> A line that has been set as a breakpoint changes color based on your current Editor Format settings. To change these, select <u>T</u>ools, <u>O</u>ptions and select the Editor Format page.

The same three actions can also be used to remove a breakpoint, since breakpoints are toggle items. If you've placed several breakpoints in your application and want to remove them all at once, you can do so by selecting <u>D</u>ebug, <u>C</u>lear All Breakpoints (or by pressing Ctrl+Shift+F9).

You need to set a breakpoint at the MsgBox statement in the time tracking application. Use the following steps to do this:

1. If the Code window for the Frame1_Click procedure is not open, open frmSplash from the Project Explorer. Double-click the frame to display the Frame1_Click procedure.

2. Locate and select the following line:

```
gsMyName = InputBox("Please enter your name: ")
```

3. Set a breakpoint for this line by selecting Debug, Toggle Breakpoint. The line changes color and a circle is displayed beside it in the margin indicator bar (see Figure 7-2).

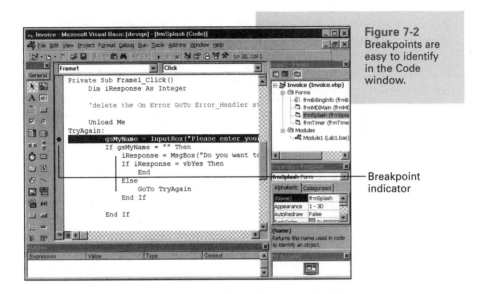

Figure 7-2
Breakpoints are easy to identify in the Code window.

4. To clear this breakpoint (and all other breakpoints if you happen to have any), select Debug, Clear All Breakpoints.

5. To set a breakpoint directly using the margin indicator bar, click the margin indicator bar next to the following line:

```
iResponse = MsgBox("Do you want to leave the application?", vbYesNo)
```

Now that you've set a breakpoint in this procedure, you're ready to debug the procedure using tools such as *stepping* and the Immediate window. Several tools are available to assist you in locating errors in your applications. Two of the most useful tools—especially when you're trying to debug If and Select Case statements —work hand-in-hand with breakpoints. These are the Step Into and Step Over menu items on the Debug menu; the following section explains how they work.

Stepping Through Your Code

In the previous section you set a breakpoint for the MsgBox statement of the Frame1_Click procedure. A breakpoint stops execution of the application *before* executing the line that contains the breakpoint. What you need to do next is to step though your code, starting with the MsgBox line, to observe what happens.

There are two ways to do this, *Step Into* and *Step Over*. Both stepping methods allow you to see line-by-line execution of the application so you can trace the flow of logic statements (such as If) and inspect variable and property values.

There's just one difference between the two types of stepping. If you're debugging a procedure that calls one or more other procedures and you do not want to step through any called procedures, use Step Over. Step Over does not do line-by-line execution of called procedures. If you want to observe line-by-line execution of all statements, including the statements in any called procedures, use Step Into.

You've already set the breakpoint for this procedure, so the application will run uninterrupted to that point and then stop to let you see what's going on. To step through your procedure, complete the following steps:

1. Press F5 to run the application.
2. Click the frame on the splash screen. This calls the Frame1_Click procedure. The input box that lets you enter your name is displayed.
3. Click the Cancel button. The Code window is displayed with the MsgBox statement highlighted (see Figure 7-3).

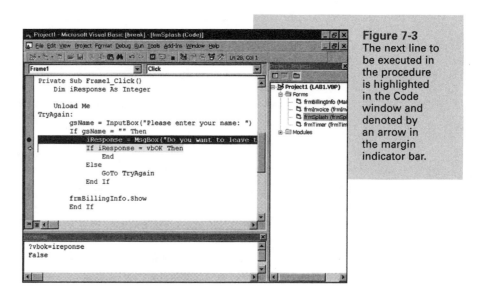

Figure 7-3
The next line to be executed in the procedure is highlighted in the Code window and denoted by an arrow in the margin indicator bar.

4. Select Debug, Step Into to execute the highlighted statement.
5. The message box is displayed. Select Yes.

6. Press F8 to continue stepping through the procedure. Pressing F8 is equivalent to selecting <u>D</u>ebug, Step <u>I</u>nto. This takes you to the first line of the `If` statement.

7. To see if `iResponse` is being handled as equal to `vbOK`, press F8.

8. Notice that the next line to be executed is the `Else` statement. This means that `iResponse` is being handled as not equal to `vbOK`.

9. Position your pointer over the `iResponse` variable. A ToolTip is displayed telling you that `iResponse = 6`.

10. Select <u>R</u>un, <u>E</u>nd to end the application execution.

To further test your application, you can use the Immediate window while you're stepping through the procedure. This allows you to test the value of a variable such as `iResponse`.

Using the Immediate Window

The Immediate window expands your debugging capabilities. This window is automatically opened and displayed below the Code window when the application enters break mode. Tasks you can do with the Immediate window include:

- Printing variable and property values while an application is running
- Changing the value of a variable or property while an application is running
- Typing new statements and immediately executing them
- Copying and pasting existing code lines and immediately executing them
- Calling a procedure as you would in program code
- Viewing debugging output while an application is running

Printing Values in the Immediate Window

When you're running an application you can, as you saw earlier, learn the value of a variable by positioning your pointer above the variable name while in break mode. Another way to track the value of a variable (or a property) is by using the Immediate window. There are three ways to print values to the Immediate window:

- Use the `Print` method in the Immediate window
- Use a question mark (?) in the Immediate window (this is shorthand for the `Print` method)
- Add a `Debug.Print` statement directly in a procedure

Using the `Print` Method in the Immediate Window

You can use the `Print` method (or the question mark) to test the values of variables and properties. To print the value of the `iResponse` variable in the Immediate window, use the following steps:

1. Press F5 to run the application.

2. Click the frame on the splash screen. This calls the `Frame1_Click` procedure, and the input box that lets you enter your name is displayed.

3. Click the Cancel button. The Code window is displayed with the `MsgBox` statement highlighted.

4. Select <u>D</u>ebug, Step <u>I</u>nto to execute the highlighted statement.

5. The message box is displayed. Select <u>Y</u>es.

6. Press F8 (or select <u>D</u>ebug, Step <u>I</u>nto) to continue stepping through the procedure. This takes you to the first line of the `If` statement.

7. To print the value of `iResponse` in the Immediate window, activate the Immediate window by clicking it and then type the following line:

   `? iResponse`

8. Press Enter to see the value of `iResponse`. The resulting value is displayed on the next line of the Immediate window (see Figure 7-4).

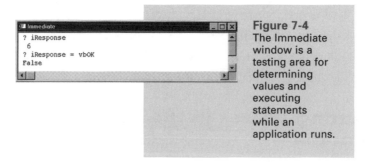

Figure 7-4
The Immediate window is a testing area for determining values and executing statements while an application runs.

9. You can use the Immediate window to test your application further. Type the following line in the Immediate window:

   `? iResponse = vbOK`

10. Press Enter. The result of this statement is `False`, which gives you a clue about where the problem is in the procedure.

11. Select <u>R</u>un, <u>E</u>nd to end the application.

> **If you want to execute a statement that has been used previously in the Immediate window, just move the insertion point to that line and press Enter.**

Printing from Application Code

The disadvantage to the previous approach of using the Immediate window is that you have to find a point in the application's execution where you can access the Immediate window. You might prefer instead to use the `Debug.Print` statement. This statement is added directly to a procedure and sends text to the Immediate window. You can examine the text after the application runs. To use `Debug.Print` with the time tracking application, complete the following steps:

1. Select <u>D</u>ebug, <u>C</u>lear All Breakpoints to remove any breakpoint that's currently set.

2. Modify your `Frame1_Click` procedure so that it matches the following (changes are in bold):

```
Private Sub Frame1_Click()
    Dim iResponse As Integer

    Unload Me
TryAgain:
    gsMyName = InputBox("Please enter your name: ")
    If gsMyName = "" Then
        iResponse = MsgBox("Do you want to leave the application?",
➥vbYesNo)
        Debug.Print "The value of iResponse is " & iResponse
        If iResponse = vbOK Then
            End
        Else
            GoTo TryAgain
        End If
    End If
    frmBillingInfo.Show
End Sub
```

3. Run the application by pressing F5.

4. Click the frame on the splash screen. This calls the `Frame1_Click` procedure, and the input box that lets you enter your name is displayed.

5. Click the Cancel button.

6. The message box is displayed. Select <u>Y</u>es.

7. The input box is displayed again. (This is the problem you're debugging.) Type your name and press Enter.

8. The Billing Information form is displayed. Click Cancel to end the application.

9. Look at the contents of the Immediate window. As Figure 7-5 shows, you can see that the value of iResponse is 6.

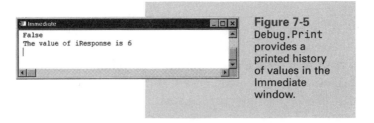

Figure 7-5
Debug.Print provides a printed history of values in the Immediate window.

Tip   **You do not need to remove `Debug.Print` statements from your application before compiling it. These statements are automatically removed during the compile process.**

Using Watches

You probably have a good idea by now what the problem is with this procedure. Before you correct the problem, however, try one more debugging technique called *watch expressions*. Watch expressions are user-defined expressions that let you observe the behavior of a variable or an expression. Watch expressions are created by selecting Debug, Add Watch at design time or in break mode at runtime. A watch expression can be any valid VB expression.

You can create three types of watch expressions. The first is Watch Expression, which is used to monitor an expression without affecting the execution of the application. The second is Break When Value is True. If you want to see, for example, when iResponse becomes equal to vbOK, use this type. The last type is Break When Value Changes—when this is selected, program execution automatically breaks when the value of the expression changes.

To use a watch expression to provide the value of iResponse, follow these steps:

1. If the `Frame1_Click` procedure is not already displayed, access it.
2. Select <u>D</u>ebug, <u>A</u>dd Watch to display the Add Watch dialog box (see Figure 7-6).

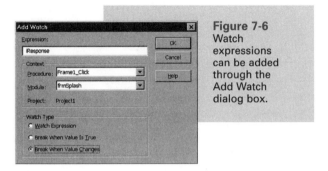

Figure 7-6
Watch expressions can be added through the Add Watch dialog box.

3. In the <u>E</u>xpression text box, type **iResponse**. The items in the Context frame allow you to control where this variable is a watch expression. Since this is a variable with local scope, no changes need to be made to these items.
4. Select the Break When Value <u>C</u>hanges option button.
5. Click OK.
6. Press F5 to run the application.
7. Click the frame to display the input box.
8. Click Cancel.
9. Select Yes in response to the prompt about exiting the application. This assigns a value to `iResponse`. Since you've created a watch expression that breaks when the value of `iResponse` changes, the execution breaks and the Watch window is displayed (see Figure 7-7).

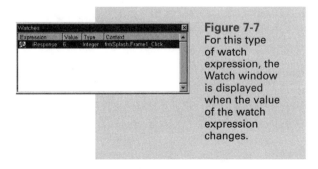

Figure 7-7
For this type of watch expression, the Watch window is displayed when the value of the watch expression changes.

10. Press F5 to continue the execution of the application.

11. Type your name in the input box and press Enter.

12. Click Cancel to end the application.

If you've created a watch expression and need to modify it, you can select Debug, Edit Watch. This displays the Edit Watch dialog box that allows you to change the setup of the watch expression.

If you want to quickly create a watch expression, highlight the expression in the Code window and select Debug, Quick Watch (or press Shift + F9).

Correcting the Error

At this point you're definitely ready to correct the error in the time tracking application. The problem is that the message box being displayed has Yes and No buttons on it, but the If statement is looking for vbOK. iResponse can never equal vbOK. Use the following steps to correct the problem:

1. If the Frame1_Click procedure is not currently displayed, access it.

2. Right-click the watch expression listed in the Watch window. Select Delete Watch to remove it.

3. Modify the Frame1_Click procedure so that it matches the following (changes are in bold):

```
Private Sub Frame1_Click()
    Dim iResponse As Integer

    Unload Me
TryAgain:
    gsMyName = InputBox("Please enter your name: ")
    If gsMyName = "" Then
        iResponse = MsgBox("Do you want to leave the application?",
➥vbYesNo)
    'Delete the Debug.Print statement that is currently located here.
        If iResponse = vbYes Then
            End
        Else
            GoTo TryAgain
        End If
```

```
    End If

    frmBillingInfo.Show
End Sub
```

Notice that you've just deleted one line and changed another line.

4. Run the application by pressing F5.

5. Click the frame to display the input box.

6. Click Cancel.

7. Select <u>Y</u>es in response to the message box. The application's execution correctly terminates.

Error Handling

Debugging is the process of dealing with all the problems you can predict and correct. But what about things you cannot control and cannot predict? Unless your application is very small, there's no way for you to predict every possible thing that can happen while your application runs. You cannot control the operating system or hardware platform, and you definitely cannot control the user. To paraphrase a popular saying, users do the darnedest things!

To handle unexpected scenarios you need to write an *error handler*. This is a routine for trapping and dealing with errors in your application. There are three basic steps to creating an error handler:

1. Set an error trap. This involves telling the application where to branch when an error occurs.

2. Write an error-handling routine (this is where you branch when an error occurs).

3. Provide an exit from the error-handling routine.

There are two basic reasons to include error handling in your applications. One is to create robust applications. This means runtime errors are dealt with so that a sudden termination, commonly known as a *crash*, does not occur. An application that crashes does not endear itself to the user. The other reason is to allow for graceful exits in the event that your error handler cannot resolve the problem. Whenever possible, you want to save the user's work before ending the application.

Setting an Error Trap

To set an error trap, you need to use the `On Error` statement in each procedure that might encounter errors. The `On Error` statement tells VB what to do in the case of an error. Only one error trap at a time can be enabled in a given procedure.

There are two different approaches to handling errors. One is *in-line error handling*. In this case, you use one of the statements listed in Table 7-1.

Table 7-1 Summary of On Error Statements	
Statement	**Description**
On Error Resume	If a runtime error occurs, execution resumes at the statement that caused the error.
On Error Resume Next	If a runtime error occurs, execution resumes at the statement after the one that caused the error.

In-line error handling is not the preferred way to handle errors. A better way is to use an error trap that jumps to an error-handling routine. This gives you the flexibility to respond to a variety of errors. To set an error trap that jumps to an error-handling routine, use the `On Error GoTo` *line* statement, where *line* represents the line label preceding the error-handling code. The following is a basic skeleton of a procedure that includes an error-handling routine:

```
Sub With_Error_Handler()
    On Error GoTo ErrorHandler
    'The body of the procedure goes here.
    'The next statement, Exit Sub or Exit Function (whatever is appropriate),
    'goes before the line label for the error handler. This is done so that
    'if there are no errors, the error-handling routine is skipped.
    Exit Sub
'The next line is the line label for the error-handling routine.
'Don't forget to end the line label with a colon.
ErrorHandler:
    'The code for the error handler goes here.
    .
    .
    .

End Sub
```

The code for the error-handling routine processes the error that was generated, by evaluating the error and determining a course of action. This evaluation process is done with either an `If` statement or a `Select Case` statement. You should always include an `Else` statement to handle all unanticipated errors.

To disable an error handler, use an `On Error GoTo 0` statement in the procedure after the initial `On Error` statement. This is useful if you're testing an application and do not want to see or deal with errors.

As part of the `If` or `Select Case` statement, you need to test the value of the `Err` object's *Number* property. The `Err` object contains information about runtime errors. Its *Number* property can be used to return the numeric value specifying a particular error. Once you've determined what the error is, you have four options:

To do this action	Use this statement
Return to the statement that caused the error	Resume
Return to the line after the one that caused the error	Resume Next
Go to a line label in the procedure	Resume *line*
End the procedure or application	End

To add an error-handling routine to the `Frame1_Click` procedure of the time tracking application, complete these steps:

1. If the `Frame1_Click` procedure is not currently displayed, access it.

2. Modify this procedure so that it matches the following (changes are in bold):

```
Private Sub Frame1_Click()
    Dim iResponse As Integer

    On Error GoTo Error_Handler

    Unload Me
TryAgain:
    gsMyName = InputBox("Please enter your name: ")
    If gsMyName = "" Then
        iResponse = MsgBox("Do you want to leave the application?",
➥vbYesNo)
        If iResponse = vbYes Then
            End
        Else
            GoTo TryAgain
        End If
    End If
```

```
        frmBillingInfo.Show
    Exit Sub
Error_Handler:
    Select Case Err
    Case 7
        MsgBox "Out of Memory" & Chr(13) & "Close nonessential
➥applications."
        Resume
    Case 35 To 51
        MsgBox "Contact the Help Desk."
        Exit Sub
    Case 482
        MsgBox "Check printer for error."
        Dim iPrintResponse As Integer
        iPrintResponse = MsgBox("Do you wish to try to print again?",
➥vbYesNo)
        If iPrintResponse = vbYes Then
          Resume
        Else
          Resume Next
        End If
    Case Else
        MsgBox "Unrecoverable error. Exiting application."
        End
    End Select
End Sub
```

3. Save frmSplash.

> Use the `Error` function if you want to use the text of an error
> message in a message box. Your statement should look similar
> to this:
>
> `MsgBox Error(Err)`
>
> Search for Trappable Errors in online help to get a list of the
> error numbers your error handler should trap.

Creating a Centralized Error Handler

Rather than including an error-handling routine in each of your procedures, you
should create a *centralized error handler.* This is a separate function that processes
each error that's generated and then, based on the error number, initiates an
action. Each procedure still requires an `On Error` statement. This statement

branches to an area of the application that has a `Select Case` statement to process the results returned by the centralized error handler. There are five possible cases for this `Select Case` statement:

Case	Action
1	Perform a Resume
2	Perform a Resume Next
3	Perform a Resume *line*
4	Exit the procedure
5	End the application

For each error, a value from 1 through 5 is returned from the centralized error handler function to the local procedure.

To add a centralized error handler, use the following steps:

1. Open `Module1` from the Project Explorer.
2. Select <u>T</u>ools, Add <u>P</u>rocedure to display the Add Procedure dialog box (see Figure 7-8).

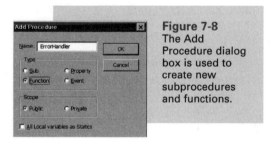

Figure 7-8
The Add Procedure dialog box is used to create new subprocedures and functions.

3. In the <u>N</u>ame text box, type **ErrorHandler**.
4. For Type, select <u>F</u>unction.
5. Click OK to create the function.
6. Type the following code for this function:

```
Function ErrorHandler(iErrNum) As Integer
    Select Case iAction
    Case 5
        'Invalid procedure call
        MsgBox Error(iErrNum) & " Contact Help Desk."
        iAction = 2
    Case 7
        'Out of memory
```

```
            MsgBox "Close all unnecessary applications."
            iAction = 1
        Case 11
            'Division by zero
            MsgBox "Zero is not a valid value."
            iAction = 1
        Case 48, 49, 51
            'Error in loading DLL
            MsgBox iErrNum & " Contact Help Desk."
            iAction = 5
        Case 57
            'Device I/O error
            MsgBox "Insert Disk in Drive A."
            iAction = 1
        Case Else
            MsgBox "Unrecoverable Error."
            iAction = 5
        End Select

        ErrorHandler = iAction
    End Function
```

7. Open frmInvoice from the Project Explorer.

8. Double-click the cmdPrint button to open the Code window. The cmdPrint_Click procedure is displayed.

9. Modify this procedure to match the following (changes are in bold):

```
Private Sub cmdPrint_Click()
    Dim x As Object
    On Error GoTo ErrHandler

    cmdPrint.Visible = False
    cmdCancel.Visible = False

    'Change the BackColor of the current form.
    Me.BackColor = &HFFFFFF

    'Change the BackColor of all controls.
    For Each x In frmInvoice.Controls
        x.BackColor = &HFFFFFF
    Next

    PrintForm
    End
    Exit Sub
ErrHandler:
    Dim iErrorAction As Integer
    iErrorAction = ErrorHandler(Err)
    Select Case iErrorAction
```

```
        Case 1
            Resume
        Case 2
            Resume Next
        'This procedure doesn't need Case 3 which is resuming to a line.
        Case 4
            Exit Sub
        Case 5
            End
        End Select
    End Sub
```

10. Save frmInvoice and Module1.

By branching to a centralized error handler function and then performing the Resume, Resume Next, or other necessary statement in the local procedure, you're assured that VB resumes in the correct location. Yet this allows for custom code—such as a message—to be placed in the local procedure's error routine. This code needs to be placed in all procedures where you want to support error handling.

One great aspect of having a centralized error handler is that you only need to create the Select Case with all the error numbers once. In fact, you might want to place this function in its own module. Then you can add the module to all your applications, thereby reusing the code over and over. If you discover a new error you need to trap, just add it to this module and all your future applications will support that error. Another advantage of a centralized error handler is that it allows for consistent error messages, because you always reference the same function.

Saving Your Project

Whenever you make changes you know you want to keep, you need to save the form that contains those changes. As you learned earlier, each form is its own file, so if you make changes on multiple forms you need to save multiple files. If you add a form or module to your application, you need to save the project so that a reference to that form or module file is included in the project definition. You might want to have VB save files for you automatically. On the Environment tab of the Options dialog box is a group of option buttons to allow you to set the save options for VB. Three options are available:

- **Save Changes**—If you want VB to automatically save any changes you've made without prompting you, use this option. The changes are saved when you run the application by selecting Run or pressing F5.

- **Prompt To Save Changes**—If you want VB to display a dialog box asking if you want to save changes to your project when you run it, use this option.

- **Don't Save Changes**—Select this option if you do not want to save changes each time you run your application.

To have your changes saved automatically each time you run the application from the VB development environment, for example, complete the following steps:

1. Select <u>T</u>ools, <u>O</u>ptions to display the Options dialog box.
2. Select the Environment tab.
3. Select the <u>S</u>ave Changes option button.
4. Click OK.

Making Your Project an EXE File

You application has been tested and debugged, so you're ready to make your project an *EXE file* (often called an *executable file*). This is simply a matter of selecting Ma<u>k</u>e ProjectName.exe on the <u>F</u>ile menu.

Caution

> This method of creating an EXE file is useful if you plan to run the application on only your own system. If you want to run it on other systems, you should use the Application Setup Wizard as discussed in Chapter 12, "Testing the Invoice System."

To make the time tracking application an EXE file, follow these steps:

1. Select <u>F</u>ile, Ma<u>k</u>e LawTrack.exe to display the Make Project dialog box (see Figure 7-9).

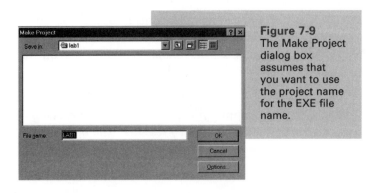

Figure 7-9
The Make Project dialog box assumes that you want to use the project name for the EXE file name.

2. In the File name text box, type **Time**.

3. Click OK. In a few seconds the EXE file is created.

4. Minimize Visual Basic.

5. Right-click the desktop to display its pop-up menu; select New.

6. Select Shortcut to display the Create Shortcut dialog box.

7. Click the Browse button. Locate and select the EXE file you just created.

8. Click Open to use that file with this shortcut.

9. Click Next to display the Select a Title for the Program dialog box.

10. Click Finish to create the shortcut.

11. Double-click the newly created icon on your desktop to launch the time tracking application.

12. Click the frame to display the input box that prompts you for your name.

13. Enter your name and press Enter to display the Billing Information form.

14. Enter data in this form and click OK.

15. Select Yes in response to the message box that asks if you want to preview the invoice.

16. Click Print to print the invoice and end the application.

Summary

You have successfully created your first complete VB project! In this project you reviewed and refreshed your previous VB knowledge and added to that knowledge. You're now ready to tackle more advanced topics such as MDI design and Automation, which are discussed in detail in the next project.

Project 1 Summary

The time tracking system allowed you to build on the basic knowledge of Visual Basic you already had, and gave you a good foundation for working with the other projects in this book. By completing this project you learned how to design an application interface, receive input from a user, and apply that input to other parts of the application. You gained experience with the use of controls and objects. You built logic into the application to process the results of user input and to perform different actions based on that input.

After building the application, you learned several ways to test and debug it. You also learned to write an error-handling routine so that your application could process errors based on their type.

Once your application was tested and debugged, you went through the process of saving your project and form files and making the project an EXE file.

HANDS ON
PROJECT 2

2

THE
INVOICE SYSTEM

- Reusing forms from another application
- Using MDI (multiple document interface)
- Understanding special coding considerations for the MDI environment
- Working with menus
- Adding a toolbar to your application
- Working with status bars
- Controlling Microsoft Word using Automation
- Controlling Microsoft Excel using Automation
- Using the Object Browser
- Using the Application Setup Wizard

Project Overview

The invoice system builds on your previous knowledge of VB. This project takes you through the process of upgrading an application. Once you have completed this project, you will know how to reuse forms from another application.

During this project you will convert the time tracking application into an MDI application. In the process you will learn MDI skills such as which properties to work with to create child forms and how to create multiple instances of a child form.

You will master ways to create status bars, toolbars, and menu systems for your applications. Best of all, you will introduce whole new sets of functionality to your applications by learning to use Automation to exploit the features of other applications from VB.

CHAPTER 8

What is the Invoice System?

The invoice system you're going to create during this project is actually an extension of the time tracking system created in the first project. Recall that at the completion of the first project you could print an invoice. You might have noticed, however, that no data for the invoice was saved. In this project you'll extend the first application so that it saves the data. The new application will store the invoice information into a Microsoft Excel workbook. Instead of using the `PrintForm` statement, you'll use Excel as the report generator for the invoices (see Figure 8-1).

ON THE

CD

The completed project can be found on the CD included with this book.

You'll also add the capability to generate "reminder" letters (see Figure 8-2) to be sent to accounts that are past-due. This is a feature found in many commercial accounting applications. These letters will be generated in Microsoft Word 97 so that you can utilize the formatting capabilities of a full-featured word processor. You'll use your VB application to initiate a query of the data in Excel and then use that information to create the letter in Word. All your user needs to do is to select a menu option in your application to have all of this done.

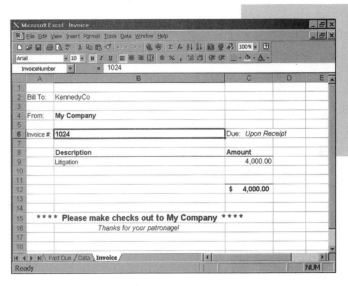

Figure 8-1
By using Excel to generate the invoice, you'll have more control over the invoice's look through Excel's formatting features.

Note

To complete every part of this project, you'll need Microsoft Word 97 and Microsoft Excel 97.

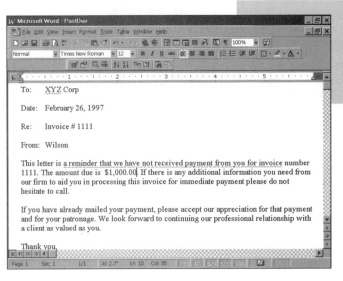

Figure 8-2
You'll use three applications to create this letter: Visual Basic, Excel, and Word!

When this application is complete, you'll have the following: a way to prompt the user for the information needed to generate an invoice, a way to print the invoice, an Excel file with the invoice data in it, and a letter generator. By building this application you'll become more proficient in several tools and techniques used by intermediate-to-advanced VB programmers, and you'll be able to build more sophisticated applications.

You'll need to address some new interface issues. One is the fact that the previous application you created moved from form to form. When you ran it, the application didn't look like other Windows applications you've used. Most Windows applications have a main form that houses the other forms used by the application. Your new application for the second project will have that look. The new application will include several other interface elements, such as the menu bar and toolbar shown in Figure 8-3.

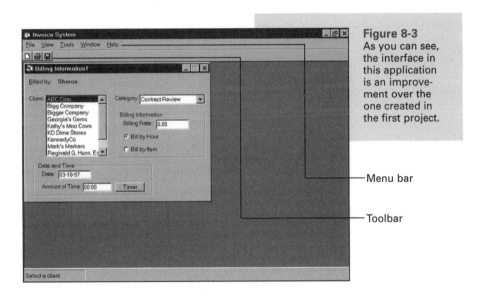

Figure 8-3
As you can see, the interface in this application is an improvement over the one created in the first project.

Menu bar

Toolbar

Invoice System Requirements

As you know, the first thing you need to do before starting any application is to review the requirements of the system. Since this is an invoicing system, some of the requirements are obvious. The application needs to generate and print invoices. What other features should this invoicing system have? The following list outlines the requirements that need to be met:

- The forms previously created for the time tracking application should be used as a foundation for the invoice application.

- Excel is to be used as the report generator that creates the printed invoices.

- Excel file format must be used to save the invoice information.

- The invoice application must let users create bar and pie charts representing information about billing categories, client activity, and invoice amounts.

- The invoice application must query the data in Excel to locate past-due items.

- The invoice application must use Word to generate the automated reminder letters.

- The interface of the invoice application must look more like a standard Windows application than the time tracking application does (the time tracking system lacks menus, toolbars, and so on).

- The invoice application must be easy for users to install.

Because of the nature of this application, you do not need to list the required data elements. They were already defined when designing the original time tracking application.

Invoice System Goals

How will creating the invoice system help you to learn VB? This project is designed to present VB concepts beyond the basics. These concepts, which should build upon your previous knowledge, are described in the following sections.

Reusing Forms from Another Application

When you're using one application as the foundation for another application, you want to be able to use the first application's forms in your new application. You might soon find that you have a library of forms to use, such as a splash screen and an About dialog box. In this project you'll add several forms from the previous application into the new application you create.

Using MDI

MDI (multiple document interface) is the type of interface you're most familiar with as a Windows user. With MDI, you have a parent window that contains child windows. An example of this is Microsoft Word, in which the main Word window contains multiple document windows. You'll use this type of interface for your new application.

You'll create a special form that becomes the *parent form* for your application. This parent form will contain other forms. You'll set the other forms' properties to make them children of the parent form.

Using Menus and Toolbars

Two key interface elements you'll use are menus and toolbars. You'll incorporate these objects into your application, and write the code associated with the menu and toolbar items.

Menus are created and maintained using the Menu Editor. Topics associated with menu creation that this project will address are menu naming conventions, menu properties, and attaching code to menu items.

Toolbars are created using a special control. You'll add this control to the project and then set its properties, add some toolbar buttons, and write code for these toolbar buttons.

By having the application use MDI and incorporate menus and toolbars, you'll create an application that mimics the look and feel of commercial Windows applications.

Controlling Another Application from Your Application

You can greatly extend the VB environment by using the features and strengths of other applications, such as Word and Excel. This is done through a process known as Automation.

Using OLE objects and Automation, you'll add the functionality of Word and Excel to the invoicing system. An *OLE object* in essence allows you to insert a small piece of another application into your VB application. *Automation* is the process of controlling one application's functionality from another application.

Using DLLs and API Calls To Extend VB

VB is a flexible language that lets you do just about anything you want to in the Windows world. But what about the things you want to do that cannot be done with VB? In that case, the *Windows API* and *DLLs* come to the rescue. You'll find out what you can do with DLLs and you'll learn how to use them.

Using the Application Wizard

VB's Application Wizard is a great tool for starting an application. In this project you'll compare the process of creating an application without the Application Wizard to that of creating one with the Application Wizard. You'll see exactly what the Application Wizard can do for you, including setting the application to be MDI, adding menus and toolbars, and even doing some of your coding!

Using the Setup Wizard

The Setup Wizard is used to create a setup program for the distribution and installation of your application. The Setup Wizard converts your project to an EXE file, determines which other files are needed by your application, compresses these files, and writes them to floppy disks. All your users need to do is to insert Disk 1 of the installation program you create, and enter Setup to install your application to their desktop. This is yet another feature of VB that gives your applications a professional look.

Summary

The second project is going to demonstrate many skills that can be used for a variety of applications. One of your goals as a VB programmer should be to create applications that not only perform well but also look good. The additional interface design elements presented in this project will help you achieve this.

Automation is becoming increasingly useful as more applications incorporate the VBA language as their macro or automation language. This gives VB programmers an ever-broadening palette of tools to use in application development. You'll learn the fundamentals of Automation in this project. Finally, you'll use the Setup Wizard to enhance the image of your application by creating a professional installation program.

CHAPTER 9

Gathering for the Invoice System

The first thing you did in the previous project was to gather information for the application; you then analyzed the information and used it in the design process. You're in the same situation now—you need to gather any information necessary to complete the analysis process. You've already identified the goals of the application (see Chapter 8, "What is the Invoice System?"), and by reviewing these goals you should be able to easily identify the forms, controls, and other objects needed to complete the application.

Because you plan to use Automation as part of the application's design, some of your work will be done in other applications (Word and Excel). The design of the invoice takes place in Excel. You need to create a worksheet that's preformatted and ready to receive values from your application. In Word, you need to create the basic text for the reminder letter and also apply any desired formatting to the document. This Word letter is used as a receptacle for data from the invoice system.

What Type of Information Do You Plan To Track?

You already determined the type of information to track with the invoice system when you completed Project 1. As a reminder, here's a list of the information tracked by this system:

- The date
- The time period (amount of time spent on a task)
- The task performed during that time period
- Whether that work is billed by the task or by the hour
- The client associated with the time spent
- The billing rate
- Who spent the time on the task

In the previous project you only used this information to design the forms needed by the application. In this project you're saving data to an Excel workbook, so you also need to use this information to design the worksheet where this data will reside when it's saved. The easiest way to organize this information in a worksheet is in columns, as shown in Figure 9-1.

ON THE CD

This file is named Invoice.xls and is found on the CD that accompanies this book.

Figure 9-1
Each column maps to a control value in the invoice system.

Client	Billing Category	Total Time	Hour or Item?	Billing Rate	Total Amount Billed	User Name	Date	Paid
Mark's Markers	Contract Review	1.00	Hour	55.00	55.00	Kennedy	3-17-97	No
XY2 Inc.	Employment Contract	2.00	Hour	55.00	110.00	Kennedy	11-14-96	No
KD Dime Stores	Retail Lease	2.00	Hour	100.00	200.00	Hunter	12-4-96	Yes
Georgia's Gems	Retail Lease	4.50	Hour	100.00	450.00	Hunter	1-12-97	Yes
Bigger Company	Retail Lease	22.00	Hour	100.00	2200.00	Hunter	1-20-97	No
Simone Widgets	Litigation	25.00	Hour	125.00	3125.00	Thomas	2-14-97	No
Mark's Markers	Employment Contract	5.00	Hour	55.00	275.00	Kennedy	10-13-96	Yes
Reginald G. Hunn, Esquire	Will	7.00	Item	75.00	75.00	Padgett	11-12-96	Yes
Georgia's Gems	Contract Review	3.00	Hour	55.00	165.00	Kennedy	12-9-96	Yes
KennedyCo	Litigation	45.00	Hour	125.00	5625.00	Thomas	2-25-97	No
Kathy's Moo Cows	Litigation	55.00	Hour	125.00	6875.00	Brown	1-15-97	Yes
Kathy's Moo Cows	Retail Lease	6.00	Hour	100.00	600.00	Hunter	1-11-97	No
ABC Corp.	Litigation	16.00	Hour	125.00	2000.00	Jesup	9-20-96	Yes
Susan Wilson	Divorce	10.00	Item	200.00	200.00	Padgett	10-1-96	Yes
Georgia's Gems	Contract Review	12.50	Hour	55.00	687.50	Wilson	2-8-97	No
XY2 Inc.	Litigation	55.00	Hour	125.00	6875.00	Brown	1-4-97	No
Bigg Company	Employment Contract	3.00	Hour	55.00	165.00	Wilson	12-6-96	Yes
Reginald G. Hunn, Esquire	Litigation	16.50	Hour	125.00	2062.50	Thomas	9-30-96	Yes
Mark's Markers	Retail Lease	20.00	Hour	100.00	2000.00	Hunter	11-4-96	No
Bigger Company	Contract Review	22.00	Hour	55.00	1210.00	Kennedy	2-7-97	No
Joe Johnson	Divorce	10.00	Hour	75.00	750.00	Padgett	1-9-97	Yes
XY2 Inc.	Retail Lease	18.50	Hour	100.00	1850.00	Hunter	2-25-97	Yes
Joe Johnson	Will	15.00	Item	450.00	450.00	Padgett	12-7-96	Yes

You might have noticed one column in Figure 9-1 that did not exist in the previous list of data elements. The Paid column has been added as a data element so that the user can get a list of past-due accounts. For this project you can safely assume that another system is handling the data for this column, and you're just using it for the purpose required by the invoice system.

Organizing the User Input

Let's return to the list of questions presented in Chapter 2, "The Visual Basic Development Environment," to document the purpose of the application. These questions are always a good starting point for the analysis process:

- **What is the purpose of the application I am writing?**

  This application allows a user to enter task and time-spent information for billing purposes. Once this data is entered, an invoice can be printed. With this application the user also can query the data to locate past-due items. Once the past-due items are located, the application automatically generates reminder letters for the appropriate clients.

- **Is the application replacing a current process?**

  Yes, in two ways. It is replacing the original paper process and it is extending the previous automated process achieved by the time tracking application.

- **Are there paper forms that I am automating?**

  This system still replaces the original tracking form and the paper-based invoice. It also enhances the previous automated invoice. The reminder letters are new, automated paper forms.

- **Who will use the application?**

  The users are attorneys who must track their billable hours and create invoices to send to their clients.

- **What type of data will the user enter in the application?**

  The data entered in this application will be directly applied to the invoice that's created upon completion of billing information input. This includes the user's name, client's name, billing category, date of the invoiced item, billing rate, amount of time spent on the item, and the total amount billed.

- **What will the data be used for?**

  The collected data is used for the creation of invoices to be sent to clients. It also is used to generate reminder letters for past-due accounts.

- **What types of output will the application produce?**

  The two types of output from this application are invoices for billable time and reminder notices for past-due accounts.

Determining the Number of Forms for Your Application

The next step of the analysis process is to identify the forms needed by the application. You already know about five of the forms because this application is building on the time tracking application. You also know that the new application is going to be an MDI application. This means that you need a parent form to act as a container for the other forms. You also need a form to preview the past-due notice. That means the application needs a total of seven forms, as listed below (existing form names are noted in parentheses):

- Startup splash screen (`frmSplash`)
- Form prompting the user for his or her name (`InputBox` function)
- Parent form
- Form containing the remainder of required user input (`frmBillingInfo`)
- Form for timer feature (`frmTimer`)
- Form to display a billing preview (`frmInvoice` was used in the time tracking application, but in the invoice application you must create a new one)
- Form to display a preview of the past-due notice

As you can see from the list, three new forms need to be completed. Two of them—the main form and the form to display the preview of the past-due notice—are completely new. The other form is replacing the existing `frmInvoice`. Since you're using Excel to print the invoice, you'll want to display the invoice the same way Excel formats it. Besides form creation, you also need to create templates for the invoice and the reminder letter. This requires up-front work in both Excel and Word.

Determining Additional Needed Objects

You're going to reuse most of the forms and controls you had in the time tracking system. There are just a few additional objects needed by the invoice system. There new objects are the menus and toolbar buttons being added to the application. Table 9-1 briefly describes these objects.

Table 9-1	Menu and Toolbar Buttons Needed for Invoice System	
Object Name	**Control Type**	**Description**
mnuFile	Menu	Top-level menu
mnuFileNew	Menu	Creates new invoice form
mnuFileSave	Menu	Saves information entered in invoice form
mnuFilePrint	Menu	Prints invoice form
mnuFileExit	Menu	Exits application
mnuView	Menu	Top-level menu
mnuStatusBar	Menu	Toggles status bar on and off
mnuTools	Menu	Top-level menu
mnuToolsPastDue	Menu	Generates reminder letters
mnuWindow	Menu	Top-level menu
mnuCascade	Menu	Cascades child forms
mnuTile	Menu	Tiles child forms
mnuHelp	Menu	Top-level menu
mnuHelpAbout	Menu	Displays About box
btnNew	Toolbar button	Equivalent to mnuFileNew
btnPrint	Toolbar button	Equivalent to mnuFilePrint
btnSave	Toolbar button	Equivalent to mnuFileSave

Notice the descriptions of the toolbar buttons—each is equivalent to a menu action. This is because toolbar buttons should be shortcuts to menu items. You never should have a toolbar button perform an action that cannot also be done through the menu system.

Toolbar buttons are created just like other controls, by using tools from the toolbox. In this project you'll learn how to use the Menu Editor to create the menu system. It's important to remember that menus are objects and therefore have properties and events like other objects do.

Extending Visual Basic by Using Other Applications

Visual Basic is extendable in several ways. One way is through *ActiveX controls*. There are numerous tools on the market that you can incorporate into your application. These components give your application new capabilities—ranging from text editing to scientific analysis—that would otherwise require you to do extreme amounts of coding. A lot of the capabilities found in these third-party tools are already on your desktop if you own Microsoft Office. Want to include financial analysis in your application? These functions are available through

Excel. Want to add a grammar checker? No problem . . . use Word. How about generating slide shows based on user input? Sounds like a job for PowerPoint! If you and your users already have Microsoft Office and other OLE-compliant applications, why not use them? They're already paid for and they offer familiar interfaces to your user.

Anything you can do with Word, Excel, PowerPoint, or Project can also be done in your VB applications by using *Automation* (this is the process of controlling one application through another). Now that Visual Basic for Applications (VBA) is the Automation language for these and other products, Automation is even easier.

Selecting Your Tools: Word and Excel

Note   **To complete every part of this project, you'll need Microsoft Word 97 and Microsoft Excel 97.**

For the invoice system, you'll use VB to automate two Microsoft Office products. One is Word, which you'll use to generate the reminder letters. The application will take information the user types in, test to see which clients have accounts that are not current, and print the necessary letters.

The second application is Excel, which will be the data repository for the invoice information. Excel will also serve as a report generator, creating the actual invoices. Another feature of Excel that your application will exploit is its charting ability. You could use VB's Chart control, but why do that when the data is already stored in Excel?

Summary

This project has two major goals. The first is to provide you with additional VB skills, such as designing an MDI application, Automation, menu creation, and toolbar design. The second is to give you an idea of what it's like to upgrade an existing application. By completing this project in the next three chapters, you'll get an idea of how to add new features that are both desirable and useful to your end user.

CHAPTER 10

Designing the Invoice System

You need to address two major considerations as part of the design phase for the invoice system: the look of the application and the approach. In the analysis for this application it was determined that the look of the application needed to be upgraded beyond that of the time tracking system. By converting this application to an MDI environment and adding a toolbar and menu bar, you'll address the appearance requirements. In this chapter, you'll make the application an MDI application.

As far as the approach of the application goes, the invoice system will rely heavily on Automation. In this chapter, you'll complete the background work needed to accomplish the Automation process.

What is Automation?

One of the goals of this application is to demonstrate the use of *Automation*. Working with Automation often requires that you do work in applications outside of the VB environment. In the applications that you plan to control through

Automation, you're going to set up a *template*. This template is then used as a receptacle for data input from the user of your VB application. You need to set up templates in both Excel and Word.

As mentioned earlier, Excel is not only going to serve as a report generator, but also is going to store the data for your application. Using the native VB environment, you can only save to the following file formats:

- Text
- RTF (Rich Text Format)
- Access database (MDB file)

Using Automation, however, you can support any file format that an OLE-compliant application supports. You can save to an extremely wide variety of file formats, including—but not limited to—the following formats:

Automation, previously known as OLE Automation, is a technology that allows you to incorporate the functionality of Windows applications into your VB code. To use Automation you must own a copy of the application whose functionality you want to incorporate into your application, and that application must support Automation.

- Microsoft Excel
- Lotus 1-2-3
- Borland Quattro Pro
- Borland dBase
- DIF (Data Interchange Format)
- SYLK (Symbolic Link)
- Microsoft Word
- Corel WordPerfect
- Microsoft Works
- HTML Document
- Microsoft Project
- Microsoft PowerPoint

If you are familiar with Automation and OLE, you may notice that some file formats listed above are not from applications that support Automation. The reason you can save to these formats is because some other application that does support Automation can save to these formats. For example, Excel can save to a Lotus 1-2-3 file format.

Creating the Past-Due Reminder Document in Word

The first thing you'll do in terms of working on the design of the invoicing system is to create the template for the reminder letter in Word. The Word application has been selected for a number of reasons. The first is that it's a state-of-the-art word processor offering any editing feature you'll need for the invoice system. The second is that it's an extremely popular word processor. Finally, you know that you won't have any trouble using Word, because it fully supports Automation.

> **Tip**
>
> **If you do not want to create this document yourself, you can find it on the CD accompanying this book. The file is** `D:\examples\Lab2\PastDue.doc` **(assuming that drive D is your CD-ROM drive).**

Okay, you're ready to start the template creation. Realizing that this is not a book about Word, this part of the project emphasizes only those features of Word that make doing Automation easier. It is assumed that you have a basic working knowledge of Word.

Let's review the general process that needs to occur to achieve automatic generation of the reminder letters. You need to create a document with the standard text of the reminder letter. The invoice application queries data to find out which clients are late paying their invoices. Then part of the data stored for a particular invoice needs to be strategically inserted into a reminder letter. The following data should be inserted in the letter:

- The client's name
- The invoice number
- The amount due
- The name of the user who generated the invoice

A bookmark is a named location within a Word document that is used for reference purposes. When you define a bookmark, you specify its location and name.

Your first idea of how to accomplish this is probably to use mail merge. While you certainly could do so, that would create more work than you need to do. Instead, you can use bookmarks to mark where you want to insert text. To create the reminder document, follow these steps:

1. Start Microsoft Word.
2. Type **To:** and press the Tab key.
3. Select <u>I</u>nsert, Bookmar<u>k</u> to display the Bookmark dialog box (see Figure 10-1).
4. In the <u>B</u>ookmark Name text box, type **ClientName1**.
5. Click <u>A</u>dd to add the bookmark to the document at the current location. Press Enter.

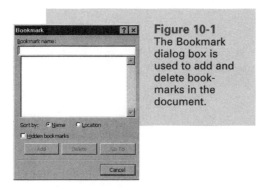

Figure 10-1
The Bookmark dialog box is used to add and delete book-marks in the document.

6. Type **Date:** and press the Tab key. Select Insert, Date and Time to display the Date and Time dialog box. Select Month dd, yyyy and click OK.

7. Press Enter. Type **Re:** and press the Tab key.

8. Type **Invoice #:**.

9. Select Insert, Bookmark to display the Bookmark dialog box. In the Bookmark Name text box, type **Invoice1**. Click Add to add the bookmark to the document at the current location. Press Enter.

10. Type **From:** and press the Tab key.

11. Select Insert, Bookmark to display the Bookmark dialog box. In the Bookmark Name text box, type **UserName1**. Click Add to add the bookmark to the document at the current location. Press Enter.

12. Type the following text:

    This letter is a reminder that we have not received payment from you for invoice number

13. Type a space after the word number. Select Insert, Bookmark to display the Bookmark dialog box. In the Bookmark Name text box, type **InvoiceNumber2**. Click Add to add the bookmark to the document at the current location. Press Enter.

14. Add a period to complete the sentence, type a space, and type the following text to begin the next sentence:

    The amount due is

15. Type a space after the word is. Select Insert, Bookmark to display the Bookmark dialog box. In the Bookmark Name text box, type **AmountDue**. Click Add to add the bookmark to the document at the current location. Press Enter.

16. Add a period to complete the sentence, type a space, and type the following text as the next sentence:

If there is any additional information you need from our firm to aid you in processing this invoice for immediate payment, please do not hesitate to call.

Press Enter and then type the following paragraph:

If you have already mailed your payment, please accept our appreciation for that payment and for your patronage. We look forward to continuing our professional relationship with a client as valued as you.

Press Enter and then type the following text:

Thank you,

17. Press Enter. Select Insert, Bookmark to display the Bookmark dialog box. In the Bookmark Name text box, type **UserName2**. Click Add to add the bookmark to the document at the current location. Press Enter. Figure 10-2 shows how the entire letter looks.

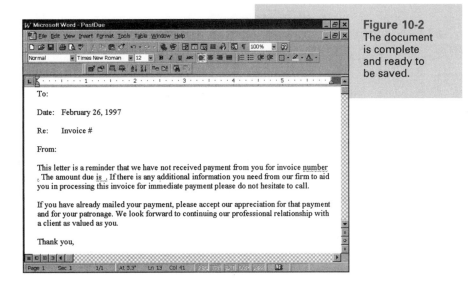

Figure 10-2
The document is complete and ready to be saved.

18. Select File, Save to display the Save dialog box.

19. Select the location where you want to save the file. (You might want to save it to the same directory as your VB project files.)

20. Type **PastDue** for the File Name and click Save to save the document.

21. Exit Word.

As mentioned earlier, you can get a similar end result using mail merge, but with more work required on your part. Bookmarks are a great tool in this type of situation—they are the easiest way to get to a specific part of a document. Trying to tell VB to go, for example, to the fifth word in the second paragraph of the third page is a challenge, to say the least. A bookmark is much faster to create and much easier to reference in code.

Setting Up the Invoice and Past Due Sheets in Excel

You need to do two things in Excel for this application. First, set up the Invoice sheet. On this sheet you'll enter the static text for the invoice, format the cells, enter any necessary formulas, and name cells for easier referencing from code. Second, create the Past Due sheet. This sheet is used during the process that queries the data in the workbook to locate past-due invoices.

Setting up the Invoice Worksheet

For this project, it is assumed that you've had some experience with Excel. To set up the invoice as a worksheet in Excel, use the following steps:

1. Start Excel.
2. Select File, Open to display the Open dialog box.
3. From the CD accompanying this book, select `D:\examples\Lab2\Invoice.xls` (assuming that drive D is your CD-ROM drive).
4. Click Open to open the file.
5. There is currently a single worksheet, named Data, in this workbook. You need to add another sheet. Select Insert, Worksheet to do this.
6. Right-click the tab of the newly created sheet to access its shortcut menu. Select Rename. Type **Invoice** and press Enter.
7. In cell A2, type **Bill To:**.
8. In cell A4, type **From:**. In cell B4, type **My Company**.
9. In cell A6, type **Invoice #:**.
10. In cell B8, type **Description**. In cell C8, type **Due: Upon Receipt**.
11. In cell B15, type ******Please make checks out to My Company******.
12. In cell B16, type **Thanks for your patronage!**.
13. In cell C12, type **=SUM(C9:C10)**.

14. Right-click cell C12 to display its shortcut menu. Select Format Cells to display the Format Cells dialog box.

15. Select the Number tab. From the Category list box, select Accounting. Click OK to format the cell.

16. Continue formatting the invoice so that it resembles the invoice worksheet shown in Figure 10-3. Table 10-1 lists the format settings for the cells of this worksheet.

Table 10-1   Format Settings for the Invoice Worksheet

Cell(s)	Format Settings
A1:A2, B1, C1, C6	Arial, 10 point, Normal
B4, C12	Arial, 10 point, Bold
B8:C8	Arial, 10 point, Bold, Border on bottom
B9:C11	Arial, 9 point, Normal
C11	Border on bottom
B15	Arial, 12 point, Bold, Centered
B16	Arial, 10 point, Italic, Centered

A named cell replaces the absolute cell reference in formulas. An absolute cell reference is given in row/column format (for example, A2). An example of a formula using this type of reference is =B1*A2 —as you can see, this is not the friendliest-looking formula. If you named A2 something like `TaxRate` *and named* `B1` *something like* `SalesPrice`*, though, you could use* `=SalesPrice* TaxRate`*, which is much easier to read.*

Figure 10-3
The Invoice worksheet is formatted to give it a professional look.

17. Select cell B2. Select the Name box located on the same line as the formula bar. Type **ClientName** and press Enter. This creates a named cell. (Be sure to press Enter or the new cell name won't be saved.)

18. Name the cells listed in Table 10-2.

Table 10-2	Named Cells on the Invoice Worksheet
Cell	**Name**
B6	InvoiceNumber
B9	Category
C9	AmountDue

19. Select File, Save As. Save the Invoice.xls file to the directory where your Project 2 files are located.

Named cells serve the same purpose in Excel as bookmarks do in Word—they give you an easy way to refer to and access particular locations from your VB code. Named cells are not required for your VB application to work, but they make your code more readable (for example, it's easier to remember why you're writing a value to AmountDue than to C9)!

Creating the Past Due Worksheet

Excel uses filters to display rows that meet certain criteria that you select or enter. Advanced filters allow you to filter based on more sophisticated criteria that can include multiple conditions for a single column, multiple criteria for multiple columns, and conditions that incorporate the use of a formula.

The next thing you need to do in Excel is to set up a sheet for entering criteria when you query for the past-due invoices. Use the following steps to do this:

1. Select Insert, Worksheet to add the new worksheet.

2. Right-click the tab of the newly created sheet to access its shortcut menu. Select Rename. Type **Past Due** and press Enter.

3. Select the Data sheet.

4. Highlight A1:J1.

5. Select Edit, Copy.

6. Select the Past Due sheet. Select cell A1 and press Enter to paste the selection.

7. Save the workbook.

8. Exit Excel.

You've added the Past Due worksheet so that you'll have an area to build the query needed to generate the reminder letters. In the next chapter, when you start writing the Automation code, you'll use an advanced filter. Advanced filters require an area for the criteria.

Preparing for the Upgrade

This project is an example of upgrading an application—you're upgrading the existing time tracking system and turning it into the invoice system. To do this you're going to reuse some forms and modules from the time tracking system. Once you have these forms added to the project, you'll need to adjust the values of some properties for a few of the old project's objects.

Adding Files to the Project

You want to add three of the forms you used for the time tracking system to the invoice system. You also need the module you used for that project. The easiest way to do this is to copy the form files to a new directory and then build the project from there. The main reason to copy these files is so that you can make changes to the copied forms and module without affecting the original time tracking application. To achieve this, use the following steps:

1. Using the method you prefer, copy the following files from the directory containing your Project 1 files to the directory containing your Project 2 files: `frmSplash.frm`, `frmTimer.frm`, `frmBillingInfo.frm`, `Lab1.bas`, and `Time.bmp`.

2. Start Visual Basic. Click OK to start a Standard EXE project file.

3. Right-click the Project Explorer to display its shortcut menu. Select <u>A</u>dd.

4. Select <u>A</u>dd File to display the Add File dialog box (see Figure 10-4).

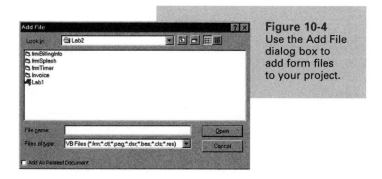

Figure 10-4
Use the Add File dialog box to add form files to your project.

5. Locate and select the directory where your Project 2 files are located.

6. Select `frmBillingInfo` and click <u>O</u>pen to add this file to the project.

7. Right-click the Project Explorer to display its shortcut menu. Select <u>A</u>dd.

8. Select <u>A</u>dd File to display the Add File dialog box. Select `frmSplash` and click <u>O</u>pen to add this file to the project.

9. Right-click the Project Explorer to display its shortcut menu. Select <u>A</u>dd.

10. Select <u>A</u>dd File to display the Add File dialog box. Select `frmTimer` and click <u>O</u>pen to add this file to the project.

11. Right-click the Project Explorer to display its shortcut menu. Select <u>A</u>dd.

12. Select <u>A</u>dd File to display the <u>A</u>dd File dialog box. Select Lab1.bas and click <u>O</u>pen to add this file to the project.

Adjusting Properties

Once you've added the files to the project, you can assign the necessary new values for certain properties. Use the following steps to do this:

1. Open frmSplash from the Project Explorer.

2. In the Properties window, locate and select the *Picture* property.

3. Click the selection button for this property. Locate and select the directory where your Project 2 files reside.

4. Select Time.bmp and click <u>O</u>pen. The image on the form doesn't change, but you're now referencing the file in the local directory.

5. Right-click Form1 from the Project Explorer to display its shortcut menu. Select <u>R</u>emove Form1 to delete this form from the project.

6. Select <u>F</u>ile, Sa<u>v</u>e Project to display the Save Project dialog box.

7. In the File <u>N</u>ame text box, type **Invoice** and click <u>S</u>ave to save the project.

8. Select <u>P</u>roject, Project1 Prop<u>e</u>rties to display the Project Properties dialog box shown in Figure 10-5.

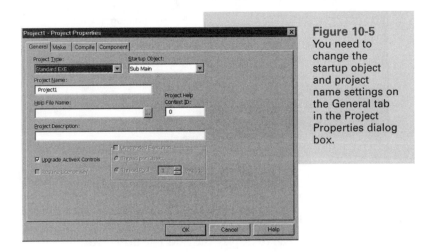

Figure 10-5
You need to change the startup object and project name settings on the General tab in the Project Properties dialog box.

9. Select frmSplash from the <u>S</u>tartup Object drop-down list.

10. Enter **Invoice** in the Project <u>N</u>ame text box.

11. Select the Make tab (see Figure 10-6).

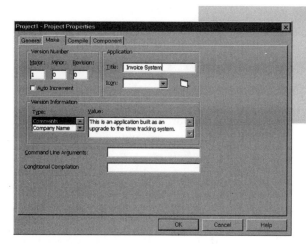

Figure 10-6
On the Make tab you need to change the title and the version information comments.

12. Enter **2** in the M_inor text box.

13. Enter **InvoiceSys** in the _Title text box.

14. Select Comments from the Type list.

15. In the _Value text box, enter the following comment:

This is an application built as an upgrade to the time tracking system.

16. Click OK to save the changes.

17. Press F5 to run the application.

18. Verify that the correct product name is displayed in the splash screen (see Figure 10-7). Click the frame to proceed.

Figure 10-7
The splash screen reflects the changes just made in the Project Properties dialog box.

19. Click Cancel to end the application.

20. Click <u>Y</u>es to confirm that you want to exit.

21. Select <u>F</u>ile, Sa<u>v</u>e Project to save the changes.

Using Multiple Document Interface (MDI)

SDI is a windowing environment in which only one document can be open at a time. In this environment, one window flows to another window in a linear progression. MDI is a windowing environment in which one main window contains as many other windows as the program requires.

One of the design features to support in the invoice application is the requirement that it be an MDI application. Your application is currently a *single document interface (SDI)* application. SDI is a very common approach to interface design. Several applications you've probably worked with use SDI, including Paintbrush, Solitaire, Media Player, and Calculator. As you can see from these examples, applications that use SDI are typically not as sophisticated as those that use MDI. By making the invoice system an MDI application, you're giving your users several benefits. One is that the application looks more like the other commercial applications they've worked with, which gives users an additional comfort level with your application.

Another benefit of the MDI environment is that you'll allow users to open more than one billing information window at a time. This is a pretty major enhancement. Many users like to work on multiple things at once—now your application is going to more closely reflect the way they work.

In the MDI environment, you'll have a main form called the *MDI parent form* or *MDI container*. The forms that reside in the MDI parent form are called *child forms*. Microsoft Word, shown in Figure 10-8, is an excellent example of an MDI application. You can see that it has an MDI parent form that owns the menu bar and toolbar for the application. Within the parent window are several documents —the child forms.

Complete the following steps to see child forms in action:

1. Open Microsoft Word. Word starts with one new document.

2. Click the New toolbar button. Another document opens.

3. Click the New toolbar button again. A third document opens.

4. Select <u>W</u>indow, <u>A</u>rrange All. This tiles the windows.

5. Try to drag the Document2 window out of the boundaries of the Microsoft Word window. You cannot do so, because the Microsoft Word window is the MDI parent form. The Document2 window is the child form, and a child form is forced to remain inside of its parent.

6. Close Word.

MDI parent forms provide a workspace for all the child forms in your application. Child forms are the forms contained in an MDI parent window when the application is running.

There are two basic steps in creating an MDI application:

1. Create the MDI parent form.
2. Create the child forms.

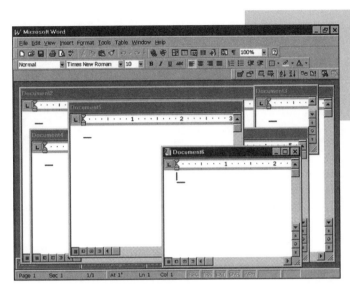

Figure 10-8
Microsoft Word is a great example of an application that utilizes MDI.

Creating an MDI Parent Form

The first step in this process is to create an MDI parent form. This special type of form is added through the Project menu. MDI parent forms act very much like regular forms at runtime; however, the behavior of an MDI parent form and its child forms will differ from regular forms when you minimize or maximize them. Here are some aspects of their behavior:

- Child forms, meaning forms with the *MDIChild* property set to True, are displayed within the MDI parent form.

- If a user maximizes a child form, the content of the child form's *Caption* property is added to the MDI parent form's *Caption* property so that both names are displayed in the MDI parent form's title bar.

- If a child form is minimized, it shrinks to a small title bar at the bottom of the MDI parent form. The child form does not appear as a button on the Windows taskbar.

- When the MDI parent form is minimized, the MDI parent form and all its child forms shrink to a single button on the Windows taskbar.

To add an MDI parent form to your application, use the following steps:

1. Select <u>P</u>roject, Add MD<u>I</u> Form to display the Add MDI Form dialog box (see Figure 10-9).

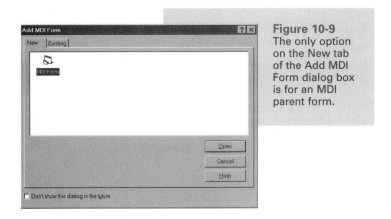

Figure 10-9
The only option on the New tab of the Add MDI Form dialog box is for an MDI parent form.

2. Click <u>O</u>pen to add the MDI parent form (see Figure 10-10).

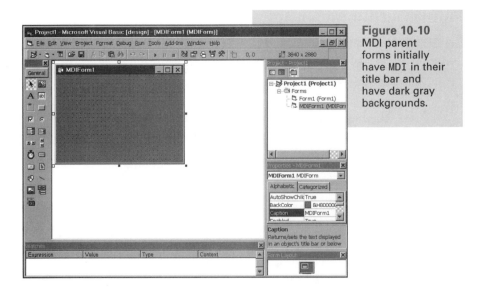

Figure 10-10
MDI parent forms initially have MDI in their title bar and have dark gray backgrounds.

3. One of the first things you'll notice about the newly created MDI parent form is its color. Unlike the other forms you've been working with (whose background color is light gray), this form's background color is dark gray.

This is typical of MDI parent forms. If you want to verify this, go into a commercial MDI application such as Word or Excel and close or minimize all the child windows. The background of the parent in those applications is dark gray.

4. Select the *Name* property from the Properties window. Type **frmMDIMain**.

5. Select the *Caption* property. Type **Invoice System**.

6. Select <u>F</u>ile, Sa<u>v</u>e Project to save the changes to the project. The Save File As dialog box is displayed because a new form has been added to the project. Click <u>S</u>ave to save the file as `frmMDIMain.frm`.

Something has changed on the menu system now that you've created your MDI parent form. Complete these steps to see what it is:

1. Select the <u>P</u>roject menu. Notice that the Add MD<u>I</u> Form menu item is now dimmed and unavailable. This is because you can have only one MDI parent form per project.

2. Click the form to deselect the <u>P</u>roject menu.

Maximizing the MDI Form Using the *WindowState* Property

When you're working with an MDI application, you often want it to be maximized when it starts. This is done using the *WindowState* property. *WindowState* is a runtime property that can be used to set the visual state of a form window. Table 10-3 lists the available values for this property.

Table 10-3 Values for the *WindowState* Property		
Value	**Constant**	**Description**
0	VbNormal	Normal (the default)
1	VbMinimized	Minimized (represented as an icon)
2	VbMaximized	Maximized (enlarged to full-screen size)

You need to have `frmMDIMain` display automatically in a maximized state; but first you need to make sure it shows at all. As the application currently stands, `frmMDIMain` is never shown. There are two ways that you can display `frmMDIMain`. One way is to make it the startup form. Before deciding to use this method, though, think about other MDI applications. More often than not, the splash screen is displayed and then the main MDI parent form is displayed. This is the approach you're going to use. Complete the following steps:

1. If frmMDIMain is not currently displayed, open it from the Project Explorer.

2. Double-click this form to access the Code window. The Form_Load procedure is displayed.

3. Type the following line of code for this procedure:

```
Me.WindowState = vbMaximized
```

4. Now you need to write the code to show frmMDIMain. Open frmSplash from the Project Explorer.

5. Double-click the frame to open the Code window. The Frame1_Click procedure is displayed.

6. Modify the procedure so that it matches the following (changes are in bold):

```
Private Sub Frame1_Click()
    Dim iResponse As Integer
    'delete the On Error GoTo Error_Handler statement

    Unload Me
TryAgain:
    gsMyName = InputBox("Please enter your name: ")
    If gsMyName = "" Then
        iResponse = MsgBox("Do you want to leave the application?",
➥vbYesNo)
        If iResponse = vbYes Then
            End
        Else
            GoTo TryAgain
        End If
    End If

    'delete the frmBillingInfo.Show line that was here
    frmMDIMain.Show
    'Delete from here to End Sub statement
End Sub
```

7. Press F5 to run the application.

8. Click the frame on the splash screen to display the input box.

9. Enter your name in the input box and click OK. frmMDIMain is displayed, as shown in Figure 10-11.

10. Close the application by clicking the Close button in the upper-right corner of the window.

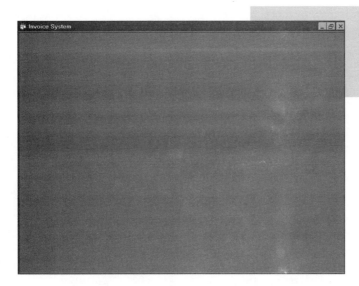

Figure 10-11
The MDI parent form is displayed in a maximized state.

Creating Child Forms

You have the MDI parent form created, but when you run the application you have nothing else. As it stands, there's no way to display the other forms of the application. You need to create the child forms. This sounds like a lot of work, but all you actually need to do is set each child form's *MDIChild* property to True.

In the invoice system, only one form currently needs to become a child form. That form is frmBillingInfo. To make it a child form, follow these steps:

1. Open frmBillingInfo from the Project Explorer.
2. Select the *MDIChild* property from the Properties window.
3. Set this property's value to True.

You still need to write code to display frmBillingInfo. Use the following steps:

1. Open frmMDIMain from the Project Explorer.
2. Double-click the form to open the Code window. The MDIForm_Load procedure is displayed.
3. Modify the MDIForm_Load procedure so that it matches the following:

```
Private Sub MDIForm_Load()
    Me.WindowState = vbMaximized
    frmBillingInfo.Show
End Sub
```

4. Press F5 to run the application.
5. Click the frame on the splash screen to display the input box.

6. Enter your name in the input box and click OK. The Billing Information form is displayed as a child form of the MDI parent form (see Figure 10-12).

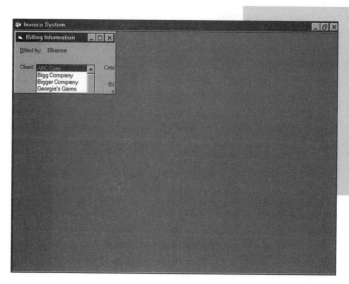

Figure 10-12
When displaying `frmBillingInfo` as a child form, you need to write code to compensate for the default size of the form; otherwise, the child form might be displayed too small.

7. Close the application by clicking the Close button in the upper-right corner of the parent window.

As you probably noticed, `frmBillingInfo` is displayed too small. This can be easily corrected with code, as shown in the following steps:

1. Open `frmBillingInfo` from the Project Explorer.

2. Double-click the form to open the Code window. The `Form_Load` procedure is displayed.

3. You need to add lines to this procedure to set the *Height* and *Width* properties. Modify the procedure so that it matches the following (changes are in bold):

```
Private Sub Form_Load()
    lblBilledBy.Caption = gsMyName
    With lstClient
        .AddItem "ABC Corp."
        .AddItem "XYZ Inc."
        .AddItem "KD Dime Stores"
        .AddItem "Bigg Company"
        .AddItem "Bigger Company"
        .AddItem "Simons Widgets"
        .AddItem "Mark's Markers"
```

```
        .AddItem "Reginald G. Hunn, Esquire"
        .AddItem "Georgia's Gems"
        .AddItem "KennedyCo"
        .AddItem "Kathy's Moo Cows"
        .Selected(0) = True
    End With

    With cboCategory
        .AddItem "Divorce"
        .AddItem "Will"
        .AddItem "Retail Lease"
        .AddItem "Contract Review"
        .AddItem "Living Trust"
        .AddItem "Residental Lease"
        .AddItem "Employment Contract"
        .AddItem "Litigation"
        .ListIndex = 0
    End With

    optByHour.Value = True
    mskDate.Text = Format(Date, "mm-dd-yy")
    txtAmountOfTime.Text = "00:00"
    txtBillingRate = "0.00"

    Me.Height = 3996
    Me.Width = 5496

End Sub
```

4. Press F5 to run the application.

5. Click the frame on the splash screen to display the input box.

6. Enter your name in the input box and click OK. The Billing Information form is displayed as a child form (see Figure 10-13).

7. Click Cancel to end the application.

Another thing you might want to consider for your child form in this application is disabling the user's ability to maximize the window. If a user maximizes the Billing Information form, it becomes less attractive (see Figure 10-14).

You probably also want to disable the user's ability to resize the child form (again to maintain the best appearance). The two properties you need to set are *MaxButton* (to False) and *BorderStyle* (to Fixed Single). Complete the following steps to set these properties for frmBillingInfo:

1. Open frmBillingInfo from the Project Explorer.

2. Select *MaxButton* from the Properties window.

3. Set its value to **False**.

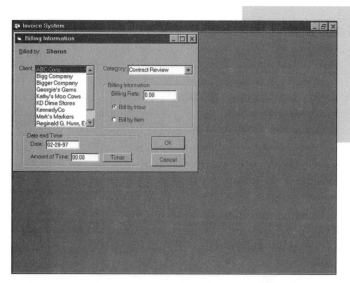

Figure 10-13
Adding two lines of code to the Form_Load procedure has corrected the form size problem.

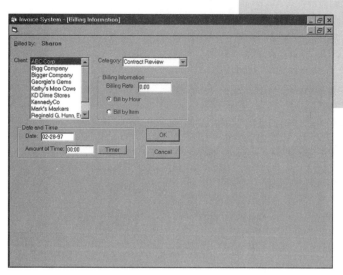

Figure 10-14
Some child forms should not be maximized due to cosmetic reasons.

4. Set *BorderStyle* to **1 - Fixed Single**.

5. Press F5 to run the application.

6. Click the frame on the splash screen to display the input box.

7. Enter your name in the input box and click OK. The Billing Information form is displayed as a child form, as shown in Figure 10-15.

8. Click Cancel to end the application.

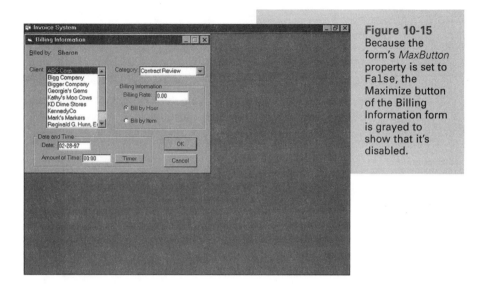

Figure 10-15
Because the form's *MaxButton* property is set to False, the Maximize button of the Billing Information form is grayed to show that it's disabled.

MDI parent forms and child forms are differentiated from regular forms in the Project Explorer (see Figure 10-16). MDI parent forms have an icon next to them that shows a large, solid form behind a smaller, dimmed form. The icon for child forms is the opposite—a small, solid form in front of a larger, dimmed form. As you can see from the invoice system, an application can be a mixture of an MDI parent form, regular forms, and child forms.

Child form

MDI parent form

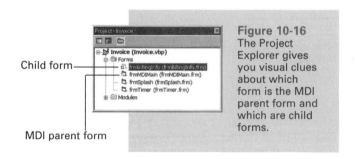

Figure 10-16
The Project Explorer gives you visual clues about which form is the MDI parent form and which are child forms.

Creating Multiple Instances of a Child Form

Think of most of the MDI applications you've worked with. Do they have only one child form? No, they allow you to display several child forms. You need to modify your invoice application so that it can have multiple child forms. The big question is how to create multiple instances of a child form. You accomplish this by using the Dim statement's optional New keyword. New allows for the creation of a new instance of an object—in this case, a child form. The syntax for creating an instance of a child form is as follows:

```
Dim varname As New NameOfChildForm
```

varname is the name that will be used to refer to the new instance of the child form in code. *NameOfChildForm* is the name of the child form that is used to create the new child form instance. Once the new instance of the child form has been created, you need to show it using the Show method. To add the capability to create multiple child form instances to the invoice application, follow these steps:

1. Open frmMDIMain from the Project Explorer.

2. Double-click the form to open the Code window. The frmMDIForm_Load procedure is displayed.

3. Select Click from the Code window's Event box to display the frmMDIForm_Click procedure.

4. Type the following code into this procedure:

```
Dim frmNewBill As New frmBillingInfo
frmNewBill.Show
```

Caution

> Normally you should not place this type of code in the Click event of a form, but you're going to do it now because this is an easy place to locate the code. In the next chapter, you'll cut this code and paste it into a menu.

5. Press F5 to run the application.

6. Click the frame on the splash screen to display the input box.

7. Enter your name in the input box and click OK. The Billing Information form is displayed as a child form.

8. Click the MDI parent form (not the Billing Information form). A new instance of the child form is displayed.

9. Click the MDI parent form again to display another instance of the child form (see Figure 10-17).

10. Click Cancel on any Billing Information form to end the application.

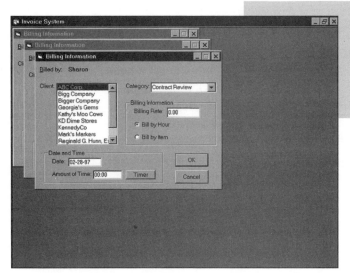

Figure 10-17
Creating multiple
instances of a
child form
required only
two lines of
code.

Working with the Caption Property of Child Forms

When you clicked the MDI parent form to create two new instances of the child form, you might have noticed a small issue with the captions of the new child forms. They're all the same! Needless to say, this could cause confusion for your user. To deal this issue, you just need to add some new VB code. Use the following steps to add this code to your application:

1. If the Code window is not open for frmMDIMain, open it.

2. If the MDIForm_Click procedure is not displayed, select Click from the Event box.

3. Modify the MDIForm_Click procedure so that it matches the following (changes are in bold):

```
Private Sub MDIForm_Click()
    Dim frmNewBill As New frmBillingInfo
    giFormCount = giFormCount + 1
    frmNewBill.Caption = frmNewBill.Caption & giFormCount
    frmNewBill.Show
End Sub
```

4. Select Load from the Event box. Modify the MDIForm_Load procedure to match the following (changes are in bold):

```
Private Sub MDIForm_Load()
```

```
    Me.WindowState = vbMaximized
    giFormCount = 1
    frmBillingInfo.Caption = frmBillingInfo.Caption & giFormCount
    frmBillingInfo.Show
End Sub
```

5. Open `Module1` from the Project Explorer.

6. Add the following line of code to the `General Declarations` area of the module:

   `Public giFormCount As Integer`

7. Press F5 to run the application.

8. Click the frame on the splash screen to display the input box.

9. Enter your name in the input box and click OK. The Billing Information form is displayed as a child form.

10. Click the MDI parent form (not the Billing Information form). A new instance of the child form is displayed—notice its title bar text.

11. Click the MDI parent form again to display another instance of the child form (see Figure 10-18).

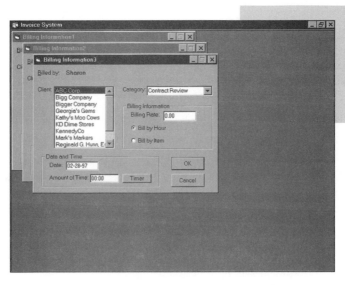

Figure 10-18
Each new child form now increments the number at the end of the title bar caption.

12. Click Cancel on any Billing Information form to end the application.

The `giFormCount` variable is used to keep track of the next number that is available to use for newly created forms. `giFormCount` is incremented and then appended to the *Caption* property of that form.

There is some work remaining to make the invoice system even more of an MDI application (for example, you need to get rid of the OK and Cancel buttons on all the child forms), but that will be done as you learn to work with menus in the next chapter.

Summary

This chapter demonstrated that when you plan to use Automation as part of your development platform, you must do some work outside of the VB environment. In this chapter you set up a Word document to be used as the starting point for the invoice system's reminder letter. You also created the structure for the invoice statement in Excel. You'll learn how to use Automation from your VB application in the next chapter.

You were given a lot of hands-on experience with MDI parent forms and child forms in this chapter. You also got an opportunity to see some of the code required to make this type of interface work. You'll build on your MDI knowledge and further enhance the application's interface in the next chapter.

CHAPTER 11

Building the Invoice System

Interestingly enough, the little things will matter most to your application's users. Often a user is more excited about a simple status bar than another feature you've spent 80 hours programming. This is why it is important to enhance the interface of your application as much as possible with elements such as status bars, menus, and toolbars. These things are important to your users, and in this chapter you'll work with all of them.

You'll also work with Automation, a technology that's becoming increasingly important. With Automation in this project you're writing data and filtering data, as well as printing and saving files. This chapter shows you just a few of the things you can do with Automation. At this point you're probably thinking, "Show me the code!" This chapter will require you to enter and analyze detailed code listings.

Enhancing Your Application's Interface

Certain interface elements are signatures of a professional application. One is a status bar. A few years ago you rarely saw a status bar, but now it's hard to find a commercial application without one.

 A *status bar* is a special window that the application uses to display status information such as current page position or date and time; it's typically located at the bottom of an MDI parent form.

Adding a Status Bar to Your Application

Most commercial applications provide feedback to the user through a status bar located at the bottom of the MDI form. To do this, you add a status bar control to the MDI parent form. Status bars are often divided into panels, with each panel providing different information.

Word is an example of an application that provides substantial feedback through its status bar. Complete the following steps to see how this works:

1. Open Microsoft Word.
2. Select File, Open. The Open dialog box is displayed.
3. Open the C:\Program Files\DevStudio\VB\License.Doc file.
4. Press the Page Down key repeatedly. As you move through the document, the status bar gives you updated information about your location.
5. Look at the right end of the status bar. OVR is grayed out—this means that overtype mode is disabled.
6. Select Tools, Options to display the Options dialog box.
7. Select the Edit tab.
8. Place a checkmark in the Overtype Mode check box.
9. Click OK to apply the change. Notice that OVR is now black at the right end of the status bar, indicating that overtype mode is enabled.
10. Select Tools, Options to display the Options dialog box.
11. Remove the checkmark from the Overtype Mode check box.
12. Click OK to apply the change. Notice that OVR is grayed out again.
13. Exit Word and return to Visual Basic.

To control the text in the status bar, you use each panel's *Text* property. The status bar control is a control available through the Microsoft Windows Common Controls 5.0 component. To add this component to your project, follow these steps:

1. Right-click the toolbox to display its pop-up menu.
2. Select Components to display the Components dialog box.
3. Place a checkmark beside Microsoft Windows Common Controls 5.0.
4. Click OK to add the component to the project. If you have the Immediate window open, you might need to close it so that you can see all the tools you've added to the project. Figure 11-1 shows the expanded toolbox.

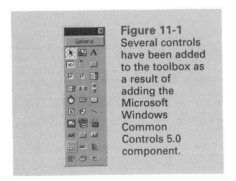

Figure 11-1
Several controls have been added to the toolbox as a result of adding the Microsoft Windows Common Controls 5.0 component.

With the expanded toolbox, you can place a status bar control on the MDI form of the invoice application. Follow these steps:

1. Select the Status Bar tool from the toolbox.
2. Open `frmMDIMain` from the Project Explorer.
3. Draw a rectangle at the bottom of the form to represent the status bar control. Don't worry about being exact in the placement of this control. It automatically snaps to the bottom of the form and spans the width of the form.
4. Adding panels to the status bar is not done with a toolbox control, but by setting property values. What's even stranger is that you cannot set the property values for the panels through the Properties window. You have to do it through the Property Pages dialog box. Right-click the new status bar and select Properties to display the Property Pages dialog box (see Figure 11-2).
5. Select the Panels tab.
6. Type **Enter Billing Information** in the Text text box.
7. Type **1800** in the Minimum Width text box.
8. Click OK to save the changes. Figure 11-3 shows the form with its status bar.

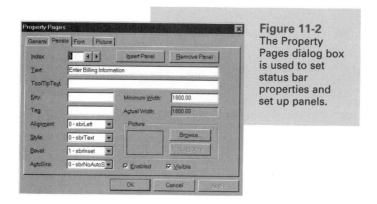

Figure 11-2
The Property
Pages dialog box
is used to set
status bar
properties and
set up panels.

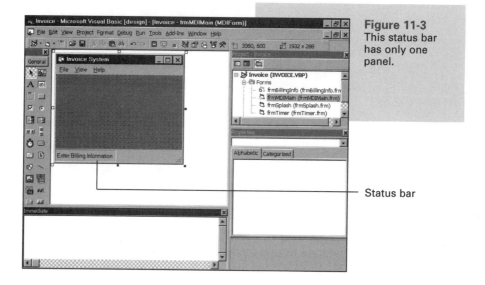

Figure 11-3
This status bar
has only one
panel.

Status bar

Note   **A status bar can have a maximum of sixteen panels.**

To change the text displayed in a status bar, you set the *Text* property for each of the status bar's panels. Panels are identified by their index numbers, which are set on the Panels tab of the Property Pages dialog box. A control's GotFocus event is a good place to add the code to control the *Text* property. Use the following steps to add status bar text to the invoice application:

1. Open frmBillingInfo from the Project Explorer.

2. Double-click lstClient to open the Code window.

3. Select `GotFocus` from the Event box to display the `lstClient_GotFocus` procedure.

4. Add the following line to this procedure:

   ```
   frmMDIMain.staMain.Panels(1).Text = "Select a client."
   ```

5. Select `cboCategory` from the Object box.

6. Select `GotFocus` from the Event box to display the `cboCategory_GotFocus` procedure.

7. Add the following line to this procedure:

   ```
   frmMDIMain.staMain.Panels(1).Text = "Select a billing category."
   ```

8. Save the module as `staMain`. Press F5 to run the application.

9. Click the frame of the splash screen to display the input box.

10. Type your name and press Enter. The MDI parent form of the invoice application is displayed.

11. Look at the status bar. `Select a client.` is the currently displayed text.

12. Select the Category drop-down list. Notice the status bar text.

13. Close the application by clicking the Close button in the upper-right corner of the MDI parent form.

You can continue to customize the status bar text for each control on the form if you want to. Now that you understand how to work with status bar text, the next section will discuss working with menus.

Menus

An interface element that you are used to seeing in most applications is a *menu bar*. Even Solitaire and Notepad have menu systems!

Complete the following steps to examine the Notepad menu bar:

1. Select Programs from the Windows Start menu.

2. Select Accessories, Notepad. The Notepad applet opens.

3. Notice that even this simple applet has a basic menu structure, including a File menu, an Edit menu, a Help menu, and a Search menu.

4. Click File. Notice the standard File menu items: New, Open, Save, Save As, Page Setup, Print, and Exit.

5. Exit Notepad and return to Visual Basic.

This is the next thing you'll add to enhance the look of the invoice system. When you add a menu bar to your application, you actually add a *menu control.*

Examples of typical menus are File and Help. These menus (called *top-level menus*) are not commands, and should not perform actions themselves. Instead, these menus include commands within their structure. In some applets you might see a File menu with only one command in it: Exit. In complicated applications, top-level menus often branch to submenus (and certain submenus even have their own submenus). As far as menu design is concerned, a *submenu* is any item that's located in a menu hierarchy below a top-level menu, including both commands (which lead to actions) and names (which lead to actual submenus).

The Menu Editor, shown in Figure 11-4, is used to create a menu control. The Menu Editor allows you to name a menu, set the menu's *Caption* property, and set several other properties.

Tip

You're not limited to using the Menu Editor when you want to set properties for a menu control. Once the control has been created, you can also use the Properties window to set the control's properties.

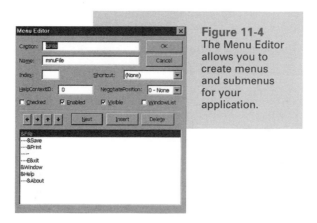

Figure 11-4
The Menu Editor allows you to create menus and submenus for your application.

The invoice application to which you're adding a menu system is an MDI application, so you need to deal with a couple of extra issues. Think about other MDI applications you've used. Which window has the menu bar? In MDI applications, the MDI parent form has the menu bar. Technically speaking, you *can* give a child form a menu bar. In that case, the menu bar on the MDI child form supplants the menu bar on the MDI parent when the child form is active.

> **Caution**
>
> Having a different menu bar display when a certain child form becomes active is disconcerting for your users! Because of this, you want to add menus to only the MDI parent form.

To add menus to the invoice application, use the following steps:

1. Open frmMDIMain from the Project Explorer. Make sure that the frmMDIMain object is displayed (not the Code window). The Menu Editor can only be accessed when a form is displayed.

2. Select <u>T</u>ools, <u>M</u>enu Editor to display the Menu Editor.

3. The first thing to enter is the caption for the menu you're creating. Just as you would expect, the *Caption* property of a menu is the text that appears for this object in the menu bar. For top-level menus, the caption should be one word without any spaces. Spaces are permissible for submenu captions. The first menu you're creating is the File menu. Type **File** and press the Tab key to move to the next field.

4. Type **mnuFile** in the Na<u>m</u>e text box.

5. Press Enter. You're now ready to create another menu or submenu. In this case, you need to create a submenu. In the Ca<u>p</u>tion text box, type **New** and then press the Tab key.

6. Type **mnuFileNew** in the Na<u>m</u>e text box.

7. Click the right-arrow button located near the <u>N</u>ext button. In the menu list found at the bottom of the Menu Editor, notice that New is indented— this means that it's a submenu.

> **Tip**
>
> There are two schools of thought on the naming conventions for menus. One, which is used in this project, dictates that you include the menu hierarchy in the name. mnuFileNew is an example of this. The other, which is used in the final project of this book, dictates that you include only the current menu item's name (as in mnuNew). Each approach has an advantage. Using the menu hierarchy acts as documentation in that when you look at a menu's name, you know exactly where it falls within the menu system. Not using the menu hierarchy can be a better approach if you think you might rearrange your menu system.

Note The maximum number of submenu levels you can create for each menu is four.

8. Continue creating the menu system using the menu items in Table 11-1.

Table 11-1	Invoice Menu System Settings	
Caption Value	*Name* Value	Description
Save	mnuFileSave	Submenu of the File menu
Print	mnuFilePrint	Submenu of the File menu
Exit	mnuFileExit	Submenu of the File menu
Help	mnuHelp	A top-level menu—use the left-arrow button to outdent this item in the hierarchy
About	mnuHelpAbout	Submenu of the Help menu

9. Click OK to save the menu.
10. Press F5 to run the application.
11. Click the frame of the splash screen to display the input box.
12. Type your name and press Enter. The MDI parent form of the invoice application is displayed.
13. Click the File menu. You can see its four submenus: New, Save, Print, and Exit.
14. Click the Help menu. You can see the About submenu.

Caution Don't click any of the submenus. Because you haven't written code for them, they don't do anything at this point.

15. Close the application by clicking the Close button in the upper-right corner of the MDI parent form.

Note

If you have a menu item that, when selected, displays a dialog box or input box, you should end its name with an ellipsis (...). For example, many File menus have a Print Setup... menu item. The ellipsis is a visual clue to users that this command needs additional information from them to complete its work. When they choose this command, they'll be prompted for the necessary information—typically through a dialog box.

Adding Keyboard Access and Shortcut Keys

As you can see, creating a menu in VB is really easy. Take a look at your menu bar. Notice anything odd about the menus? They don't have keyboard access. Take a look at VB's File menu. The "F" is underscored. This means that "F" is used for *keyboard access*—the user can select the File menu by pressing Alt+F. To denote the keyboard access key for a menu item, precede that character with an ampersand (&) in the control's *Caption* property.

Tip

If you wish to add keyboard access to other controls, such as option buttons and command buttons, just include the ampersand in their *Caption* properties. For controls that do not have *Caption* properties, use the *Caption* property of the label for that control.

If you select VB's File menu, you'll see that some of the commands—such as Save and Print—have *shortcut keys*. These provide the user with an alternative method to access these frequently used commands so that they do not need to use the menu system. To specify shortcut keys for menu items, use the *Shortcut* property. When selecting shortcut keys, look at other applications and notice what they are using for shortcut keys. Whenever possible, be consistent across your applications. Use the following steps to add keyboard access and shortcut keys to the invoice application's menu system:

1. Select Tools, Menu Editor to display the Menu Editor.
2. Change the Caption of the File menu to **&File**.
3. Select New from the Menu List.

4. Change its caption to **&New**.

5. From the Shortcut drop-down list, select Ctrl+N.

6. Change the remainder of the captions for the menu items to match those in Table 11-2. Figure 11-5 shows the completed menu system displayed in the Menu Editor.

Table 11-2	Keyboard Access and Shortcuts for the Menu System	
Menu	**New Caption**	**Shortcut**
Save	&Save	Ctrl+S
Print	&Print	Ctrl+P
Exit	E&xit	none
Help	&Help	none
About	&About	none

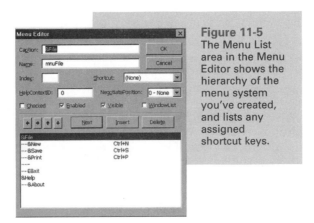

Figure 11-5
The Menu List area in the Menu Editor shows the hierarchy of the menu system you've created, and lists any assigned shortcut keys.

7. Click OK to save the changes. The keyboard access characters are now displayed (see Figure 11-6).

Look at the menu bar now. Each character preceded by an ampersand is now available for keyboard access. You may wonder why you used "x" instead of "E" as the keyboard access for the Exit menu. You did so because "x" is the standard keyboard access key for the Exit menu item in Windows applications (you can check this out in VB, Word, or another application). When in doubt about which characters to use for keyboard access, just study other applications. Users have come to expect certain characters to be used for certain commands.

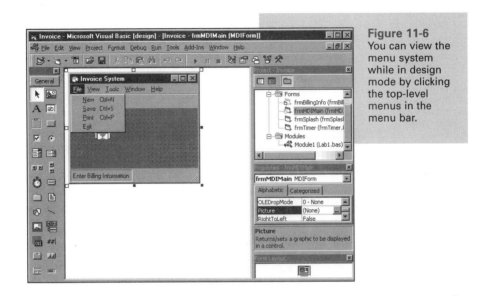

Figure 11-6
You can view the menu system while in design mode by clicking the top-level menus in the menu bar.

Look at VB's menu bar. The File and Format menus begin with the same letter, but they have different keyboard access characters. Top-level menus should always have unique keyboard access characters. Submenu items within a menu can have the same keyboard access characters, but this is not recommended for usability reasons.

Using Separator Bars

A separator bar is a horizontal line displayed between items on a menu to present the menu items in logical groups.

Select VB's File menu. Notice that all the save-related menu items are grouped and all the print-related items are grouped. They're visually segregated by a line that separates them from other menu items. To add a separator bar to your menu system, use these steps:

1. Select Tools, Menu Editor to display the Menu Editor.
2. Select E&xit from the Menu List.
3. Click Insert to add a blank item to the Menu List.
4. Type a hyphen (-) in the Caption text box. VB will convert the hyphen automatically into a line that has the length needed to span the menu.
5. Type **mnuSep1** in the Name text box. Even though you'll never refer to the separator bar in code, VB requires you to name it.
6. Click OK to save the changes.
7. Press F5 to run the application.
8. Click the frame of the splash screen to display the input box.

9. Type your name and press Enter. The MDI parent form of the invoice application is displayed.

10. Click the File menu. Notice the shortcut keys and the separator bar (see Figure 11-7).

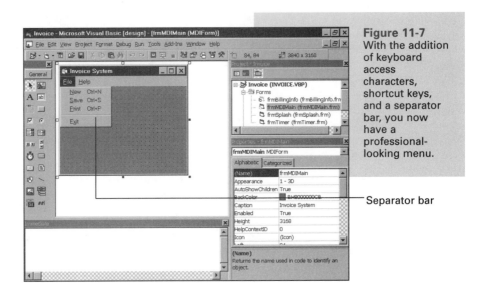

Figure 11-7
With the addition of keyboard access characters, shortcut keys, and a separator bar, you now have a professional-looking menu.

Separator bar

11. Close the application by clicking the Close button in the upper-right corner of the form.

Adding Code to Menu Objects

You might be thinking at this point, "I have a great-looking menu that doesn't do anything!" That's true, but it's easily corrected. The first thing you'll do is add code for the Exit menu:

1. From `frmMDIMain`, while in design mode, click File, Exit to open the Code window. The `mnuFileExit_Click` procedure is displayed.

2. Enter the following line of code in this procedure:
   ```
   End
   ```

3. Select `MDIForm` from the Code window's Object box.

4. Select `Click` from the Event box to display the `MDIForm_Click` procedure.

5. Cut all the code from this procedure to the Clipboard.

6. Select `mnuFileNew` from the Object box to display the `mnuFileNew_Click` procedure.

7. Paste the code from the Clipboard into this procedure. The end result should look like the following:

```
Private Sub mnuFileNew_Click()
    Dim frmNewBill As New frmBillingInfo
    giFormCount = giFormCount + 1
    frmNewBill.Caption = frmNewBill.Caption & giFormCount
    frmNewBill.Show
End Sub
```

8. Open `frmBillingInfo` from the Project Explorer.

9. Remove the OK and Cancel buttons from this form.

10. Press F5 to run the application.

11. Click the frame of the splash screen to display the input box.

12. Type your name and press Enter. The MDI parent form of the invoice application is displayed.

13. Select <u>F</u>ile, <u>N</u>ew to add a new form (see Figure 11-8).

14. Select <u>F</u>ile, E<u>x</u>it to end the application.

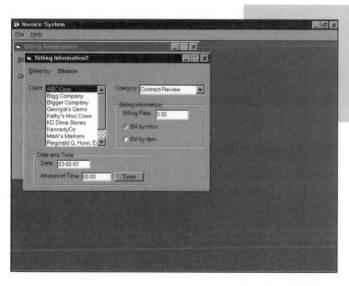

Figure 11-8
Selecting <u>F</u>ile,
<u>N</u>ew allows
you to create
multiple Billing
Information
forms.

Enabling and Disabling Menu Items

As a user of Windows applications, you're aware that when a menu item is unavailable, it's *dimmed* (also referred to as *grayed out*). The property that determines this is the *Enabled* property. When *Enabled* is set to `True`, the menu item is available for use; when *Enabled* is set to `False`, the menu item is unavailable. In the invoice system you want to disable the <u>S</u>ave and <u>P</u>rint commands when no forms are open. To make this happen, complete the following steps:

1. Open `frmBillingInfo`. Select `Form` from the Code window's Object box.

2. Select `Unload` from the Event box to display the `Form_Unload` procedure.

3. Add the following lines of code to the form:

```
giFormCount = giFormCount - 1
    If giFormCount = 0 Then
        With frmMDIMain
            .mnuFileSave.Enabled = False
            .mnuFilePrint.Enabled = False
        End With

    End If
```

4. Select `Load` from the Event box to display the `Form_Load` procedure.

5. Add the following code at the top of this procedure:

```
With frmMDIMain
    .mnuFileSave.Enabled = True
    .mnuFilePrint.Enabled = True
End With
```

6. Press F5 to run the application.

7. Click the frame of the splash screen to display the input box.

8. Type your name and press Enter. The MDI parent form of the invoice application is displayed.

9. Select <u>F</u>ile, <u>N</u>ew to add a new form.

10. Close both forms.

11. Select the <u>F</u>ile menu. Notice that <u>S</u>ave and <u>P</u>rint are disabled (see Figure 11-9).

12. Select <u>N</u>ew to add a form.

13. Select the <u>F</u>ile menu. Notice that <u>S</u>ave and <u>P</u>rint are now enabled.

14. Select E<u>x</u>it to end the application.

Working with a Menu Control's *Checked* Property

Occasionally you'll see a menu that acts as a *toggle menu*. This type of menu is denoted by a checkmark. When the menu item is toggled on, a checkmark is displayed next to the menu item. When the menu item is toggled off, the checkmark is not displayed. An example of a toggle menu item is <u>S</u>tatus Bar on the <u>V</u>iew menu. You can toggle the display of the status bar on and off. To add this capability to the invoice application, complete these steps:

Figure 11-9
Two menu items,
Save and Print,
are currently
unavailable.

1. Open frmMDIMain from the Project Explorer.
2. Select Tools, Menu Editor to display the Menu Editor.
3. Select &Help from the Menu List.
4. Click Insert to add a blank menu.
5. Type **&View** in the Caption text box.
6. Type **mnuView** in the Name text box and press Enter.
7. Click Insert to add a blank menu item.
8. Type **&Status Bar** in the Caption text box.
9. Type **mnuViewStatusBar** in the Name text box.
10. Click to place a checkmark in the Checked check box.
11. Click the right-arrow button to indent the menu item.
12. Click OK to save these changes to the menu system.
13. Select View, Status Bar to display the mnuViewStatusBar_Click procedure.
14. Enter the following text in this procedure:

```
mnuViewStatusBar.Checked = Not mnuViewStatusBar.Checked
    If mnuViewStatusBar.Checked = False Then
        staMain.Visible = False
    Else
        staMain.Visible = True
    End If
```

15. Press F5 to run the application.

16. Click the frame of the splash screen to display the input box.

17. Type your name and press Enter. The MDI parent form of the invoice application is displayed.

18. Notice that the status bar is currently displayed. Select View. Notice that there's a checkmark next to Status Bar. Select Status Bar and then notice that the status bar is no longer displayed.

19. Select View, Status Bar and verify that the status bar is displayed again.

20. Select File, Exit to end the application.

Creating a Window Menu

When you're using an MDI application, you expect to see a Window menu. On the Window menu is a list of the currently opened windows. This list is used to navigate the application's open windows. Another thing you expect to be able to do through the Window menu is arrange the open windows. To add a standard Window menu to the invoice system, complete these steps:

1. Open `frmMDIMain` from the Project Explorer.

2. Select Tools, Menu Editor to display the Menu Editor.

3. Select `&Help` from the Menu List.

4. Click Insert to add a blank menu.

5. Type **&Window** in the Caption text box.

6. Place a checkmark in the Window List check box.

7. Type **mnuWindow** in the Name text box and press Enter.

8. Click Insert to add a blank menu item.

9. Type **&Cascade** in the Caption text box.

10. Type **mnuWindowCascade** in the Name text box.

11. Click the right-arrow button to indent this menu item. Click Next.

12. Click Insert to add a blank menu.

13. Type **&Tile** in the Caption text box.

14. Type **mnuWindowTile** in the Name text box.

15. Click the right-arrow button to indent this menu item.

16. Click OK to save these changes to the menu system.

17. From `frmMDIMain` select Window, Cascade to display the `mnuWindowCascade_Click` procedure.

18. Type the following code in this procedure:
    ```
    frmMDIMain.Arrange vbCascade
    ```

19. Select `mnuWindowTile` from the Object box to display the `mnuWindowTile_Click` procedure.

20. Type the following code in this procedure:

    ```
    frmMDIMain.Arrange vbTileHorizontal
    ```

21. Press F5 to run the application.

22. Click the frame of the splash screen to display the input box.

23. Type your name and press Enter. The MDI parent form of the invoice application is displayed.

24. Select File, New three times to add three new forms.

25. Select the Window menu. Notice the list of open windows.

26. Select Tile to tile the windows.

27. Select Window, Cascade to cascade the forms.

28. Select File, Exit to end the application.

That's all you're going to do with menus for now. Later in this chapter you'll go back and write code for the Save and Print menu items.

Toolbars

Since you already have the basic menu system, you can easily add a *toolbar* to your application. Toolbars contain toolbar buttons that give users an alternative to using the menu system for frequently used commands.

The great thing about toolbar buttons is that they reuse the code you've already written for menu items. All you need to do is to call these menu procedures from the `ButtonClick` event procedure of the toolbar.

An image list control contains a collection of list image objects. Each list image object in the collection is referred to by a unique index or key.

Using the Image List Control

Before you create your toolbar, you should add an image list control to the MDI form. This control is needed by the toolbar to store the images used by the toolbar buttons. The image list control is only displayed on the form in design mode. This type of control is not meant to be used alone; it acts as a holding place for images that are to be used by other controls (such as a toolbar).

Tip

The image list control is available through the Microsoft Windows Common Controls 5.0 component.

To add an image list control to the invoice application, complete these steps:

1. Open `frmMDIMain` from the Project Explorer.

2. Place an image list control on the form.

3. Select the *Name* property from the Properties window. Enter **imlMain** as the name of this control.

4. Right-click `imlMain` and select Properties to display the Property Pages dialog box. Select the Images tab (see Figure 11-10).

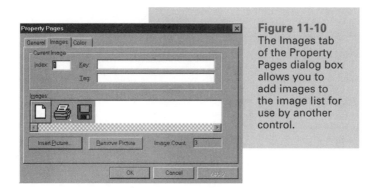

Figure 11-10
The Images tab of the Property Pages dialog box allows you to add images to the image list for use by another control.

5. Click the Insert Picture button to display the Select Picture dialog box. The images designed to be used as toolbar button images are located in `\Program Files\DevStudio\VB\Graphics\Bitmaps\Tlbr_w95`. Go to this directory to see a listing of graphic files.

6. Select the New file from the file list and click Open to select the image.

7. Click the Insert Picture button to display the Select Picture dialog box.

8. Select the Save file from the file list and click Open to select the image.

9. Click the Insert <u>P</u>icture button to display the Select Picture dialog box.

10. Select the Print file from the file list and click <u>O</u>pen to select the image.

11. Click OK to save the new settings.

Adding the Toolbar

After you've selected images for your toolbar buttons, you can add the toolbar itself. The toolbar control is used as a container for toolbar buttons. The toolbar buttons are going to use the image list control to select their button images. Use the following steps to add a toolbar to frmMDIMain:

Tip The toolbar control is available through the Microsoft Windows Common Controls 5.0 component.

1. Select the toolbar control from the toolbox.

2. Draw a toolbar at the top of frmMDIMain.

3. Select the *Name* property from the Properties window. Enter **tlbMain** for the name of this control.

4. Right-click the toolbar and select P<u>r</u>operties to display the Property Pages dialog box (see Figure 11-11).

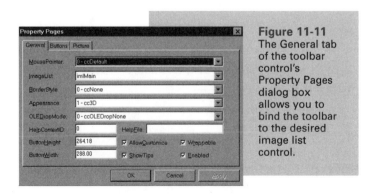

Figure 11-11
The General tab of the toolbar control's Property Pages dialog box allows you to bind the toolbar to the desired image list control.

5. Select im1Main from the <u>I</u>mageList drop-down list.

6. Select the Buttons tab (see Figure 11-12).

7. Click I<u>n</u>sert Button to add the first button to the toolbar.

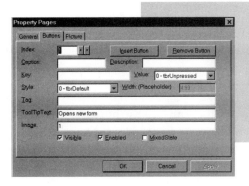

Figure 11-12
The Buttons tab of the toolbar control's Property Pages dialog box is used to add buttons to the toolbar.

8. Type **New** in the ToolTip Text text box.
9. Type **1** in the Image text box.

Note

If you had used a key to identify your image, you would enter the key's name in the <u>K</u>ey text box instead of entering a value in the Image text box.

10. Click the <u>A</u>pply button.
11. Click I<u>n</u>sert Button to add the next button to the toolbar.
12. Type **Print** in the ToolTip Te<u>x</u>t text box.
13. Type **2** in the Image text box.
14. Click the <u>A</u>pply button.
15. Click I<u>n</u>sert Button to add the last button to the toolbar.
16. Type **Save** in the ToolTip Te<u>x</u>t text box.
17. Type **3** in the Image text box.
18. Click OK to save these settings. The toolbar now contains toolbar buttons (see Figure 11-13).

Adding Code to the Toolbar

All the code for working with the toolbar buttons goes into one procedure, the toolbar's `ButtonClick` event procedure. Within this procedure you'll have a `Select Case` statement that has a case for each button in the toolbar. To add the necessary code to your application, follow these steps:

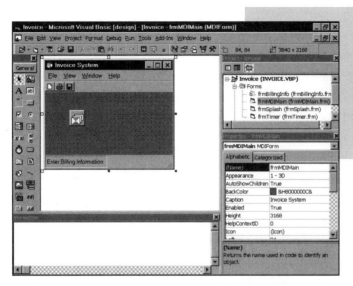

Figure 11-13
The toolbar for the invoice system now has three toolbar buttons. The image list control will not be displayed at runtime.

1. Before you start adding code for the toolbar, add some code for the Save and Print menu items so that you can test the associated toolbar buttons. Click File, Save to open the Code window. The `mnuFileSave_Click` procedure is displayed. Enter the following code for this procedure:

```
MsgBox "Save was selected."
```

2. Select `mnuFilePrint` from the Object box. The `mnuFilePrint_Click` procedure is displayed. Enter the following code for this procedure:

```
MsgBox "Print was selected."
```

You will replace the code lines entered in Steps 1 and 2 with more functional code later in the chapter.

3. Select `tlbMain` from the Object box. The `tlbMain_ButtonClick` procedure is displayed. Enter the following code for this procedure:

```
Select Case Button.Index
    'New button
    Case 1
        mnuFileNew_Click
    'Print button
    Case 2
        mnuFilePrint_Click
```

```
                'Save button
                Case 3
                     mnuFileSave_Click
            End Select
```

4. Press F5 to run the application.

5. Click the frame of the splash screen to display the input box.

6. Type your name and press Enter. The MDI parent form of the invoice application is displayed.

7. Position the pointer over the first toolbar button. Notice the ToolTip.

8. Click the first toolbar button. A new form is created.

9. Click the second toolbar button. The print message box is displayed. Click OK.

10. Select File, Exit to end the application.

EXERCISE

Take a couple of minutes right now to experiment with the File menu items and toolbar buttons by clicking each of them and seeing what happens. All objects except the ones that use the `mnuFileNew_Click` procedure (the New toolbar button and the New submenu) should display message boxes. This was done to avoid runtime errors. You'll add the actual required functionality later.

As you can see from this part of the project, the great thing about creating a toolbar is reusing your menu code! In the next part of the project you'll learn the skills you need to write the actual procedures for the Save and Print menu items.

Controlling Another Application from Your VB Application

Automation is the process of controlling a second application from a first application by having the first one use the second one's objects, properties, events, and methods.

One of the most significant enhancements to VB over the years has been the capability to control another application. Previously known as *OLE Automation*, the technique now called *Automation* has come into its own with the steady increase of applications that support both Automation and *Visual Basic, Application Edition* (also known as *Visual Basic for Applications* or *VBA*).

Automation affords an incredible array of features that you can incorporate into your applications. If you like something that Word does, then use it! If you love pivot tables in Excel, then go ahead—include them in your VB application.

A controller application controls a server application. A server application provides its objects, events, properties, and methods by exposing them to the controller application.

With the advent of VBA, you have the advantage of not needing to learn a new language so that you can automate another application. When Excel had its own macro language, for example, you had to know VB and also learn the Excel macro language. You'll find that much of your VB knowledge these days transfers directly to the VBA environment. There are some differences in syntax between the two environments, but you'll adapt to them quickly.

In the invoice system, VB acts as a controller application, and the other applications (in this case, Word and Excel) act as server applications. A server application exposes its objects so that they can be manipulated by the controller application.

Adding a Reference to an Object Library

Most applications that support Automation provide an *object library*. An object library is a file that has an OLB file extension. It provides information to the controller application about available objects in the server application. To use the object library information, you need to reference the OLB file from your controller application. For the invoice system, you need to add two object library references, one to Word and one to Excel. Use the following steps to add these references to your project:

1. Select Project, References to display the References dialog box (see Figure 11-14).

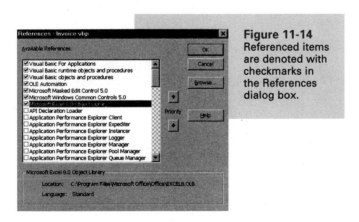

Figure 11-14
Referenced items are denoted with checkmarks in the References dialog box.

2. Locate Microsoft Excel 8.0 Object Library in the Available References list box.

3. Place a checkmark next to the Excel object library.

4. Locate Microsoft Word 8.0 Object Library in the Available References list box.

Tip

If you do not have Word 97 installed on your system, the Word portions of the invoice system will not work. Word 97 (Word 8.0) is the first version of Word that uses VBA. Prior to this release, Word used WordBasic as its automation language.

5. Place a checkmark next to the Word object library.

6. Click OK to add these references to your project.

Viewing an Object Library's Contents

The Object Browser allows you to view an object library's exposed objects. The Object Browser lists all properties, events, and methods for the exposed objects. The following exercise shows you how to view the object libraries referenced in the previous section.

1. Select View, Object Browser to display the Object Browser window (see Figure 11-15).

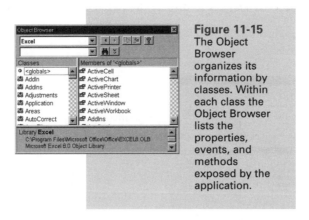

Figure 11-15
The Object Browser organizes its information by classes. Within each class the Object Browser lists the properties, events, and methods exposed by the application.

2. Select Excel from the Project/Library list (the first drop-down list) to display the contents of the Excel object library.

3. Select Worksheet from the Classes list to see the members of the Worksheet class.

4. Select the second Calculate member from the Members list. The green box icon next to this member denotes that it's a method or function.

EXERCISE

5. Press F1. Help information for this member is displayed. Notice the title bar of this window—you're displaying Excel Visual Basic Help. This is one of the advantages of referencing a library. You can press F1 to get context-sensitive help without leaving VB.

6. Close the Help window.

7. Close the Object Browser window.

Writing Code To Automate Excel

The first thing you're going to automate in Excel is the save process. To create the code to be executed when the user selects File, Save, follow these steps:

1. Open frmMDIMain from the Project Explorer.

2. Select File, Save from the form's menu bar to access the mnuFileSave_Click procedure.

3. Delete the MsgBox statement from this procedure.

4. Enter the following code in the same procedure:

```
Dim sngBilledTime As Single, sngMinutes As Single, sngHours As Single
Dim iResponse As Integer
Dim sErrorMessage As String
Dim x As Excel.Application

Set x = CreateObject("Excel.Application")
With x
    .Workbooks.Open filename:="C:\Prima\VB5\prog files\Lab2\Invoice.xls"
    .Worksheets("Data").Range("A2").Select
    .Selection.Sort Key1:=.Range("B2"), Order1:=xlDescending,
➡Header:=xlGuess
    .Range("A3").Select
    .Selection.EntireRow.Insert
    .Range("A3").Select
    .Range("A3").Value = frmBillingInfo.lstClient.Text
    .Range("B3").Value = .Range("B2").Value + 1
    .Range("C3").Value = frmBillingInfo.cboCategory.Text
    sngMinutes = Val(Right(frmBillingInfo.txtAmountOfTime.Text, 2))
    sngHours = Left(frmBillingInfo.txtAmountOfTime.Text,
➡(InStr(1, frmBillingInfo.txtAmountOfTime.Text, ":") - 1))
    Select Case sngMinutes
        Case Is >= 0 And sngMinutes < 15
            If sngHours > 0 Then
                sngBilledTime = sngHours
            Else
```

```
                  sngBilledTime = 0.5
            End If
        Case Is >= 15 And sngMinutes <= 30
            sngBilledTime = sngHours + 0.5
        Case Is > 30 And sngMinutes <= 59
            sngBilledTime = sngHours + 1
    End Select
    .Range("D3").Value = sngBilledTime
    If frmBillingInfo.optByHour.Value = True Then
        .Range("E3").Value = "Hour"
    Else
        .Range("E3").Value = "Item"
    End If
    .Range("F3").Value = frmBillingInfo.txtBillingRate.Text
    .Range("G2").Select
    .Selection.Copy
    .Range("G3").Select
    .ActiveSheet.Paste
    .Application.CutCopyMode = False
    .Range("H3").Value = frmBillingInfo.lblBilledBy.Caption
    .Range("I3").Value = frmBillingInfo.mskDate.Text
    .ActiveWorkbook.Save
    .Application.Quit
End With

Set x = Nothing
Unload frmBillingInfo
```

5. Press F5 to run the application.

6. Click the frame of the splash screen to display the input box.

7. Type your name and press Enter. The MDI parent form of the invoice application is displayed.

8. Select XYZ Corp. for Client and Litigation for Category. Enter **75** for the billing rate and **3:00** for the amount of time spent on the task.

9. Select File, Save to save these changes to the Invoice.xls file. The billing information form is no longer displayed.

10. Select File, Exit to end the application.

11. Start Excel.

12. Open Invoice.xls. Notice the added row (see Figure 11-16).

13. Exit Excel.

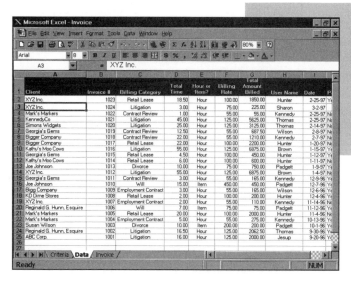

Figure 11-16
The information from the Billing Information form has been saved to the `Invoice.xls` file (to the third row of the worksheet).

Now examine the `mnuFileSave_Click` procedure in detail. Some of the code should look familiar to you. The procedure has its foundation in the `cmdOK_Click` procedure that was assigned to the OK button that used to reside on the form. The first three lines declare some typical variables:

```
Dim sngBilledTime As Single, sngMinutes As Single, sngHours As Single
Dim iResponse As Integer
Dim sErrorMessage As String
```

`sngBilledTime`, `sngMinutes`, and `sngHours` are used to determine and store the amount of time spent on the billable item. The next `Dim` statement is different from any you've done before:

```
Dim x As Excel.Application
```

Because the Excel object library has already been referenced by the project, you can create a fully qualified variable declaration. This increases the speed and performance of your application. You could have declared the variable as an Object data type, but there are performance issues with that approach. When you declare a variable of the Object data type, VB uses late binding. When you declare an object variable of a specific class — for example, `Excel.Application` — VB uses early binding. This speeds up object references and often speeds the application's overall performance.

Note ⬛ ***Binding* is the process of resolving the reference to the object library made by some type of object variable declaration.**

ANALYSIS

Once you've declared the object variable, use the `CreateObject` function in a `Set` statement to create a new object and assign an object reference to an object variable:

```
Set x = CreateObject("Excel.Application")
```

To save work, use the `With` statement:

```
With x
```

At this point in the procedure, you're controlling Excel. The first thing you do is open the file you want to work with. To open a file in Excel, use the `Open` method of the Workbooks collection. (A *workbook* is a file in the Excel environment.) Once the workbook is opened, select the worksheet and set of cells—referred to as a *range*—that you want to work with:

```
.Workbooks.Open filename:="C:\Prima\VB5\prog files\Lab2\Invoice.xls"
.Worksheets("Data").Range("A2").Select
```

You've selected Range A2, a single-cell range, and now you need to execute a *sort*. The data is sorted in descending order based on the invoice numbers that are located in Column B:

```
.Selection.Sort Key1:=.Range("B2"), Order1:=xlDescending, Header:=xlGuess
```

This places the newest invoice at the top.

Once the rows are sorted, you move to the second row of data. Then a row is inserted so that it can receive the data from `frmBillingInfo`. If you're wondering why you don't select the first row of data (which would be Row 2 in this case, because Row 1 contains headings), it's to work around a formatting obstacle. If you insert a row between Row 1 and Row 2, the new row adopts the formatting of Row 1, which has a blue background and yellow text. A quick and easy way to handle this is to insert the blank row between Rows 2 and 3. You don't have to worry about how this affects the data, because you always sort the data before adding another record. Once the new row is inserted, you select the first cell in the row using the `Range` object:

```
.Range("A3").Select
.Selection.EntireRow.Insert
.Range("A3").Select
```

The next three lines of code write information from `frmBillingInfo` to the worksheet:

```
.Range("A3").Value = frmBillingInfo.lstClient.Text
.Range("B3").Value = .Range("B2").Value + 1
.Range("C3").Value = frmBillingInfo.cboCategory.Text
```

The next section of code is a modified version of the code originally used for the form's now-deleted OK button. This code calculates how much time has been spent on the billing task and rounds it up:

```
sngMinutes = Val(Right(frmBillingInfo.txtAmountOfTime.Text, 2))
sngHours = Left(frmBillingInfo.txtAmountOfTime.Text,
➥(InStr(1, frmBillingInfo.txtAmountOfTime.Text, ":") - 1))
Select Case sngMinutes
Case Is >= 0 And sngMinutes < 15
        If sngHours > 0 Then
    sngBilledTime = sngHours
        Else
    sngBilledTime = 0.5
        End If
Case Is >= 15 And sngMinutes <= 30
        sngBilledTime = sngHours + 0.5
Case Is > 30 And sngMinutes <= 59
        sngBilledTime = sngHours + 1
End Select
.Range("D3").Value = sngBilledTime
```

Next you test the value of the optByHour option button on frmBillingInfo. Based on the value of this option button, you write either **Hour** or **Item** in cell E3. This was also modified from the code originally used by the OK button on frmBillingInfo:

```
If frmBillingInfo.optByHour.Value = True Then
        .Range("E3").Value = "Hour"
Else
        .Range("E3").Value = "Item"
End If
```

After the appropriate text is written to cell E3, you write the billing rate to cell F3:

```
.Range("F3").Value = frmBillingInfo.txtBillingRate.Text
```

The next five lines of code perform a copy-and-paste action. You want to copy the formula in cell G2 to cell G3. The formula in G2 is an IF function evaluating the text in Column F to see if it says Hour or Item, and calculating the total billable amount. If the text in Column F says Hour, then the amount of time is multiplied by the billable hourly rate. If it says Item, then just the billable rate is used. Notice the statement that sets *CutCopyMode* to False. If you do not do this, Excel will not turn off the marquee (a moving border around the item that is to be pasted):

```
.Range("G2").Select
.Selection.Copy
.Range("G3").Select
.ActiveSheet.Paste
.Application.CutCopyMode = False
```

You write the appropriate data to the last two cells:

```
.Range("H3").Value = frmBillingInfo.lblBilledBy.Caption
.Range("I3").Value = frmBillingInfo.mskDate.Text
```

Once the cells are written to, you want to save the changes, quit Excel, and terminate the `With` statement:

```
.ActiveWorkbook.Save
.Application.Quit
End With
```

The last things to do in terms of the Automation are: set the object variable to the reserved word `Nothing` to dissolve the association of the object variable with its object, and unload the form. You do so with the last two lines of code:

```
Set x = Nothing
Unload frmBillingInfo
```

If you're familiar with Excel, you can use the Macro Recorder to record most of this process and then cut-and-paste the resulting code into VB. You can use this code as a foundation for your procedure.

Automating Word and Excel To Create Reminder Letters

The next system requirement you need to implement is the past-due letter function. This requires the use of both Word and Excel. You need Excel because that's where the data resides. You'll use Excel's advanced filter feature to locate the desired record. Two worksheets, Past Due and Data, come into play at this point. Data, as the name implies, is where the invoice information resides. Past Due has the criteria area needed by the past-due letter. Once the record has been located, you'll write the appropriate information to the Word document you set up in the last chapter. To finalize this feature, use the following steps:

1. Open `frmMDIMain` from the Project Explorer.

2. Select Tools, Menu Editor to display the Menu Editor.

3. Select &Window from the Menu List and click Insert to add a blank menu item.

4. Type **&Tools** in the Caption text box.

5. Type **mnuTools** in the Name text box and press Enter.

6. Click Insert to add a blank menu item. Click the right-arrow button to indent this menu item.

7. Type **&Past Due Letters** in the Caption text box.

8. Type **mnuToolsPastDue** in the Name text box and press Enter.

9. Click OK to save the changes.

10. Select Tools, Past Due Letters from `frmMDIMain` to access the `mnuToolsPastDue_Click` procedure.

11. Enter the following code in this procedure:

```
Dim x As Excel.Application
Dim y As Word.Application
Dim sDate As String
Dim oResults As Object
Dim iNumRows As Integer

Set x = CreateObject("Excel.Application")
Set y = CreateObject("Word.Application")

sDate = InputBox("Input the date you wish to find Past due items for in
➥m/d/yy format: ")
With x
    .Workbooks.Open filename:="C:\Prima\VB5\prog files\Lab2\Invoice.xls"
    .Worksheets("Past Due").Range("I2").Value = sDate

    .Range("A1").CurrentRegion.Select
    iNumRows = .Selection.Rows.Count
    .Range("A1").Select
    .Selection.Offset(iNumRows + 4, 0).Select

    .Range("A1:J23").AdvancedFilter Action:=xlFilterCopy, CriteriaRange:=
➥Sheets("Past Due").Range("A1:J2"), CopyToRange:=Selection,
➥Unique:=False
    .Range("A1").Select
    .Selection.Offset(iNumRows + 5, 0).Select

End With

With y
    .Documents.Open filename:="C:\Prima\VB5\prog files\lab2\PastDue.doc"
    .Selection.GoTo What:=wdGoToBookmark, Name:="ClientName"
    .Selection.TypeText Text:=x.Selection.Value
    .Selection.GoTo What:=wdGoToBookmark, Name:="InvoiceNumber1"
```

```
    x.Selection.Offset(0, 1).Select
    .Selection.TypeText Text:=x.Selection.Value
    .Selection.GoTo What:=wdGoToBookmark, Name:="UserName1"
    x.Selection.Offset(0, 6).Select
    .Selection.TypeText Text:=x.Selection.Value
    .Selection.GoTo What:=wdGoToBookmark, Name:="InvoiceNumber2"
    x.Selection.Offset(0, -6).Select
    .Selection.TypeText Text:=x.Selection.Value
    .Selection.GoTo What:=wdGoToBookmark, Name:="AmountDue"
    x.Selection.Offset(0, 5).Select
    .Selection.TypeText Text:=Format(x.Selection.Value, "$###.00")
    .Selection.GoTo What:=wdGoToBookmark, Name:="UserName2"
    x.Selection.Offset(0, 1).Select
    .Selection.TypeText Text:=x.Selection.Value
    .Application.PrintOut
    MsgBox "Printing is complete."
    .ActiveDocument.SaveAs filename:="C:\Prima\VB5\prog files\lab2\" &
➡x.Range("B2").Value
    .Application.Quit
End With

With x
    .ActiveWorkbook.Close savechanges:=False
    .Application.Quit
End With

Set y = Nothing
Set x = Nothing
```

12. Select File, Save frmMDIMain.frm from the Visual Basic menu.

13. Press F5 to run the application.

14. Click the frame of the splash screen to display the input box.

15. Type your name and press Enter. The MDI parent form of the invoice application is displayed.

16. Select Tools, Past Due Letters.

17. Type **1/4/97** for the date in the input box and press Enter.

18. The letter is now being generated. This may take a few moments. When it's done, a message box will inform you that the letter has printed. The letter should look like the one shown in Figure 11-17.

19. Select File, Exit to end the application.

To: XYZ Inc.

Date: February 26, 1997

Re: Invoice # 1012

From: Brown

This letter is a reminder that we have not received payment from you for invoice number 1012. The amount due is $6875.00. If there is any additional information you need from our firm to aid you in processing this invoice for immediate payment please do not hesitate to call.

If you have already mailed your payment please accept our appreciation for that payment and for your patronage. We look forward to continuing our professional relationship with a client as valued as you.

Thank you,

Brown

Figure 11-17
The printed letter contains the filtered data resulting from the date entered.

It's time to examine the code for the `mnuToolsPastDue_Click` procedure in detail. The first two variables define fully-qualified variables that perform early binding:

```
Dim x As Excel.Application
Dim y As Word.Application
```

The `sDate` variable stores the date entered by the user. The `iNumRows` variable stores the number of rows of current data.

```
Dim sDate As String
Dim iNumRows As Integer
```

The `CreateObject` function is used in a `Set` statement to create a new object and assign an object reference to an object variable. This is done for Excel and Word, since you're using both applications:

```
Set x = CreateObject("Excel.Application")
Set y = CreateObject("Word.Application")
```

The user needs to be prompted for the date to be used. This is done with an input box that saves the result to the `sDate` variable:

```
sDate = InputBox("Input the date you wish to find Past due items for in
➥m/d/yy format: ")
```

The first `With` statement deals with Excel operations. First, the `Invoice.xls` file is opened; next, the desired date is written to the criteria area that will be used during the filtering operation:

```
With x
    .Workbooks.Open filename:="C:\Prima\VB5\prog files\Lab2\Invoice.xls"
    .Worksheets("Past Due").Range("I2").Value = sDate
```

`CurrentRegion` is an extremely useful tool that's used in the next code line:

```
.Range("A1").CurrentRegion.Select
```

It returns a `Range` object that represents the current region. The current region is a range bounded by any combination of blank rows and columns. This is used because you don't know if you have 10 rows or 10,000 rows. Using `CurrentRegion` addresses this concern.

`Selection.Rows.Count` returns the number of rows in the selection (in this case, it's all your rows of data). This number is saved to the `iNumRows` variable. Cell A1 is selected again to act as a starting point. Using the `Offset` property, you make the selected cell four rows beneath your data:

```
iNumRows = .Selection.Rows.Count
.Range("A1").Select
.Selection.Offset(iNumRows + 4, 0).Select
```

Once this area is selected, it's used to accept a copy of the row or rows that you've filtered from the data. The `AdvancedFilter` method is used to find the rows that match the date entered by the user and have a value of `No` in their Paid column. The resulting row or rows get copied to the range selected in the previous lines of text, as shown in the next lines of code:

```
.Range("A1:J23").AdvancedFilter Action:=xlFilterCopy, CriteriaRange:=
➥Sheets("Past Due").Range("A1:J2"), CopyToRange:=Selection,
➥Unique:=False
```

You select A1 to serve as a starting point again. This time the selection is offset by the total number of rows of data plus five more rows. This is because the `AdvancedFilter` method copies the header row as well as any rows that match the filter. This means that you must go an extra row to reach the needed data:

```
.Range("A1").Select
.Selection.Offset(iNumRows + 5, 0).Select
```

```
End With
```

Now it's time to work with Word. The first thing you do is open the `PastDue.doc` document:

```
With y
    .Documents.Open filename:="C:\Prima\VB5\prog files\lab2\PastDue.doc"
```

After the file is opened, you go to the first bookmark. At this bookmark you write the value of the currently selected cell:

```
.Selection.GoTo What:=wdGoToBookmark, Name:="ClientName"
.Selection.TypeText Text:=x.Selection.Value
```

From this point on, you repeat the process of going to a bookmark in Word, selecting the next cell to the right in Excel, and writing the contents of the cell to the document:

```
.Selection.GoTo What:=wdGoToBookmark, Name:="InvoiceNumber1"
x.Selection.Offset(0, 1).Select
.Selection.TypeText Text:=x.Selection.Value
.Selection.GoTo What:=wdGoToBookmark, Name:="UserName1"
x.Selection.Offset(0, 6).Select
.Selection.TypeText Text:=x.Selection.Value
.Selection.GoTo What:=wdGoToBookmark, Name:="InvoiceNumber2"
x.Selection.Offset(0, -6).Select
.Selection.TypeText Text:=x.Selection.Value
.Selection.GoTo What:=wdGoToBookmark, Name:="AmountDue"
x.Selection.Offset(0, 5).Select
.Selection.TypeText Text:=Format(x.Selection.Value, "$###.00")
.Selection.GoTo What:=wdGoToBookmark, Name:="UserName2"
x.Selection.Offset(0, 1).Select
.Selection.TypeText Text:=x.Selection.Value
```

Once all the text is written to the document, you're ready to print it:

```
.Application.PrintOut
MsgBox "Printing is complete."
```

The next line of code saves the document with the same name as the invoice. After that, you exit Word:

```
.ActiveDocument.SaveAs filename:="C:\Prima\VB5\prog files\lab2\" &
        ➥x.Range("B2").Value
.Application.Quit
End With
```

Close the `Invoice.xls` file without saving changes, and then exit Excel:

```
With x
.ActiveWorkbook.Close savechanges:=False
.Application.Quit
End With
```

The last thing to do in terms of the Automation is to set the object variables to the reserved word `Nothing` to dissolve the association of each object variable with its object. The last two code lines accomplish this:

```
Set y = Nothing
Set x = Nothing
```

You might want to expand this procedure as a way to experiment with and practice your VB programming skills. One way to expand it is to add a way to deal with the issue of multiple rows retrieved by the filter—figure out a way to print multiple letters if that happens. Another way you might want to challenge yourself is by incorporating an error-handling system for this application.

Summary

This chapter introduced several very important VB topics. You learned how to add a status bar, menu system, and toolbar to your application, and how to provide code for these objects. You also got extensive hands-on experience with Automation using two server applications, Excel and Word. Now that you've worked with these techniques, you can incorporate them into your own applications. In the next chapter you'll go through the necessary steps to test the invoice application. Once the testing phase is over you'll go through the process of preparing the application for distribution.

CHAPTER 12

Testing the Invoice System

This chapter helps you test and distribute the invoice system. The application development itself is basically complete. Through the testing process you want to verify that it performs as you intended. Once the application has been tested, you'll be ready to distribute the application. To do this you'll use the Application Setup Wizard. This wizard walks you through the process of creating distribution disks and a setup program.

Testing the Application

In Project 1 you went through the basics of testing an application. As your applications become more and more sophisticated, the importance of testing increases. The invoice system has many more things to test than the time tracking system did. For example, you need to test each menu item and toolbar button. You need to make sure that data is being written correctly and that files are being saved. Every action that the user can perform while interacting with your application needs to be tried as part of the testing process.

Creating a Testing Checklist

The invoice system is a moderately simple application. You have a parent form that only needs to track one child form. In spite of this, you still have numerous actions to test. As the number of forms, controls, menus, and toolbar buttons grows in an application, so does the time required for testing. Not only the quantity but also the complexity of the testing increases.

You shouldn't rely on your memory to test an application. Just using your memory to track whether or not you've tested all the menus or all the controls on a form doesn't build a reliable testing environment. A good tool to use when testing an application is a *testing checklist*. This checklist should include everything you need to verify, test, and try in your application—this includes both cosmetic and functional behaviors. Here's an example of a testing checklist that you can use as a foundation for building your own customized checklist:

✔ **Do all menus have unique keyboard access?**

Verify that you do not have duplicate keyboard access characters on the top-level menus (File, Format, and so on).

Verify that you do not have duplicate keyboard access characters within a submenu structure (Save, Save As, and so on).

✔ **Do the standard menu items (Save, Print, Help, and so on) have shortcut keys assigned to them?**

Verify that the shortcut keys are available and that they are the standard ones. Shortcut keys are not an area to express your creativity. For example, Ctrl+V should always be the shortcut for the Paste menu item.

✔ **Does each caption for a menu item that branches to a dialog box end in an ellipsis (...)?**

The Common User Access (CUA) standard states that when a menu item needs additional information—typically requested in the form of a dialog box—that control's caption should end with an ellipsis. This is a commonly overlooked area when testing an interface.

✔ **If this is an MDI application, did you include a Window menu with its *WindowList* property set to True?**

Users expect a window list to appear in the Window menu. Verify that it appears.

✔ **Do any of the child forms of an MDI application have menus?**

If so, do you have a really good reason for doing this? If you do not have an extremely good reason, remove the menus from the child forms.

✔ **Do controls have keyboard access?**

Users do not want to have to press the Tab key several times to get to a particular control on a form.

✔ **Did you include a status bar?**

Users have come to expect this interface element in their applications.

✔ **Has the status bar text been tested?**

Tab through all the controls on a form to verify the status bar text for each control. Move through the menu system also to verify that the correct text for each menu item is displayed in the status bar.

✔ **Do all toolbar buttons have ToolTips?**

Move your pointer over each toolbar button. Is the ToolTip displayed and is its text correct?

✔ **Have all toolbar buttons been tested?**

Click each toolbar button and notice the resulting behavior. Is it what you intend?

✔ **Do all dialog boxes have default and cancel buttons?**

All dialog boxes should have one command button with its *Default* property set to True and one command button (occasionally this is the same button) with its *Cancel* property set to True. Users may become frustrated if they press Enter or Escape and nothing happens.

✔ **Is the tab order correct on all forms?**

When you press the Tab key to move through the controls on a form, are the controls accessed in the order you expect?

This type of checklist can be used by you or someone else to test your application. You might want to create this checklist as a spreadsheet (see Figure 12-1) so that it's in an easy-to-use grid format. In conjunction with this list you might want to provide testers a list of commonly used shortcut keys and keyboard access characters so that they can verify these are used in your application. You can create this list once and then use it to test all your future applications. Table 12-1 lists commonly used access characters and Table 12-2 lists commonly used shortcut keys.

The best person to test an application is not the programmer. You are frankly the last person who should test an application that will be distributed to multiple users. You're likely to miss things just because you've been looking at the application for so long. Whenever possible, let someone else test your application.

Figure 12-1
Using a spreadsheet as a checklist allows you to come up with a standardized approach to testing.

Form	Toolbars			Menus						Status Bar		Forms		Dialog Box		MDI	
	Toolbar (Y/N)	Toolbar Tips?	Toolbar Buttons Tested?	Menu Bar (Y/N)	Menu Items Tested?	Keyboard Access for Menus?	Use of Standard Access Char.?	Use of Standard Shortcut Keys?	Do Menu Items That Need More Info. Have an Ellipsis?	Status Bar (Y/N)	Status Bar Text Verified?	Tab Order Correct?	Controls Have Keyboard Access	Is This a Dialog Box?	If So, Does It Have Default and Cancel Btns.?	MDI Application (Y/N)	Window Menu and Window List (Y/N)
frmSplash	N			N						Y	Y	N/A	N/A	Y	N		
frmMDIMain	Y	Y	Y	Y	Y	Y	Y	Y	N/A	Y	Y	N/A	N/A	N		Y	Y
frmBillingInfo	N			N						N		N	N	N			

Table 12-1 Commonly Used Access Characters

Menu Item	Access Character
File	F
New	N
Open	O
Save	S
Save As	A
Page Setup	u
Print Preview	v
Print	P
Exit	x
Edit	E
Undo	U
Cut	t
Copy	C
Paste	P
View	V
Tools	T
Options	O
Window	W
Cascade	C
Tile Vertically	V
Tile Horizontally	H
Help	H
Contents	C
Index	I
About	A

Table 12-2 Commonly Used Shortcuts

Menu Item	Shortcut
New	Ctrl+N
Open	Ctrl+O
Save	Ctrl+S
Print	Ctrl+P
Undo	Alt+Backspace
Cut	Ctrl+X
Copy	Ctrl+C
Paste	Ctrl+V
Help Topics	F1

Completing the Testing Process

You are ready to test the invoice application. Recall the checklist presented earlier in the chapter, because you will evaluate the application based on that checklist:

1. Press F5 to start the application.

2. Click the frame to display the input box.

3. Enter your name and press Enter to display the main part of the application. Normally you would test this input box by doing various things—not typing anything and clicking OK, clicking the Cancel button, and so on—but this input box was tested thoroughly in the last project.

Tab order is the order in which controls receive focus on a form as a user presses the Tab key. Focus determines which object has the attention of the system. The object with focus is the object that the user can currently interact with through the keyboard.

4. Test the tab order of the Billing Information form. The first thing to notice is whether or not the Client list box has the focus (it should). Press the Tab key. The next control to receive focus is the Category drop-down list box. So far, there are no problems.

5. Press the Tab key again. You expect the next control to receive focus to be the Billing Rate text box. This is not the case. The Bill by Hour option button gets the focus. The tab order needs to be corrected, so make note of this. You do not need to further test the tab order because you already know that it needs to be corrected.

6. As you tab through the controls, is the correct text being displayed in the status bar? You only added status bar text for the first two controls on this form. In real life you would correct this by adding status bar text for the rest of the controls, but that's unnecessary for the purposes of this project.

7. Take a look at the controls on this form. They do not have keyboard access characters. Make a note to correct this.

8. Navigate the menu system. Does it have keyboard access characters? It does, so you don't need to correct anything in that area. Does it use standard shortcut keys? It does.

9. Select File, New to add another form. This function works.

10. On the new form, select KD Dime Stores for the client and Employment Contract for the category. Set the billing rate to **100** and the amount of time to **2:00**.

11. Select File, Save. What happens? At this point you see something very unexpected. The first Billing Information form disappears. This is because with the code currently written, the first form loaded has its contents written to the Invoice.xls file and then is unloaded. This is definitely not your intention, so this is a major bug that needs to be corrected. Make a note about this.

12. Select File, Print. All that happens when this menu is selected is that a message box is displayed. Make a note that you need to go back and write meaningful code for the Print menu item.

13. Don't worry about testing the Tools, Past Due Letters menu item. That was tested extensively in the last chapter.

14. Select File, Exit to end the application.

In Step 2 you may have felt uncomfortable with the fact that a user has to click a frame to continue the application. This is not very intuitive, but it's the way the splash form template is set up. If you prefer to add an OK button to this form, you can cut the code from the `Frame1_Click` procedure and paste it to the OK button's `Click` procedure. Or you can add a timer to the control to display the splash screen for a certain length of time and then automatically unload the form. In this case, cut the code from `Frame1_Click` and paste it to the form's `Unload` event procedure.

You now have several things to fix and debug in your application. The following items were noted during the testing process:

- The tab order on `frmBillingInfo` is incorrect.
- The controls on `frmBillingInfo` need keyboard access characters.
- The File, Save operation does not work correctly.
- The File, Print operation needs to be written.

Setting the Tab Order and Keyboard Access

As you saw during testing, tab order is the order in which controls receive focus when the user presses the Tab key. An incorrect tab order can be disconcerting to the user. By default, VB assigns a tab order to controls as you create them on a form. Each new control is placed last in the tab order. The property determining a control's placement in the tab order is the *TabIndex* property. If you change a control's *TabIndex* property to adjust its location in the tab order, VB automatically renumbers the *TabIndex* setting of other controls on that form as necessary.

Note Controls that have their *Visible* or *Enabled* property set to `False` are skipped in the tab order because they cannot receive focus.

Note

The following types of objects do not support the *TabIndex* property: menu, timer, data, image, shape, and line.

There are two approaches for resetting a form's tab order. The first way is more intuitive. Start with the first control and set its *TabIndex* property to **0** (tab indexing starts with 0). Select the second control and set its *TabIndex* to **1**, and so on. This approach can be problematic with forms that have a large number of controls. About halfway through setting the *TabIndex* property for your controls, you might find yourself wondering, for example, if the last number was 17 or 18. Then you have to select the last control you worked with, look up the value of its *TabIndex* property, and then return to the control you were working with.

The second way takes advantage of the fact that VB automatically adjusts tab order numbering following insertions and deletions. Start with the last control in the tab order. Set its *TabIndex* property to **0**. Select the next-to-last control in the tab order and set its *TabIndex* to **0**. Continue moving backward through the tab order, always setting *TabIndex* to **0**. This is how the method works: When you set the *TabIndex* value of the next-to-last control to 0, the *TabIndex* value of the last control becomes 1. When you set the next control's *TabIndex* value to 0, the next-to-last control's *TabIndex* value becomes 1 and the last control's *TabIndex* value becomes 2. Using this approach, you don't have to worry about what the current number should be when setting the *TabIndex* property. The only number you need to remember is 0!

You also need to assign keyboard access characters to the controls. You do this by using the *Caption* property just as you did for menu items. Precede the character that is to be the keyboard access with an ampersand (&). Some controls, like option buttons, have built-in labels. You added your own labels to other controls, such as text boxes and list boxes, that do not have *Caption* properties. To assign a keyboard access character to one of these controls, you need to set the character in the label you created for the control. Also set that label's *TabIndex* value to be one less than that of the control that's to receive focus. For example, if you have a label and a text box at the top of a form, you set *TabIndex* to **0** for the label and to **1** for the text box.

Use the following steps to set the tab order and access characters for `frmBillingInfo`:

1. Select the Timer button. Set its *TabIndex* property to **0**. Set its *Caption* property to **&Timer**.
2. Select the `txtAmountOfTime` control. Set its *TabIndex* property to **0**.

3. Select the `lblAmountOfTime` label. Set its *TabIndex* property to **0**. Set its *Caption* property to **&Amount of Time**.

4. Continue setting the *TabIndex* and *Caption* properties in the order listed in Table 12-3.

Table 12-3 TabIndex and Caption Property Settings

Control	TabIndex	Caption
mskDate	0	
lblDate	0	&Date:
optByItem	0	By &Item
optByHour	0	By &Hour
txtBillingRate	0	
lblBillingRate	0	&Billing Rate:
cboCategory	0	
lblCategory	0	Cate&gory:
lstClient	0	
lblClient	0	&Client:

5. Select File, Save `frmBillingInfo.frm` to save the changes.

Correcting the File, Save Menu Command Using the *ActiveForm* Property

Currently, when you select File, Save the first instance of the child form is saved even if another child form is active. To avoid this, you use the *ActiveForm* property of the MDI parent form. This returns the name of the active child form. To fix the bug in the invoice application, follow these steps:

1. Open `frmMDIMain` from the Project Explorer.

2. Select File, Save from this form to access the `mnuFileSave_Click` procedure.

3. Modify this procedure so that it matches the following (changes are in bold):

```
Private Sub mnuFileSave_Click()

    Dim sngBilledTime As Single, sngMinutes As Single, sngHours As Single
    Dim iResponse As Integer
    Dim sErrorMessage As String
    Dim x As Excel.Application

    Set x = CreateObject("Excel.Application")
    With x
```

```
        .Workbooks.Open filename:="C:\Prima\VB5\prog files\Lab2\
➥Invoice.xls"
        .Worksheets("Data").Range("A2").Select
        .Selection.Sort Key1:=.Range("B2"), Order1:=xlDescending,
➥Header:=xlGuess
        .Range("A3").Select
        .Selection.EntireRow.Insert
        .Range("A3").Select
        .Range("A3").Value = frmMDIMain.ActiveForm.lstClient.Text
        .Range("B3").Value = .Range("B2").Value + 1
        .Range("C3").Value = frmMDIMain.ActiveForm.cboCategory.Text
        sngMinutes = Val(Right(frmMDIMain.ActiveForm.txtAmountOfTime.Text,
➥2))
        sngHours = Left(frmMDIMain.ActiveForm.txtAmountOfTime.Text,
➥(InStr(1, frmMDIMain.ActiveForm.txtAmountOfTime.Text, ":") - 1))
        Select Case sngMinutes
            Case Is >= 0 And sngMinutes < 15
                If sngHours > 0 Then
                    sngBilledTime = sngHours
                Else
                    sngBilledTime = 0.5
                End If
            Case Is >= 15 And sngMinutes <= 30
                sngBilledTime = sngHours + 0.5
            Case Is > 30 And sngMinutes <= 59
                sngBilledTime = sngHours + 1
        End Select
        .Range("D3").Value = sngBilledTime
        If frmMDIMain.ActiveForm.optByHour.Value = True Then
            .Range("E3").Value = "Hour"
        Else
            .Range("E3").Value = "Item"
        End If
        .Range("F3").Value = frmMDIMain.ActiveForm.txtBillingRate.Text
        .Range("G2").Select
        .Selection.Copy
        .Range("G3").Select
        .ActiveSheet.Paste
        .Application.CutCopyMode = False
        .Range("H3").Value = frmMDIMain.ActiveForm.lblBilledBy.Caption
        .Range("I3").Value = frmMDIMain.ActiveForm.mskDate.Text
        .ActiveWorkbook.Save
        .Application.Quit
    End With

    Set x = Nothing
    Unload frmMDIMain.ActiveForm
End Sub
```

4. Select <u>F</u>ile, <u>S</u>ave frmMDIMain.frm to save the changes.

5. Press F5 to run the application.

6. Click the frame to display the input box.

7. Type your name and press Enter.

8. Select File, New to add another form.

9. On the new form, select KD Dime Stores for the client and Employment Contract for the category. Set the billing rate to **100** and the amount of time to **2:00**.

10. Select File, Save to save the active child form. In a few moments the active child form is unloaded.

11. Select File, Exit to end the application.

12. Start Excel.

13. Open Invoice.xls.

14. Verify that the child form information has been correctly written.

15. Close Excel.

Writing the File, Print Procedure

To print the invoice, you're going to use Excel's native print capabilities (of course, this involves Automation). Use the following steps to create a procedure to write the billing information from frmBillingInfo to an Excel worksheet and then print the worksheet:

1. Select mnuFilePrint from the Object box to display the mnuFilePrint_Click procedure.

2. Delete the MsgBox statement in this procedure.

3. Enter the following code instead:

```
Dim x As Excel.Application

Set x = CreateObject("Excel.Application")

mnuFileSave_Click
With x
    .Workbooks.Open filename:="C:\Prima\VB5\prog files\Lab2\Invoice.xls"
    With .Worksheets("Invoice")
        .Range("BillTo").Value = Worksheets("Data").Range("A3").Value
        .Range("InvoiceNumber").Value = Worksheets("Data").Range("B3").
➥Value
        .Range("Category").Value = Worksheets("Data").Range("C3").Value
        .Range("AmountDue").Value = Worksheets("Data").Range("G3").Value
        .PrintOut
    End With
```

```
        .ActiveWorkbook.Save
        .Application.Quit
    End With

    Set x = Nothing

    End Sub
```

4. Select File, Save frmMDIMain.frm to save the changes.

5. Press F5 to run the application.

6. Click the frame to display the input box.

7. Type your name and press Enter.

8. Select File, New to add another form.

9. On the new form, select KennedyCo for the client and Litigation for the category. Set the billing rate to **125** and the amount of time to **32:00**.

10. Select File, Print to save, print, and unload the form. The printed form looks like the one shown in Figure 12-2.

11. Select File, Exit to end the application.

Bill To: KennedyCo

From: **My Company**

Invoice #: **1027**   Due: *Upon Receipt*

Description	**Amount**
Litigation	4,000.00

$ **4,000.00**

* * * * **Please make checks out to My Company** * * * *
Thanks for your patronage!

Figure 12-2
The printed invoice contains information from the Billing Information form.

ANALYSIS

Most of the statements used in this procedure should be familiar to you, but let's examine them in detail. The first set of statements references the Excel application:

```
Dim x As Excel.Application

Set x = CreateObject("Excel.Application")
```

The next thing you need to do is save the invoice. (It's not a good idea to print an invoice that hasn't been recorded.) You already have a procedure named mnuFileSave_Click that does this. Rather than copying and pasting the code, just call the procedure:

```
mnuFileSave_Click
```

At this point you're ready to write the needed information to the Invoice sheet. Notice that you're writing from the third row of the Data sheet. Just as a reminder, when you save a form you insert a row between Rows 2 and 3. The record is written to the blank row, which is the new Row 3:

```
With x
    .Workbooks.Open filename:="C:\Prima\VB5\prog files\Lab2\Invoice.xls"
    With .Worksheets("Invoice")
        .Range("BillTo").Value = Worksheets("Data").Range("A3").Value
        .Range("InvoiceNumber").Value = Worksheets("Data").Range("B3").Value
        .Range("Category").Value = Worksheets("Data").Range("C3").Value
        .Range("AmountDue").Value = Worksheets("Data").Range("G3").Value
```

The `Printout` method prints a worksheet (in this case, the Invoice sheet):

```
        .PrintOut
    End With
```

At the end of the code, you save the changes, exit Excel, and set the object variable to `Nothing`:

```
        .ActiveWorkbook.Save
        .Application.Quit
End With

Set x = Nothing

End Sub
```

Using the Application Setup Wizard

The invoice application has been tested and debugged. It's time to distribute it! The easiest way to prepare your application for distribution is to use the Application Setup Wizard. The Application Setup Wizard is a utility that helps you create distribution diskettes and a setup program. To use the Application Setup Wizard, follow these steps:

You need two blank, formatted floppy disks to complete these steps.

1. Exit VB. Answer Yes if you are prompted to save files.

2. Open the Application Setup Wizard from the Visual Basic program group to display the Introduction dialog box for this wizard (see Figure 12-3).

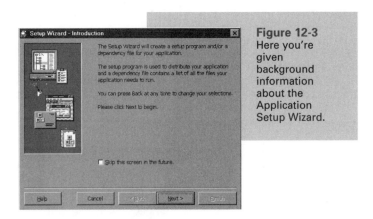

Figure 12-3
Here you're given background information about the Application Setup Wizard.

3. Click Next to display the Select Project and Options dialog box (see Figure 12-4).

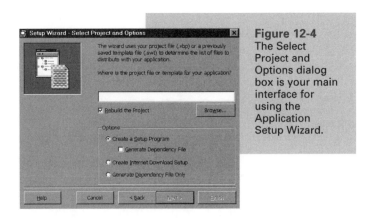

Figure 12-4
The Select Project and Options dialog box is your main interface for using the Application Setup Wizard.

4. This dialog box allows you to select the VB project you want to distribute. Click the Browse button to display the Locate VB Application's .VBP File dialog box (see Figure 12-5).

5. Locate and select the Invoice project. Click Open.

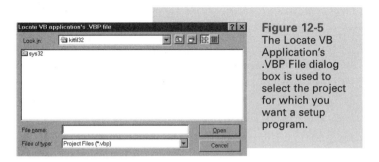

Figure 12-5
The Locate VB Application's .VBP File dialog box is used to select the project for which you want a setup program.

6. Make sure that a checkmark is in the Rebuild the Project check box. This instructs the Application Setup Wizard to create an EXE file for the invoice application whether or not the wizard finds an existing EXE, DLL, or OCX file for this project.

7. The next step is to select your options. The first option, Create a Setup Program, is the default. Associated with this option is the Generate Dependency File check box. When this is checked, the wizard generates a file that contains dependency information and includes it in the setup. Dependency files, which have a DEP extension, are used for any object of an OCX, DLL, or EXE, any ActiveX component, or any project that can be used as a component in other projects. The next option is Create Internet Download Setup. This option allows you to create an Internet download setup for only ActiveX control projects, ActiveX EXE, and ActiveX DLL projects that have public classes, including projects that contain UserDocuments. This option is not available in Visual Basic, Learning Edition. The last option, Generate Dependency File Only, generates a dependency file with the same name as your project and a DEP extension, and places this file in the same directory as your project. Select Create a Setup Program.

8. Click Next. A message box is displayed concerning the reference this project has to EXCEL8.OLB. Click OK. Another message box is displayed concerning the reference this project has to MSWORD8.OLB. Click OK. The Distribution Method dialog box is displayed, as shown in Figure 12-6.

9. Select the Floppy Disk option button and click Next.

10. The Floppy Disk dialog box is displayed (see Figure 12-7). Select the drive you want to use, and click Next.

11. The ActiveX Components dialog box is displayed (see Figure 12-8). Here you can add any components that the wizard may have missed. Click Next.

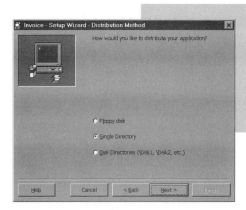

Figure 12-6
The Distribution Method dialog box allows you to select the distribution method you prefer.

Figure 12-7
The Floppy Disk dialog box is used to select the floppy drive and disk size you want.

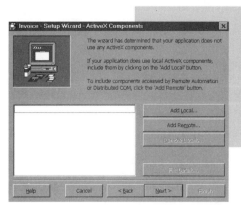

Figure 12-8
You can add local ActiveX components and remote automation components that the wizard has overlooked.

12. The Confirm Dependencies dialog box (see Figure 12-9) allows you to verify that the wizard has identified all file dependencies. Click Next.

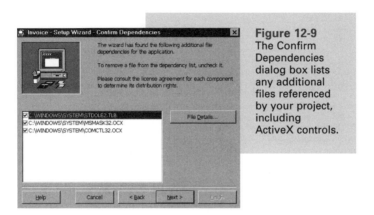

Figure 12-9
The Confirm Dependencies dialog box lists any additional files referenced by your project, including ActiveX controls.

13. The File Summary dialog box (see Figure 12-10) lists the files needed for your application to run. Click Next.

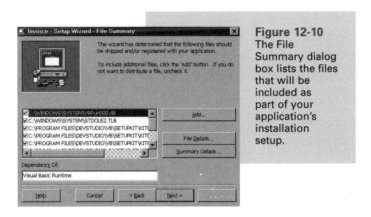

Figure 12-10
The File Summary dialog box lists the files that will be included as part of your application's installation setup.

14. The much-anticipated Finished! window is displayed (see Figure 12-11). To create the setup program, click Finish. The Working dialog box is displayed, keeping you informed of what the wizard is doing.

15. After a few moments you're prompted to insert the first of two floppy disks. Insert the disk and click OK.

16. After a few more moments you're prompted for the second floppy disk. Insert the disk and click OK.

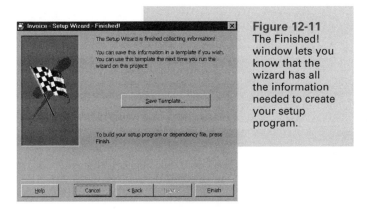

Figure 12-11
The Finished! window lets you know that the wizard has all the information needed to create your setup program.

17. When the wizard is done copying files, it displays the Setup Wizard window (see Figure 12-12). Click OK.

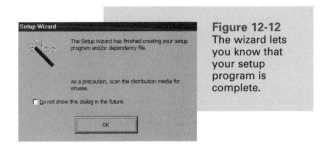

Figure 12-12
The wizard lets you know that your setup program is complete.

Before distributing any application, you should test its installation program. To install the invoice application on your system, follow these steps:

1. Insert the first disk of the setup program.

2. Click the desktop's Start button and select Run to display the Run dialog box.

3. Type **A:setup** and press Enter. After copying files, Setup displays the first screen of your setup program (see Figure 12-13). Click OK.

4. You're instructed to click the button on the next screen to start the installation process. Go ahead and click it.

5. The files are copied to your system. When this process is complete, a message box notifies you. Click OK. An icon is added to the Start menu's program list.

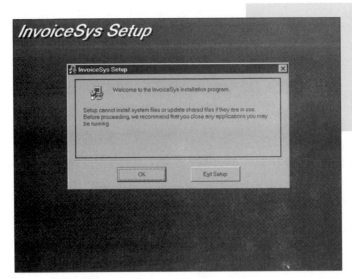

Figure 12-13
The first screen of the setup program has the familiar blue background that many installation programs use.

6. Click Start to run the application from your desktop. Select <u>P</u>rograms, Invoice to start the invoice application. The splash screen is displayed (see Figure 12-14).

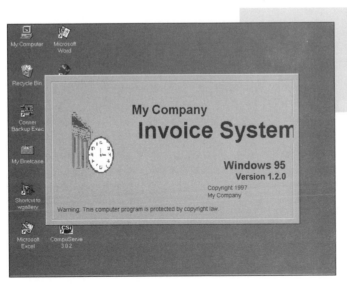

Figure 12-14
The invoice application is now installed and running on your system.

As you can see, the Application Setup Wizard is a great utility for the creation of professional-looking installation programs. You have now completed the second project.

Summary

Congratulations on your first major application upgrade! If you review how much you've done to the time tracking system to turn it into the invoice system, you'll know that you've created an upgrade with new features that should be appreciated by your end users. The interface enhancements alone would impress the typical end user. The application now looks more familiar to the user because it's an MDI application. By adding menus and a toolbar, you've greatly improved the usability of the application. And, of course, the biggest new feature is the ability to save your work using Excel!

Now that you've gained many new skills by completing the second project, you're ready to face more advanced topics such as database front-end design, which the next project discusses in detail.

Project 2 Summary

The invoice system built on the skills you learned while doing the first project. In developing the invoice system, you went through the process of upgrading an application and worked with some advanced topics and features of VB. By completing this project, you learned how to reuse forms from another application, because the invoice application used the time tracking application's forms as its foundation.

You also learned to convert an SDI application into an MDI application. You gained several skills for working with MDI applications, including setting the necessary properties for child forms. You also learned to create multiple instances of a child form by using the keyword New in your Dim statements.

You were introduced to several interface design enhancements in this project. One of these was the status bar control; another was the use of a menu system. You used the Menu Editor to create a menu system, and then wrote code for the individual menu items. You added a window list to the Window menu, and added a functional toolbar to the application.

You used Automation extensively in this project to control both Word and Excel. Once the invoice application was tested and debugged, you used the Setup Wizard to create an installation program.

HANDS ON
PROJECT 3

THE CLIENT MANAGEMENT SYSTEM

- Planning a database front end and evaluating database products
- Building your database using the Visual Data Manager
- Creating an interface with the data control
- Adding functionality using DAO (the Data Access Object model)
- Accessing data without the data control using DAO
- Creating and using queries with DAO
- Creating reports with Crystal Reports
- Accessing reports from your application
- Addressing special error-handling needs for database applications
- Compiling the application

Project Overview

Project 3, the client management system, explores some additional design and implementation considerations that you face when developing a system to interact with a database. Once you have completed this project, you will be able to plan and implement your database projects more efficiently and effectively.

During this project, you evaluate your data needs in conjunction with the system needs. You also get a chance to use the Visual Data Manager to create and manage your data source.

The project introduces several ways to implement your user interface. You can let VB do more of the work by using the data control and the Data Control Wizard, or you can create the interface without the data control and rely instead on the Data Access Object model.

Other parts of this project explore getting more out of your data with queries and developing useful reports. Some additional concerns related to error handling are discussed. The last task covered in this project is compiling your application into native C++ code instead of creating the standard VB executable. This gives you more control over the performance of your application in many instances.

CHAPTER 13

What is the Client Management System?

In the first project, you experimented with Visual Basic fundamentals to create a time tracking application. This application printed the billable time spent on a task, but didn't store the information after working with it. In most real-life applications, printing data is not the end of the process. You usually want to store important information and be able to analyze it or reuse it later.

The client management application you'll develop as the final project of the book involves the use of VB to create a front end for a database. This chapter will introduce essential VB concepts for this type of application and will outline the specific requirements for this particular application.

System Requirements for the Client Management Application

When working with clients, it is important to keep accurate records of both professional and personal information for each client. The following details might be valuable in client management tasks:

- The client's name information (like first name, last name, and title)
- The client's company information (like the name of the company and your contact's position)
- The client's mailing information (like address, city, state, and ZIP code)
- The client's electronic contact information (like phone, fax, and e-mail address)
- The client's family information (like birthdate and marital status)
- The client's legal statistics (like whether or not they have a will)
- The client's contact history (like the last time a service was performed for this client and what type of service was provided)

The application for this project needs to provide an easy method for entering, maintaining, and analyzing the client information. In particular, the application needs to provide the following functions:

- A simple mechanism for displaying a client summary to assist with client selection
- A detailed view of the client information for entry and maintenance
- A way to search for a client based on a field
- A way to narrow the list of clients to view and print
- A way to generate summary and detail reports about the clients
- A way to view client contact and service histories

Goals of the Client Management Application

As you complete the client management application, you'll gain experience with different methods for accessing, manipulating, and printing data. This project is designed to reinforce the concepts covered in the first two projects and also to introduce several new concepts. The following sections describe these new concepts.

Planning a Database Front End

Designing a database application requires several extra steps. You have to design not only the user interface, but also your database structure. You need to gather all the different types of information to be stored and maintained. This process involves a great deal of research. Brainstorming can be a useful technique for figuring out what data is needed for a system. You also should get as much input from the users as possible.

Once the list of information is finished, the list needs to be organized. The items of data need to be assigned to fields and those fields grouped into tables. This project will walk you through some fact-finding steps to assist you with defining your data needs.

Determining the Database Product

Another issue that influences the development of the application is the selection of a database to store the data. Many factors affect this decision, including the amount of data to be stored, the number of users, the required security, the operating environment, and the system support available. The selection of a database product is a complex decision. Fortunately, VB is very flexible and can access a variety of database formats. This eliminates one factor in this difficult decision.

This project will summarize some of the database products that can provide data storage for VB applications. Each environment is different, and you'll need to take your individual situation into account to best benefit your development.

Building Your Database

Once a database is chosen, the database structure has to be created. This process is different depending on your database selection. In some cases, you can use VB's *Visual Data Manager* to create and maintain the data structure.

Visual Data Manager is designed to allow you to view the fields, indexes, and queries of a database. In some cases, you also can create your database structure with it. This project will illustrate how to use Visual Data Manager to create your database structure.

Using the Data Control

Once the data structure is developed, you can develop the user interface. With VB, one way of accessing your data is to use the *data control.*

The data control makes the connection from your application to the database and a specific data set. Once the connection is made, you can use many of the controls introduced in Project 1 as tools to display field data. This process of displaying the data in a control is called *binding.*

After completing this project, you'll be able to set up the data control and bind other controls to the data control. You'll also be able to use two VB controls specifically designed to work with databases. The *DBGrid control* displays data in a spreadsheet-like view, and the *DBList control* allows you to create lists and combo boxes that can be populated with your data.

Using the Data Access Object Model

When you are managing your data, you need to navigate, locate, add, edit, and delete records. The data control provides a built in mechanism to navigate, add, and edit records, but you have to use VB and the *Data Access Object (DAO) model* to locate and delete records.

In addition to using DAO in conjunction with the data control, you can use it by itself to control all aspects of data management. This project will introduce the DAO methods, with which you'll be able to open a database, access a data set, and perform tasks on records (navigate, locate, add, edit, and delete).

You'll become familiar with the VB data access terminology. Finally, you'll learn to narrow a data set by setting up criteria to do so. This will be accomplished with *Structured Query Language (SQL)*. In the software industry, the SQL standard has been established for working with databases, and most contemporary databases use some variation of SQL in their applications.

Using Crystal Reports

VB forms and controls provide a mechanism for viewing data. Many users need to have printed reports to refer to when they are out of their offices, or to share with others who lack access to the application.

Crystal Reports is a database reporting tool. It can access all the database formats supported by VB. It offers an easy way to link to a database table, and provides a variety of report styles.

Once you've completed a report, you can use the Crystal Reports OCX to access that report from your VB application. After completing this project, you'll be able to link to your database and create, format, and access reports from the client management application.

Adding Error Handling

Debugging your VB application might locate many problems with your application, but some situations cannot be prevented. Users may attempt to access data that isn't available or may enter data that doesn't match the field specifications. If your application can be used by more than one user simultaneously, then multiple users may attempt to edit the same record. Without any programming intervention, your application will terminate unexpectedly in these situations.

These problems cannot be solved by debugging the application. As you learned in an earlier project, error handling can help manage these problems as they occur at runtime. After completing Project 3, you'll be able to use error handling to prevent an unexpected termination due to environmental factors or user errors.

Compiling Your Application

When you've completed developing the application, you don't want to ship the individual forms. You want to ship an *executable*. With previous versions of VB, executables relied on a dynamic link library for much of their functionality—VB was an interpreted language only.

VB 5 has been improved. You still can create an executable that relies on the DLL or you can compile your application, which can increase its execution speed. After completing this project, you'll be able to set up compile specifications and compile your applications.

Summary

The client management project is designed to provide a foundation of skills necessary for accessing databases with a VB application. VB offers several approaches for managing your data, and allows you to select the database that best suits your needs and environment.

If you are familiar with database programming in another language, this project will introduce the methods and properties you need to get started quickly. If you have never worked with a database before, this project will introduce you to many important aspects of planning a database application. This project also introduces the fundamentals of data access, including a look at the DAO model's SQL.

Gathering for the Client Management System

In the preceding chapter, the system requirements for the client management application were outlined. These included the necessary categories of information and the necessary program functions. Using these requirements, you're going to analyze the application's data needs and assess its user interface needs.

As with the previous two projects, the first step in Project 3 is to determine the type of data needed. Then the data can be organized into groups and the user interface can be planned.

User Input: What Type of Information Do You Plan To Track?

In the previous chapter, seven categories of client information were identified: name information, company information, mailing information, electronic contact information, family information, legal statistics, and contact history. Your first step is to break this information down into fields, as explained in the following sections.

Name Information

The first category is the client's name information. On the surface, this category seems to be very straightforward; however, the way this information will be used is a factor in determining how you break down this category. In the first project, this information was left as a single field because the only thing the user did with client names was to select them from a list.

In the client management system, names have more than one use—this affects how the data needs to be stored.

Tip

If you want to include any type of mail merge capabilities, then separating the name components is important. This also allows you to create various types of lists, such as a list showing the last name followed by the first name separated by a comma.

For this project, you need to have separate first name and last name fields. You also need to include a field to hold a prefix (such as "Mrs." or "Mr." or "Rev."). Another useful field is a salutation that indicates how you address the client; this can accommodate a nickname or whatever name you would use in a letter to the client. The salutation field will help the application's mail merge function.

Note

Some applications also include a field to hold a suffix (such as "Ph.D" or "Jr" or "III"). For this project, however, any suffix information can be included in the last name field.

Company Information

If the client is a company rather than an individual, you also need to track the company information. You need a field for the company name and another field for the client's position. You also will track what legal structure the business uses.

For this project, you'll have Company, Position, and Structure fields to track the company information. The StructureID field won't be a random entry; there will be a limited selection of valid legal structures.

Note

Some additional items you might want to add fields for when working with companies include what type of business each company is and how many years the company has been in business. Having a field to track the type of business can provide a means of establishing a specialty, and the number of years can indicate how stable the company is.

When you handle both individuals and companies as clients, creating a single report in alphabetical order can be difficult. If you use last names to alphabetize a list, then each company is displayed on the list according to its contact's last name—this makes companies very hard to locate in the list. As a solution, you can include a field that holds a string for each record to be used when you alphabetize the records for reports. This allows you to alphabetize the personal clients by last name and the companies by company name. For the client management application, you'll include a ListAs field to accomplish this.

Mailing Information

The mailing information category is fairly straightforward. You need fields for the street address, city, state, and ZIP code. For this application, they're named Address, City, State, and PostalCode.

Note

When you are tracking both personal and company clients as a group, you might want to provide two sets of address fields, one for personal addresses and the other for company addresses. If you are going to add a second set of fields for this purpose, an easier method is to call them the *primary address* and *secondary address* in your field names and documentation. You can use the primary address for mailings without having to program any logic to determine which address to use for reports.

This also allows for the possibility that one company might have more than one office. Of course, if you deal with clients who have several offices each, this approach isn't practical. In that case, you might want to consider storing addresses separately rather than with the other client information.

Depending on the type of application you're developing, you might benefit from including a County field as well as a City field. This might not affect the mailings you produce, but might provide needed information about a company's operating environment.

Electronic Contact Information

Getting hold of someone electronically has become a complex problem. A client can have a home phone number, business phone number, fax number, pager number, cellular phone number, and e-mail address. In fact, they can have more than one of each. When you design a system to track people, you have to determine which data you'll need to initiate contact.

For the client management application, you'll track only a home phone number, a business phone number, and a fax number.

E-mail has not yet become a huge communication tool for the legal profession, because it's difficult to track communication as easily with e-mail as with traditional mail or faxes. The cellular phone and pager fields have been omitted to minimize the fields needed for this application.

Family Information

When you work with people, some items of information don't directly relate to your professional contact with the clients. Many things can personalize a business relationship. You might want to keep track of a client's birthday, marital status, or the names and ages of any children they have.

For this client management application, you want to keep track of client birthdays to send each client a greeting at the appropriate time.

Tip You later could incorporate this into a marketing effort, like the reminders to undergo an insurance checkup you sometimes get from insurance agents.

For this project, you also want to keep track of each client's marital status and number of children, because that information could affect estate planning. You'll add three fields for family information: Birthdate, MaritalStatus, and Children.

Legal Statistics

Knowing if a client has a will or has incorporated a business can help the lawyer to quickly identify areas that need attention for that client. For this project, you'll use a field named Wills and another named Incorporated. The data for these fields can be just Yes or No answers.

Contact History

In the first project, you designed an application to help with time tracking, but that's only part of the tracking process for this law firm. You also want a mechanism for tracking what services have been done for a client in the past.

To track past services, you need to track the date of service. This could be the date the service was completed or initiated (or both). You also need to have a description of the type of service that was provided. So you'll use ServiceDate and Description fields. Tracking past services, however, isn't as simple as handling certain other information. A client can—in fact, you hope most clients will—have more than one service performed for them.

Each occasion you've done a service for them deserves its own ServiceDate and Description fields. Rather than create a record for each service, which would result in multiple instances of the client information, the services are easier to track in a separate table.

Another field that is helpful for client management is a place for random comments. In this project, that field is named Comments and is stored with the client information.

Organizing the User Input

In the previous projects, your analysis of user input began with a list of questions. The same questions can serve as the beginning point for this project:

- **What is the purpose of the application?**

  This application will allow users to track their clients and the services provided to those clients more effectively.

- **Is this application replacing a current process?**

  This application is replacing a manual, paper-based system.

- **Are there any paper-based forms?**

  Yes, we're automating a paper-based information sheet.

- **Who will use the application?**

  The users of this application are attorneys and other support staff who need quick access to client information.

- **What type of data will the user enter in the application?**

  This question was partially answered in the previous section and will be addressed further in the "What Type of Data is Being Stored?" section later in this chapter.

- **What will the data be used for?**

  The data will be used for quick lookups to support client contact and report generation.

- **What types of output will the application produce?**

  There will be four reports: a client listing, telephone listing, mailing labels, and a service summary report.

Determining What Forms are Needed

The requirements presented in the last chapter indicated several form needs. The first requirement was an easy mechanism for selecting what you want to work with. This needs a small form that can be left on the user's desktop for easy access.

The second requirement was a detailed view of the client information. This needs a form to detail the client information. The third requirement was the capability to search for a client based on a particular field of information. This function can be accomplished with programming from the client detail form.

The fourth requirement was the capability to narrow down the list of clients. This needs its own form. The fifth requirement was a method to generate reports. This needs a form to select a report. The final requirement was an available service history. This can be accomplished with the client detail form.

Table 14-1 lists the five forms that are needed for this application.

Table 14-1 Forms in the Client Management Application	
Form Name	**Description**
frmUsage	The Activity Selection form
frmDataCtrl	The client detail form using the data control
frmDataWizard	The client detail form created with the Form Data Wizard
frmSelect	The record selection form
frmReports	The reports form

You could create a splash form and user name prompt like the ones used in the time tracking system in Project 1. For this project, however, those forms are omitted to save time and to allow you to focus on data access.

What Type of Data is Being Stored?

Analyzing the user input for a system and identifying specific data fields is half the battle. The information then needs to be organized into groups known as *tables*. In previous projects, the type of data helped determine what type of control to use when planning your user interface.

When you start working with databases, you also need to concern yourself with what types of data can be stored in the database. All the data discussed earlier in this chapter can be classified using the standard VB text and numeric fields. Determining the specific data types cannot occur until the database itself is determined in the next chapter, but the data can be divided now.

Given the fields you've determined, you'll create a *Client table* to store all the client information. The legal structure could be stored as a text field within the Client table, but it's more space-effective to create a *Structure table* to store the possible structures. This allows a numeric value representing the legal structure to be stored in the client table—this takes less room, and provides a simple mechanism for the user to change the wording for a legal structure.

It's impossible (at least impractical and inefficient) to store multiple services within the client table—this would require multiple sets of identical fields. Even then, you'd run out of fields for clients who use many services, and you'd have space sitting around empty (and therefore wasted) for clients who use only one or two services. Instead, you'll create a *Services table* that's specifically designed to hold the service history. This table will have a field to tie the particular service rendered to the client table.

In Project 1, a table was provided to assist you with tracking the fields and forms needed. When you start working with databases, it's also helpful to keep track of which tables contain which fields.

Tip — When you're creating a database, you might want to use the naming conventions presented in Appendix A, "Recommended Naming and Programming Conventions." For tables, the recommended prefix is `tbl`.

Table 14-2 outlines the fields and tables needed for the client management application. Some additional controls are needed on other forms, but these will be discussed in later chapters. These additional controls will not be directly represented by a table in the database.

Note — The Numeric or Text Data? column will change once a database is selected.

Summary

Gathering data for an application is one of the most crucial steps in application development, especially when working with a database. If you make an incorrect decision about a field that will store data, it can cost you a great deal of time and money.

The stated application requirements are always a good starting point, but sometimes you need to look at the specific types of data to find additional data needs. The `tblStructures` table in this project, for example, was the direct result of analyzing the client information and realizing that the legal structure of the company could be better stored as a numeric value.

This chapter helped you to begin determining your database needs. The next chapter will complete the process by having you select a database and decide the field data types.

Table 14-2 Fields for the Client Management Application

Field Name	Description	Predefined Values?	Numeric or Text Data?	Standard Format?	Name of Table
Prefix	The client's title	No	Text	No	tblClients
FirstName	The client's first name	No	Text	No	tblClients
LastName	The client's last name	No	Text	No	tblClients
Salutation	The client's nickname or name for mail merge	No	Text	No	tblClients
Company	The client's company	No	Text	No	tblClients
Position	The client's position	No	Text	No	tblClients
StructureID	The company's legal structure identifier	Yes	Numeric	No	tblClients and tblStructures
Structure	The structure description	No	Text	No	tblStructures
ListAs	The name or phrase to use when alphabetizing clients	No	Text	No	tblClients
Address	The client's street address	No	Text	No	tblClients
City	The client's city	No	Text	No	tblClients
State	The client's state	No	Text	Yes, >CC	tblClients
PostalCode	The client's ZIP code	No	Text	Yes, ##### - ####	tblClients
HomePhone	The client's home number	No	Text	Yes, (###) ### -####	tblClients
WorkPhone	The client's work number	No	Text	Yes, (###) ### -####	tblClients
Fax	The client's fax number	No	Text	Yes, (###) ### -####	tblClients
Birthdate	The client's birthdate	No	Numeric	Yes, mm/dd/yyyy	tblClients
MaritalStatus	The client's marital status	Yes	Numeric	No	tblClients
Children	The number of children the client has	No	Numeric	No	tblClients
Wills	Does the client have a will?	Yes	Numeric	Yes, check box	tblClients
Incorporated	Is the client's business incorporated?	Yes	Numeric	Yes, check box	tblClients
ServiceDate	The date a service was performed	No	Numeric	Yes, mm/dd/yyyy	tblServices
Service	The service provided	No	Text	No	tblServices
Comments	Any comments about the client	No	Text	No	tblClients
ClientID	A unique identifier for the client	No	Numeric	No	tblClients and tblServices
ServiceID	A unique identifier for the service	No	Numeric	No	tblServices
ID	A unique identifier for the marital status table	No	Numeric	No	tblMaritalStatus
Description	A description of the marital status	No	Text	No	tblMaritalStatus

CHAPTER 15

Designing the Client Management System

The next step in the development process for a database application is to design the database itself. Before you can begin, you need to select a database. The first section of this chapter discusses some issues that will affect your decision.

Once you make that decision, the database structure needs to be built. The second section of this chapter introduces you to VB's Visual Database Manager, which can be used to create your database structure or just to view it as you develop your application. The second section also introduces some terminology that's essential for discussing database access from VB.

Once the database is created and populated, you can begin to develop your VB application. As you begin implementing data access, you have several choices for how to access your data—the last section explores some of your options.

Selecting a Database for Your Application

Replication is the ability to make a copy of a database and then later synchronize the copy with the original database. This allows for independent accessing of the database with the benefits of a single data source.

When you are planning your application, data storage can provide one of the toughest challenges. There are many databases to choose from, but VB doesn't present any obstacles. VB has its own *Jet engine* for database connections and it supports the *Open Database Connectivity (ODBC)* standards. This gives you access to 170 database formats, which allows you to focus on selecting the database that will best meet your data storage and data access needs.

This book is not large enough to compare and contrast all 170 database formats. To walk through the process, though, Microsoft Access and Microsoft SQL Server will be used. To determine which database is needed, consider several questions:

- How much data will be stored?
- How many users will use the system?
- What type of support is available?
- What existing systems are in place?

How Much Data Will be Stored?

Referential integrity is a set of rules developed to protect the integrity of data. It prevents a user from altering table relationships by adding data to one table in a relationship without adding matching information to the related table. It also prevents the user from deleting data involved in a relationship.

Although you cannot pinpoint the exact storage requirements for your system, you can get a rough idea. If you know that you'll have 500 records, storage requirements are less of an issue than if you expect to have 500,000 records.

Microsoft Access was developed to provide a user-friendly desktop database. It can serve as its own development environment or can be accessed from Visual Basic. When you use Access as an application development tool, you can store your data and your interface in one file. It's also capable of storing different objects in separate files and linking them.

If you are working with a lot of data, you should choose to store each table in a separate file, but you still need to keep the database product's limitations in mind. An Access file cannot exceed 1 gigabyte (G). Another Microsoft database product, Visual FoxPro, can support a table up to 2G.

If you are dealing with greater amounts of data, you need to select another product. Microsoft SQL Server is one such product. It is designed as a *client/server* database tool. Client/server applications often serve more than one user at a time, which usually means handling a greater amount of data. Microsoft SQL Server can accommodate up to 200G of information, and this number is predicted to increase in future releases.

Data validation involves verifying the data entered by a user to make sure that it meets the information needs of the system.

If you decide to go with Access and your data needs eventually grow larger than you originally planned, you aren't stuck. Access has a set of upsizing tools to assist you with moving your data to Microsoft SQL Server.

For the client management application in this project, the data requirements aren't large. This system needs to support one law firm's clients, so Microsoft Access will be more than adequate.

How Many Users Will Use the System?

The next concern is how many users are going to use the system. Both Access and SQL Server support multiple concurrent users, and both offer security, referential integrity, data validation, transaction processing, and replication.

Note   Referential integrity and data validation for Project 3 are discussed in the "Validating User Entries" and "Protecting Against Data Errors" sections of Chapter 17.

Security is a system for a database to establish user access requirements to restrict undesirable actions.

SQL Server is a client/server database tool. It offers better performance versus Access as the number of concurrent users increases. SQL Server also offers a more efficient transaction processing system, which is essential for interrelated updates. It keeps a transaction log, which is essential when a system failure occurs.

With the client management application, the number of users will be very limited, because the application is designed to track a small law firm's schedule. Only a couple of lawyers and assistants will need access to the system. Again, Access will be adequate.

What Type of Support is Available?

Another factor that may affect your decision about database products is how much support is available for data administration. Both Access and SQL Server can operate on LANs and both require some maintenance periodically.

Access files tend to increase in size as activities are performed with the database. This includes not only the addition of records, but also the creation of queries and other database-related objects. It is recommended that you periodically compact the database file to eliminate unused space. Performing this task doesn't take an Access expert, but does require other users to be out of the system.

SQL Server is better designed for a client/server, multi-user database environment. It has many standard database administration tools. It supports data replication, remote operations, e-mail notification, activity monitoring, and online backup.

SQL Server is designed to make administration of the database as painless as possible. The fact that users can remain in the system while most of the maintenance activities are occurring is a plus, especially for systems that need to be available around the clock.

What Existing Systems are in Place?

Another factor to consider when selecting a database format is what types of databases are already in use at your location. If many databases are already supported for a particular format, then maintenance routines are already in place. Adding a new database of the same format does not significantly increase the time required for maintenance. Selecting the same format also eliminates the need to learn a new product.

Time also can influence your decision when you're designing a new system. If you're trying to develop a replacement for an integrated system from another database development tool, it might take some time to complete the replacement system. With all the formats supported by VB, you can switch different parts of system without disturbing the data.

The Choice for the Client Management Application

Given the size and number of users for this system, the data needs can be met very well with Microsoft Access. Using Access also limits the need to have access to a network or to SQL Server.

Building the Databases

Once you've selected a database and planned your data structure, you need to build the database. You can use the database product you've selected to build your database or you can use Visual Data Manager, which ships with VB.

Visual Data Manager is included with VB to allow you to view your data structure—or to create a new data structure—without leaving VB. To launch Visual Data Manager, select Add-Ins, Visual Data Manager from the VB menu.

As VB attempts to open Visual Data Manager, it attempts to locate your system workgroup for Access. If VB cannot locate this workgroup, it prompts you to indicate whether you want a reference for the default workgroup added to your Visual Basic INI file. You can opt to do this or not. After you complete this step, VB opens the Visual Data Manager window (see Figure 15-1).

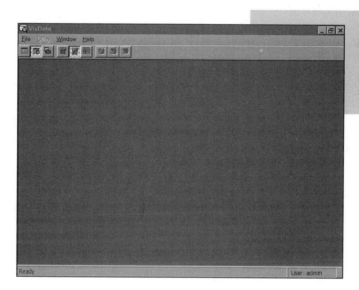

Figure 15-1
Visual Data Manager can be used to create and view data sources.

Visual Data Manager is designed to assist you with the creation and maintenance of your data sources. You can perform the following actions:

- Create a new data source file
- Open an existing data source file
- Create queries
- Import or export data
- Create database transactions
- Select a workgroup for a Jet database
- Compact or repair a Jet database
- Maintain user groups and users for a Jet database

ON THE

CD

For the client management application, you can build everything from scratch or else use the sample files located on the CD accompanying this book. To use these files, you need to copy them to your local hard drive in a directory named \Lab 3\. (Make sure there's a space between "Lab" and "3".) The files for this project are located in the \examples\Lab3\ subdirectory on the CD.

Creating Your Data Source

To use Visual Data Manager to create your data source, select <u>F</u>ile, <u>N</u>ew and then select the format you want to work with. To create the Access database for this project, select <u>M</u>icrosoft Access, Version <u>7</u>.0. This opens the Select Microsoft Access Database to Create dialog box (see Figure 15-2).

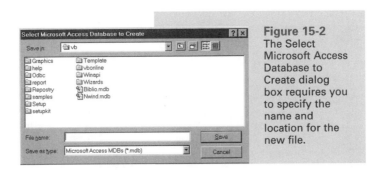

Figure 15-2
The Select Microsoft Access Database to Create dialog box requires you to specify the name and location for the new file.

Unlike word processors, Visual Basic, and many other applications you've worked with, you need to specify the database file name and location before working with it. This identifies where your structure will be created. After you enter the file name, indicate a path, and click Save, the database is created. The Database and SQL Statement windows for this new database are displayed (see Figure 15-3).

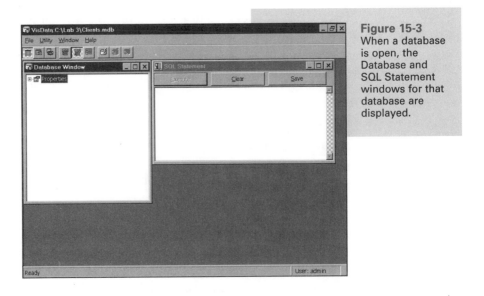

Figure 15-3
When a database is open, the Database and SQL Statement windows for that database are displayed.

The Database window displays the properties and objects for a database. If you click the plus sign (+) next to Properties, this list expands as shown in Figure 15-4.

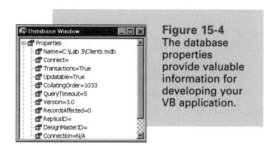

Figure 15-4
The database properties provide valuable information for developing your VB application.

The *Name* property indicates the file name and path. The *Connect* property indicates what type of database is displayed. This is not equal to a value currently because you've selected the Access format—this is the native format for the Jet engine and therefore doesn't require connect instructions.

The *Transactions* property indicates whether the database supports transactions.

A transaction is the ability to group more than one database action and treat it as a single unit. If any action fails to perform correctly, the entire group fails and the database can be rolled back (returned to the state before the transaction was executed).

The *Updatable* property indicates whether the object can be modified. The *CollatingOrder* property indicates how sorting will be arranged with this database. This allows you to support foreign languages. *QueryTimeout* indicates how many seconds the system should wait for a query executing with an ODBC database.

Version indicates which version of the DAO model (often referred to simply as DAO) is currently in use. *RecordsAffected* indicates how many records were modified with the last action query.

As mentioned earlier in this chapter, DAO supports *data replication* to better support a mobile or client/server configuration. *ReplicaID* indicates which replica this is (if you're using data replication) and *DesignMasterID* identifies which database is the base for replication.

With ODBC, you also have the ability to control your connection. The *Connection* property indicates your ODBC connection information.

After reviewing the database properties, you're ready to begin building your structure. To begin adding tables to your database, you need to point to the background of the Database window and right-click. A pop-up menu gives you the opportunity to create a new table by selecting New Table. This opens the Table Structure dialog box (see Figure 15-5).

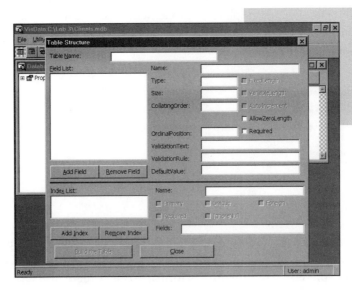

Figure 15-5
The Table Structure dialog box allows you to create the table structure.

Here you can indicate the name of the table, its fields, and its indexes; Visual Data Manager will build the table for you. For example, the client management application's first table is the one for client information. You can start by indicating the table name. Name this table `tblClients`.

 Tip

As with all VB objects, there are recommended naming conventions for data objects. For additional information, see Appendix A, "Recommended Naming and Programming Conventions."

After entering the name, you have to indicate the fields. The first field will be the ClientID field to identify the record. Each field needs to have its properties set. To add a field, click the <u>A</u>dd Field button. This opens the Add Field dialog box shown in Figure 15-6.

The *Name* property identifies the field. The *Type* property indicates the necessary data type. The types available are the data types supported by the database (in this case, Microsoft Access). The drop-down list allows you to select from `Boolean`, `Byte`, `Integer`, `Long`, `Currency`, `Single`, `Double`, `Date/Time`, `Text`, `Binary`, and `Memo`.

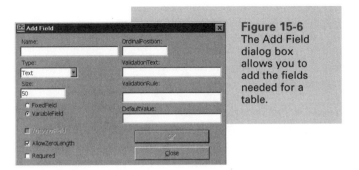

Figure 15-6
The Add Field dialog box allows you to add the fields needed for a table.

These will not always be an exact match to the Visual Basic data types. With Access, some are exact matches and several are close matches.

For ClientID, you need to select Long, because this field is going to store a number to identify the record. Rather than have the user enter this number, you want to generate it automatically. You need to select the AutoIncrField check box to make this happen. The *Required* property forces the record to fill this field as soon as each new record is created. No other property settings are needed for this field.

The next field is the Prefix field for the client's title ("Mr." or "Mrs." or whatever). The *Name* property needs to be set to Prefix and the *Type* property needs to be set to Text.

When the Text type is selected, you can indicate how many characters are expected by setting the *Size* property. By default, it assigns 50 characters. This is a bit much for a prefix, so you should cut that back to 10 or 15. This also activates the *AllowZeroLength* property, which you use to indicate whether or not the field can be left blank.

In addition to these properties, there are also some properties that are optional. You can indicate this field's *OrdinalPosition* in the list and a *DefaultValue* for the field. You can set up a *ValidationRule* for the field and *ValidationText* to be displayed when the rule isn't met.

An index is a specified order for viewing the records of a table. This usually speeds up data access.

As the fields are added, they appear in the *field list*. You need to add the remaining fields for the tblClients table. After all the fields are added, you can also add indexes.

To add an index, you use the lower portion of the New Table dialog box. You need to set several properties for each index. You click the New Index button and

A primary key is a single field that will identify the record. It is unique by nature.

then proceed to set the index's *Name* property and indicate which fields to use in the index. The *Primary* property indicates if this is the primary key for the table.

You can set the *Unique* property to True to create an index that has only unique values, but isn't acting as a primary key. You can set the *IgnoreNulls* property to True to ignore fields with no value.

ON THE

CD

For instance, we can name an index PrimaryKey, select the ClientID field, and make sure that the *Primary* and *Unique* properties are set to True. Rather than spending time creating the tables for the client management application, you can open the Client Management.MDB file. Do so by selecting File, Open Database and then browsing to locate this file on your system.

Adding Data with Visual Data Manager

A recordset is the set of records returned from a definition like the table definition for tblClients. There are three types of recordsets. For additional information, see the "Access Methods" section later in this chapter.

Once the structure is complete, you can use Visual Data Manager to add, edit, delete, or just view the contents of the database. By double-clicking any of the tables, you can open a form to work with the table data. Figure 15-7 shows the form for tblClients.

Table:tblClients ☐☐☒	**Figure 15-7**
Add Edit Delete Seek Filter Close	Visual Data Manager
Index: Company:+Company:Non-Unique	presents a form
Field NAme: Value (F4=Zoom)	for you to enter
ContactID: 4	and edit table
Prefix: Mrs.	data.
FirstName: Carol	
LastName: Parker	
Salutation: Carol	
Company:	
Position:	
StructureID: 0	
|< < 1/30 > >|	

Before double-clicking to access this form, you might want to look at the toolbar. The first three buttons allow you to select what type of recordset you want to work with.

An instant transaction is a way of initiating a transaction to bundle actions without any prior setup with code.

The next three buttons allow you to control the form development, and the last three buttons allow you to create an instant transaction. The settings for these toolbar buttons control which settings will be used to create the form. If you make changes after opening the form, the new settings are not implemented until the form is closed and reopened.

Querying Your Data

SQL *stands for* **Structured Query Language***. It is an adopted standard for getting answers to particular questions about your data.*

You can also use the SQL Statement window to query your database. If you want to see only the clients who have wills, for example, you can enter the following in the SQL Statement window and select Execute:

```
SELECT FirstName, LastName FROM tblClients WHERE Wills = True
```

Notice that you used True instead of Yes. This is an instance where there's a discrepancy between representing the field and accessing it with code. With any Yes/No field, you have to use True or False to test the field's value.

Most databases have taken standard SQL and added some custom functions. When you are working with an ODBC source, you can use a pass-though query. This turns off the syntax checking in DAO and passes the statement as is to the host database for processing.

When you select Execute, Visual Data Manager asks you if this is a pass-through query. Your response indicates whether or not you want to pass the statement through to your ODBC database for processing. In this case, the answer is No. A new form is displayed (see Figure 15-8) containing just the two fields specified in the SELECT statement and showing just two records instead of the total number of records.

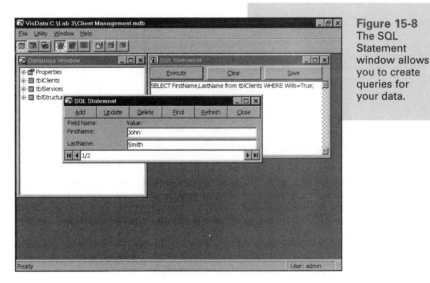

Figure 15-8
The SQL Statement window allows you to create queries for your data.

The SQL Statement window is designed for *one-time* (or *temporary*) *queries* that allow you to test a statement to determine its value. If you need to have a query stored (or saved) with the database, right-click the Database window and select New Query from the pop-up menu. This opens the Query Builder window shown in Figure 15-9.

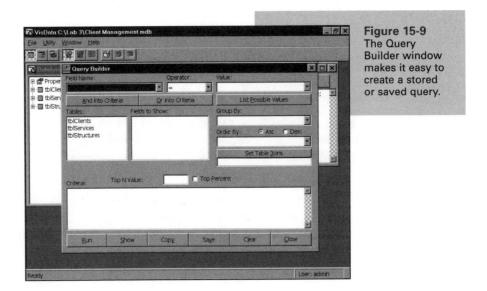

Figure 15-9
The Query Builder window makes it easy to create a stored or saved query.

Here you can select the fields you need and supply any desired criteria. If you want to save this query in the database, you need to select tblClients from the Tables list and then select the FirstName and LastName fields from the Fields to Show list. You also need to select tblClients.Wills from the Field Name drop-down list, select the = symbol from the Operator drop-down list, and type **True** in the Value text box. After everything is entered, drop the selections into place by selecting the And into Criteria button.

You then can run the query to test it. If you're satisfied with the query, you can save it with a name. When you save a query, use the qry prefix to help you identify it as a query later. (Queries also get a different icon in the Database window to help you keep track of them.) From this point on, if you click the query in the list, you'll be able to see the SQL statement you've created.

A saved or stored query is another type of database object—a QueryDef. If you will need a particular query in your application on a regular basis, you are better off creating one and storing it in your Access database. As was discussed earlier in the chapter, Access is unique in that it's capable of storing all database objects in one file. When you create a query, it takes up some space in the file. If you are creating SQL in your code, then every time it creates a QueryDef, it takes up more space. By adding the query as a stored query, you do not generate wasted space in your application.

EXERCISE

Generating wasted space in an Access database is often unavoidable, especially if you are frequently deleting records and generating queries. All databases have maintenance utilities to reclaim wasted space. The Visual Data Manager provides access to two utilities for maintaining an Access database. You can compact the database to reclaim the space, or repair the database if it has become damaged by hardware failure.

Use the following steps to compact the database:

1. Make sure that your database is closed.
2. Select File, Compact MDB, 7.0 MDB from the Visual Data Manager.
3. Select your database file from the Select Microsoft Access Database to Compact dialog box.
4. Select your database file from the Select Microsoft Access Database to Compact To dialog box.
5. Select Yes to overwrite the file when prompted for a response.
6. Select No to encrypt the database when prompted for a response.
7. Select Yes to open the database when prompted for a response.

This process will compact the database and store the compacted version with the same file name. Depending on the amount of activity prior to taking these steps, you might see a reduced file size.

Access Methods

Once the database is built, you need to access the data from your application. To access a database from VB, you use the *Data Access Object model*, known as *DAO*. DAO was introduced with VB 3.0 to provide access to Jet databases, ODBC databases, and Indexed Sequential Access Method (ISAM) databases. DAO has been improved with subsequent versions of VB to support faster access and additional formats.

With DAO, you have two choices for accessing your data. You can use the older DAO/Jet mode, or use the new ODBCDirect mode for faster access and better performance utilizing the *Remote Data Object (RDO) model*. The modes are very similar, so code built for DAO/Jet can quickly be adapted for ODBCDirect if the need arises.

To take advantage of both database access methods, you need to be familiar with the VB terminology and DAO models shown in Figures 15-10 and 15-11. DAO is very similar to the OLE concepts introduced in Project 2. The object models create a hierarchy of objects. You can reference and interact with various data objects by declaring variables to reference the top level of the hierarchy and using methods to create object variables for the objects within the hierarchy.

A workspace is an object to allow you to set up multiple working sessions.

The ODBCDirect model is very similar to part of the Jet model. Each model has a database engine as a controller, with the *Workspaces* collection to manage multiple workspaces and the *Errors* collection to track errors that occur as the data is manipulated.

The object hierarchy available under the Workspace object is where you can see the difference. The Jet model allows the developer to access workgroup security through the *Group* and *User* collections and objects.

The ODBCDirect model has the *Connection object*, which allows the developer to access information about the application's connection to the ODBC database, as well as manage the connection. This object also has the *QueryDef collection* to define pre-built SQL statements.

Both have a *Database object* to assist in the manipulation of the database. The objects below the Database object, however, differ between the two models. The Jet model is greatly influenced by the organization of the native Jet databases—it considers all objects part of the Database object.

The Jet model supports some predefined *containers* that provide information about the database, as well as QueryDefs. It has a *TableDef collection* to allow you to access the structure of a database table. (This is not universally supported across all formats accessed through this model.) It also has a *Relations collection* to allow you to retrieve information about any relationships between tables.

Both models have the *Recordset collection*. This is the object that you will spend the most time using. The Recordset collection and object represent sets of records you want to work with. They can represent a table or the results of a query. Whenever you want to display records to your user, you need to create a recordset. You also have to choose which type of recordset to create. There are three types that both models support, and each model supports one type that the other does not:

- **Table Recordset**—This type of recordset is a direct representation of a database table. You can use it to add, edit, or delete records from the database table. If you are working in a multi-user environment, any changes made by other users will be reflected in this type of recordset. If you are trying to locate records in this type of recordset, an index is required. This type is restricted to the Jet model.

Figure 15-10
The DAO model for Jet engine workspaces is used to access and modify data.

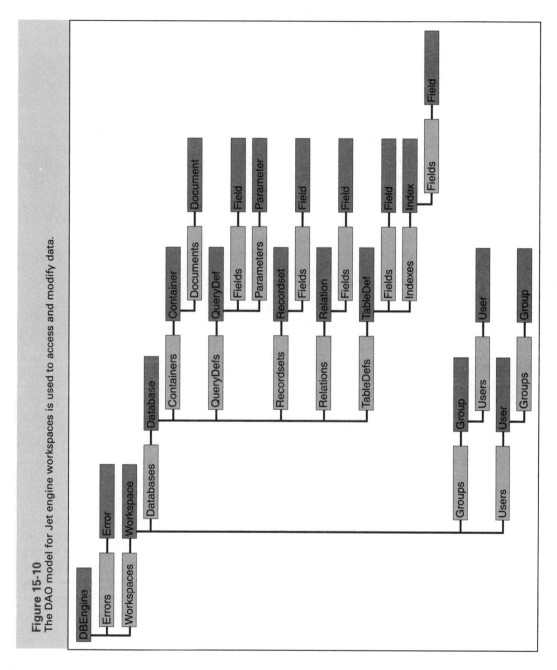

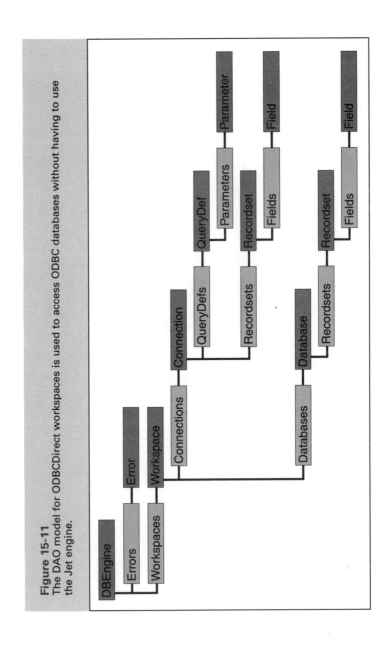

Figure 15-11
The DAO model for ODBCDirect workspaces is used to access ODBC databases without having to use the Jet engine.

- **Dynaset Recordset**—This type of recordset represents the results of a query. It can include all the fields, all the records, or a selection. It can also combine tables to create a recordset. You can use a dynaset to add, edit, and delete records from the underlying table. It takes up very little room in memory because it uses pointers to keep track of the records.

- **Snapshot Recordset**—This type of recordset represents the results of a query like the dynaset does, but the snapshot is a static representation. You can use this type of recordset only to retrieve information, and then move between records in any direction.

  It cannot support adds, edits, or deletions. One concern with a snapshot is the space needed to work with it. If the query returns a large number of records, a large chunk of memory may be required to store the snapshot, because all the returned field data must be stored in memory.

- **Forward-Only Recordset**—This type of recordset is identical to the snapshot except that it cannot be used to search for a record. Movement through this recordset is restricted to only the forward direction. This is great for any operation requiring a single pass through a set of records with no data changes.

- **Dynamic-Type Recordset**—This type of recordset is the result of a query, and it allows adds, edits, and deletions. In multi-user situations, it also dispalys changes by other users. This is similar to the Table recordset, but is restricted to the ODBCDirect model.

Selecting the correct recordset type can make a big difference in the amount of time it takes to process your data with VB. The specifics of how you create and manipulate recordsets are discussed in great detail in the next chapter.

Summary

Once the planning of the system is complete, your first step is to design the database. This requires selecting an appropriate database and building its structure.

When selecting a database, you need to consider many issues, including how many people need access to the system, how much data needs to be stored, and what resources are already in place.

Once a database is selected, Visual Data Manager is a great way to build a new data structure or view an existing one. Visual Data Manager allows you to view which fields are available as well as the data stored in those fields. It also can assist you with querying the database using SQL.

Once the database is ready, you need to know how you're going to access it from your application. VB offers two modes, each with its own data access object model, and both modes provide easy access to your data. The DAO/Jet mode is great for native Jet databases and other ISAM formats. The ODBCDirect mode has been optimized for accessing remote data sources.

CHAPTER 16

Building the Client Management System

Once the data structure is built, you're ready to develop your application. As you do so, you need to make some choices about your implementation of the DAO model. You can use the data control to make the connection to the database, use the DAO model to make the connection, or use a combination of approaches.

This chapter focuses on using the DAO model through both approaches. The first example focuses on using the data control to make the connection and provide record navigation, editing, and additions. It looks at the Data Form Designer that is designed to assist you with accessing your data. The last part of the chapter looks at adding functionality to the data control form with data objects, and also looks at providing all the same functionality as the data control with code only.

To begin the development of the client management system, you need to create a new standard EXE project with a new form. Change the *Name* property to **frmDataCtrl** and the *Caption* property to **Lab 3 - The Data Control**. As with all VB development, you should save your work regularly. You need to save your project as **Lab3** and this form as **DataCtrl**.

ON THE

CD

If you prefer to look at the whole example rather than develop this application from scratch, you can copy the files to your hard drive from the CD accompanying this book. Copy all the files from the d:\examples\Lab3\ directory to the c:\Lab 3\ directory. (Make sure there's a space between "Lab" and "3".)

Using the Data Control

The first method for integrating a database into your VB application is to use the *data control*. This control allows you to specify a database and provide a record navigator. It has built-in editing and adding capabilities.

When you want to use the data control, you need to have this new form active and then add it from the toolbox like any other control. Once the data control is added and its properties are set, you tie other controls to the data control to display the data. This process is known as *binding*. These steps create a basic data viewer and editor.

VB provides an add-in named *Data Form Designer* that can use the data control to create a form for your data source. The Data Form Designer also uses some DAO objects to provide additional database functionality.

Creating a Link to the Data

The first step is to create a link to the data source by adding the data control. Start with a new project that has a single blank form. Add the data control as you would add any other control. If you use the double-click method to create the control, it appears as shown in Figure 16-1.

Once the control is placed on the form, set some of its basic properties. For the *Name* property, the recommended prefix is dat, so name this control **datClients**.

If you want, you can change the *Caption* property. If you're familiar with Microsoft Access, you might want to display the record number and the total number of records, as in Record 1 of 50. That cannot be done automatically with the data control; it requires some code, which will be discussed later in this chapter. For now, just eliminate the *Caption* setting.

The last property to set is *Align*. This allows you to attach a control to one edge of the form. In this case, select **2 - Align Bottom**. This will keep the control at the bottom of the screen no matter what size the user makes the form.

After these properties are set, you're ready to connect to a data source and set up the type of data access that will be used. You'll use 11 properties to specify the data access for this control, as described in the following list:

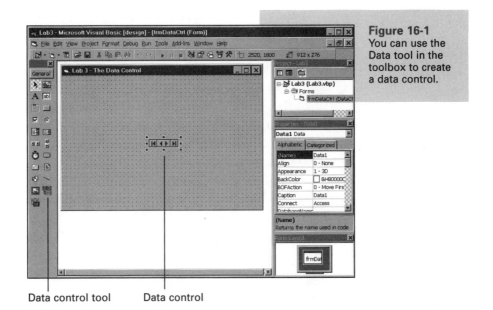

Figure 16-1
You can use the
Data tool in the
toolbox to create
a data control.

Data control tool   Data control

- The *DatabaseName* property indicates where the database is located. When your database is located on a PC or a PC network, this includes the file name as well as the path. If this database is using an ODBC source to access another type of machine, this property needs to include information about the type of system you're accessing.

  For this project, *DatabaseName* needs to point to the Client Management.MDB file.

> **You can either enter the correct path or click the Build button to the right of the property to retrieve the correct path using a standard file browser.**

- The *RecordSource* property indicates which table or query you want to use to create your recordset. If you're using a native Jet format, you can select a table or stored query from a drop-down list (entry of a SQL statement is also supported). For this project, select tblClients from the list.

- The *RecordSetType* property determines what type of recordset will be created by the data control. By default, it creates a dynaset recordset to support the control, but you can choose a different type of recordset if needed.

- The *Connect* property controls how the data is accessed. If you're not using a native Jet database, you need to use the *Connect* property to specify which format the data is stored in. This property accepts specific strings for the available formats; these can be selected from the drop-down list. For this project, don't change *Connect*, because Microsoft Access is the default.

- The *DefaultType* property allows you to indicate which mode you want to use to access your data. If your data is located in an ODBC source, you can use the Jet mode or the ODBCDirect mode (the latter optimizes for ODBC access).

- If you're using ODBCDirect mode, you also can set *DefaultCursorType* to control how the connection to the database is managed. Select the default to let the driver determine the management, or select one of the other two choices to optimize performance for a particular recordset size.

You can select to use the ODBC Cursor Library to manage the connection. This might provide better performance if the recordset to be returned is small. Choosing to use the Server Side Cursor provides better performance with larger recordsets.

- The *Exclusive* and *ReadOnly* properties indicate how the database and recordset are opened. By default, *Exclusive* is set to False, which allows you to create a multi-user application. *ReadOnly* can be set to True to speed up access to a recordset. (If you allow edits to a recordset, the database engine needs to keep track of those changes as well as which user is accessing which record at any given time. With a read-only recordset, such tracking is unnecessary.)

- If your data access needs aren't as black-and-white as simply setting the *ReadOnly* property, you can use the *Options* property. This property supports the sum of several constants to determine the type of access. You can control the behavior of other users while the current user is in the system, and can control the type of access the current user has while in the system. For example, if you have a data entry user who only enters new records, you can set *Options* to dbAppendOnly. This prevents the user from changing existing records. For a full list of constants for the *Options* property, please refer to that property's help topic in VB's online help system.

- The last two data properties are *BOFAction* and *EOFAction*. These control what happens when the user goes past the beginning or end of the recordset. (As Figure 16-2 shows, each recordset created by DAO has beginning-of-file and end-of-file markers.)

With the structure of the recordset, it's possible for a user to navigate past the BOF and EOF markers. If nothing is done, an error will occur. The *BOFAction* and *EOFAction* properties are designed to simplify the process of specifying what happens when these navigation problems occur.

With *BOFAction*, you might want to move automatically to the first record in the recordset (the default setting), or you might want to generate an error and write some error-handling code to deal with this in a special way. For this project, we want to use the default setting.

With *EOFAction*, you might want to move automatically to the last record, generate an error, or add a new record. For this project, set *EOFAction* to Add New to make it easy for the user to create a new record.

Once these properties have been set, the data control acts as a record navigation tool. There are arrows at either end of the control to move you backward or forward in the recordset:

Arrow	Function
Simple left arrow	Moves you to the previous record
Left arrow with a vertical line	Moves you to the first record in the recordset
Simple right arrow	Moves you to the next record
Right arrow with a vertical line	Moves you to the last record in the recordset

If you ran the application now, you would have a connection to your table but no way to view the data. You're ready to proceed to the next step, binding other controls to the data control.

Before the Beginning of File
BOF
Record 1
Record 2
. . .
. . .
Record n
EOF
After the End of File

Figure 16-2
The recordset has space for each record, as well as markers at the beginning and end.

Viewing the Data with Bound Controls

When you create a database application, you can connect to a database very easily with the data control. You then need to create a way to display the data. This is accomplished by using *bound controls*. A bound control has the two data properties, *DataSource* and *DataField*. *DataSource* allows you to indicate which data control you want to pull data from, and *DataField* allows you to indicate which field to display in the control. On the General tab of the toolbox, the following tools create bound controls: Label, Text Box, Check Box, Combo Box, List Box, Picture Box, and Image.

The basic process is to place the controls on the form and set essential properties like *Name* and the position properties. For *Name*, you should use the appropriate prefix (such as txt) followed by the field name for easy identification. Next, use the *DataSource* property to indicate the data control that will serve as the data source, and use the *DataField* property to indicate which field of the data control's recordset will be displayed.

For example, the first field to be displayed on the Client form is ClientID. This field is an auto-incrementing field, and should not be modified by the user. It is best represented by a label—actually, it requires two labels (one to serve as a heading and one to display the field).

The next field, Prefix, can be changed by the user. It's a text field and can be represented by a text box. You need to place a label for the heading and a text box to display the field. The *DataSource* value for the text box is the datClients control and the *DataField* value is the Prefix field.

Use the same process to set up FirstName, LastName, Salutation, Company, Position, Address, State, ListAs, and Children, which are all text fields.

PostalCode, HomePhone, WorkPhone, Fax, and Birthdate are also text fields, but they need some special attention. When they're stored in the database, they're stored without formatting. You can use the Format function to provide correct formatting, or else use one of the other controls that ships with VB.

The masked edit control, for example, is perfect for this purpose. The masked edit control has a *Format* property that allows you to specify a format for the data. You should set *Format* to "#####-####" for a masked edit control representing PostalCode. Set Format to "(###)###-####" for the controls representing telephone number fields and to **"m/d/yyyy"** for the control representing Birthdate.

Note As you learned earlier in this book, the toolbox does not include a tool for the masked edit control by default. You need to add this tool before you can create a masked edit control.

The StructureID and MaritalStatus fields also could be represented by text boxes, but those wouldn't be very valuable to the user. If you displayed a text box for StructureID, the user would have to remember the structure codes (for example, that 3 is a corporation). In an earlier project, you saw the combo box used to present a list of items. You can use combo boxes for the Client form, but two controls are specifically designed to handle lists that reside in a table. The *DB combo box* and *DB list box* are able to get their items from a data control instead of requiring you to use the AddItem method to populate these controls.

Note You need to add the appropriate tools to your toolbox before you can create DB combo box and DB list box controls.

You need to add a DB combo box and a label to the form to display the StructureID field. Set the *Name*, *DataSource*, and *DataField* properties as you have for the previous controls. Then you need to set some specific properties to populate the list. The *RowSource* property indicates which table will provide the list. For each DB combo box, you need to add another data control. For example, create one named **datStructure** pointing to the same database as the data control created earlier, and set the *RecordSource* property for this new data control to **tblStructure**. Set the *ListField* property to **Description** (this indicates which field to display in the DB combo box). Set the *BoundColumn* property to **StructureID** (this indicates which value to store in *DataField* when a choice is made).

You also need a DB combo box for the MaritalStatus field. *RowSource* points to **datMaritalStatus**, *ListField* is **Description**, and *BoundColumn* is **ID**. For both combo boxes, make sure that the style is **2 - Drop Down List**. The DB list box works the same way the DB combo box does, and has all the same properties—the DB list box just takes up a little more room.

The Wills and Incorporated fields are both Yes/No fields that translate into a Boolean field here. Each is best represented with a check box. The standard properties need to be set for these check boxes.

The last field of client information is the Comments field. This is a Memo field and can be represented on the form with a text box. You need to set the *Multi-Line* property to **True** and set the *ScrollBars* property to **2 - Vertical Scrollbars** to provide a vertical scroll bar.

Figure 16-3 shows how the form should look when you've added all these controls.

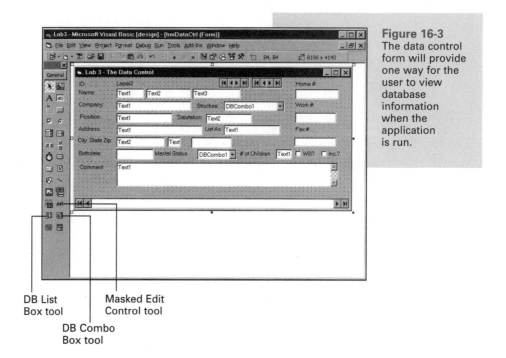

Figure 16-3
The data control form will provide one way for the user to view database information when the application is run.

DB List
Box tool

Masked Edit
Control tool

DB Combo
Box tool

Displaying Related Tables

The client management database contains client information as well as a history of what services have been performed for each client. So far you've created a form to display only the client information. If you want to display what services have been performed, you need to use an additional data control as well as other controls for the field information. This is best accomplished with another data-aware control, the *DB grid control*, which is perfect for displaying related table information on a form.

The first step is to place another data control on the form. You need to set the standard properties (including `datServices` for *Name*) and set the *Visible* property to `False` as you've done for all data controls except `datClients`. Initially point this data control to the `tblServices` table in the database; however, this will change in a moment.

The DB grid control is not a standard control, so you need to add it to your project using the method presented earlier in this book.

Place a DB grid control below the text box displaying the Comments field on the form. When it's placed on the form, the DB grid control looks like a tiny Excel workbook area. You need to set it up to display the correct data. The first step is to set its *DataSource* property to point to `datServices`.

The easiest way to set up the columns it to let the control do the work for you. Right-click the grid and select Retrieve Fields from the pop-up menu. This sets the column headings for every field in the recordset.

The results might not be exactly what you expect. You can adjust the results by right-clicking the grid and selecting Edit. This allows you to click and drag a column divider to resize the column. You can also rearrange the columns and delete unneeded columns with a few right-clicks; for each field you don't need, click to select the column header, right-click, and select Edit from the pop-up menu. When you finish, only `Service` and `ServiceDate` should be displayed.

Right-click the grid and select Properties. A special tabbed dialog box appears (see Figure 16-4) to allow you to set the DB grid box properties in a developer-friendly format.

Three properties—*AllowAdds, AllowEdits,* and *AllowDeletes*—control how much editing can be done in this control. If you wanted users to be able only to view, you would set all three to `False`. In this project, however, all three need to be set to `True` to allow the user to add, edit, and delete the service history for a client.

If you run the application now, you can view both client information and service information. Unfortunately, you see all the services listed, regardless of which client is currently displayed.

This is the first place you need to add code to get the desired visual effect for your form. The DB grid control needs to display only those records where the value of the ClientID field matches the value of the ClientID field for the current record in `datClients`.

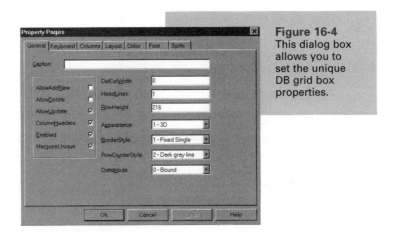

Figure 16-4
This dialog box allows you to set the unique DB grid box properties.

This is easily accomplished with code and DAO. The data control has three special events to assist you with data processing. One of these events is the Reposition event, which is triggered when a record becomes the active record. This event is the best place to display the record number in the data control, as shown in the following code:

```
Private Sub datClients_Reposition()
    datClients.Caption = "Record: " & _
        datClients.Recordset.AbsolutePosition + 1
    Dim dbServices As Database, rsServices As Recordset
    Dim strSQL As String
    strSQL = "SELECT Service, ServiceDate FROM tblServices WHERE [ClientID] = " _
        & datClients.Recordset!ClientID
    Set dbServices = OpenDatabase("c:\Lab 3\Client Management.MDB")
    Set rsServices = dbServices.OpenRecordset(strSQL, dbOpenDynaset)
    Set datServices.Recordset = rsServices
End Sub
```

The *Caption* property for the data control displays the record number by using the *AbsolutePosition* property (this keeps track of which record number is current in the recordset).

You set *Caption* to *AbsolutePosition* + 1 because, like all VB indexes, *AbsolutePosition* begins numbering with 0.

The remainder of this code uses DAO objects to solve the problem of unintentionally showing all the services. This is a preview of the "Using Data Access Objects" section later in this chapter.

You need to declare variables, including a string, for the database objects. The string, strSQL, is the SQL statement to define the ClientID for the DB grid control.

> **Access uses most of the industry standards established for SQL. If you're familiar with SQL, you should make an easy transition. If you're unfamiliar with SQL, you'll find more in-depth coverage in the "Querying the Database" section later in this chapter.**

The next two lines of code establish the DAO link to the database using the OpenDatabase and OpenRecordset methods. These methods are discussed in greater detail later in this chapter in the "Using Data Access Objects" section.

The last step is to take the resulting recordset and use it to change the recordset of the data control. This reduces the list being displayed to just those services that relate to the selected client.

With the data control and just one event, you've created a form to view your data (see Figure 16-5). It also allows you to edit your data, and can be used to add new records because *EOFAction* is set to automatically add a new record when you attempt to pass the end of the file.

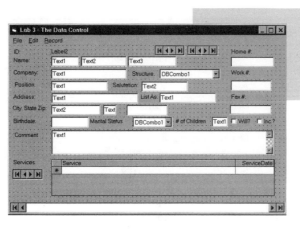

Figure 16-5
From this form you can view, edit, and add to your recordset.

EXERCISE

Earlier in this section the DB combo box was introduced to provide a selection of choices, retrieving the selection from a table. Another way to provide a selection is to use option buttons.

Unfortunately, the option button control cannot bind with a data control. If you want to use option buttons with a data control, you need to use the `Reposition` event.

To practice setting up option buttons for the marital status selection, use the following steps:

1. Create a new Standard EXE Project with a new form.

2. Set the Form's *Name* property to **frmOptions** and the *Caption* property to **Option Example**.

3. Place a data control on the form.

4. Set the following properties for this data control:

Property	Value
Name	datOptions
Align	2- Align Bottom
DatabaseName	c:\Lab 3\Client Management.MDB
RecordSource	tblClients

5. Create a frame with *Name* set to **fraOptions** and *Caption* set to **Marital Status**.

6. Create four option buttons inside the frame.

7. Set the following properties for these buttons:

Control	Property	Value
Option1	*Name*	optMarital
	Caption	Single
	Index	1
Option2	*Name*	optMarital
	Caption	Married
	Index	2
Option3	*Name*	optMarital
	Caption	Widowed
	Index	3
Option4	*Name*	optMarital
	Caption	Divorced
	Index	4

8. Add the following line of code to the datOptions_Reposition event procedure:

```
optMarital(datOptions.RecordSet!MaritalStatus) = True
```

9. Add the following lines of code to the optMarital_Click event procedure:

```
datOptions.RecordSet.edit
datOptions.RecordSet!MaritalStatus = Index
datOptions.RecordSet.Update
```

This technique gives you another choice for providing built-in options for your users. If you're going to add other record operations, you might want to take this code and call it from multiple places.

Using the Data Form Wizard

VB ships with an add-in to assist with the development of data forms. It's called the Data Form Wizard and is located on the Add-Ins menu. Through a series of prompts, this wizard gets the information from you to build the form. If you click the Add-Ins menu and this wizard doesn't appear on the menu, you need to add it.

To add the Data Form Wizard, complete these steps:

1. Select Add-Ins, Add-In Manager.

2. Select Visual Basic Data Form Wizard.

3. Click OK.

Now you are ready to use the Data Form Wizard. You need to select Add-Ins, Data Form Wizard. This launches the wizard and displays the first dialog box (see Figure 16-6). This is an introductory screen, so after you've read it once, you might want to select the Skip this screen in the future check box.

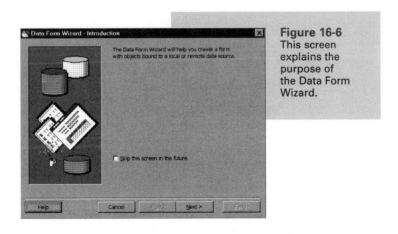

Figure 16-6
This screen explains the purpose of the Data Form Wizard.

The next screen is the Database Type selection (see Figure 16-7). Here you can select from the different data types. By default, Access is selected because it's the native Jet format.

The next screen is the Database screen (see Figure 16-8). This allows you to enter the path and file name for the database. You also can specify whether you want to see both tables and queries, or only tables.

For our purposes, you want to click B<u>r</u>owse and locate the `c:\Lab 3\Client Management.MDB` file. Leave the Record Sources as both <u>T</u>ables and Queries.

The next screen is the Form screen (see Figure 16-9). This allows you to select a style. You can select <u>S</u>ingle Record for a form based on a single recordset using

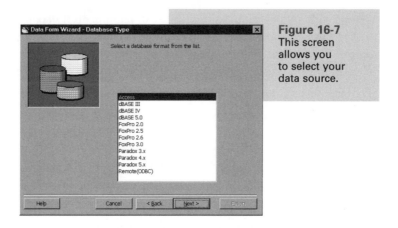

Figure 16-7
This screen allows you to select your data source.

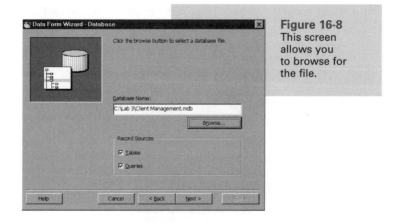

Figure 16-8
This screen allows you to browse for the file.

standard controls. The Grid (Datasheet) selection uses the DB grid control to build the recordset, and Master/Detail could accomplish something similar to what we just created, without the DB combo boxes.

The Record Source screen (see Figure 16-10) is next. This allows you to select a table or query to base the table on and select the fields you want to work with. You can also indicate a sort order.

For this example, you need to select tblClients for the Record Source. You can select ClientID, FirstName, LastName, Company, StructureID, and MaritalStatus as the fields. You can use the right-arrow button to move each field over, or use the right-chevron button to move all the fields. The left-arrow and left-chevron buttons allow you to move fields back to the list if you change your mind. You can change the order of the fields by using the Up and Down buttons in the dialog box.

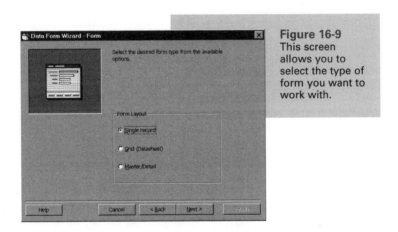

Figure 16-9
This screen allows you to select the type of form you want to work with.

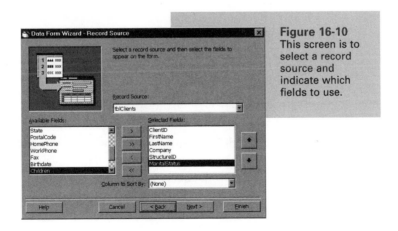

Figure 16-10
This screen is to select a record source and indicate which fields to use.

If you select the Master/Detail style, you see the Record Source screen and then you see another screen for the detail.

The next screen is the Control Selection screen (see Figure 16-11). This screen gives you an opportunity to include some additional functionality. You can include an Add button to make it easier for your users to add a record. Instead of having to go to the last record and then select the next button on the data control, users can just click the Add button.

You also can include a Delete button to help users get rid of unwanted records, or a Refresh button to let users refresh the data (this is important if you're developing for a multi-user environment). You also can add Update and Close buttons.

The last screen is the Finished! screen (see Figure 16-12). It gives you an opportunity to enter a name for the form and save the settings as your default.

Enter **frmDataWizard** as the Name. When you click the Finish button, the wizard generates the form (see Figure 16-13). For this example, many fields were omitted just to shorten the time required to generate the form.

The first thing to notice about this form is that it uses label and text box controls to display the data. It didn't set up a DB combo box for StructureID and MaritalStatus. If you select Project, Lab3 Properties, you can change the Startup Object setting to this form to let you run and see the form in action.

The command buttons are not built-in functions of the data control. These buttons are powered by code using the DAO model. Close the form after seeing how it works, and reset your startup object to frmDataCtrl.

Using Data Access Objects

Although the data control provides view, edit, and add operations, it doesn't provide a delete operation. Also, many developers feel uncomfortable with the other actions not being clearly visible since everything happens through the data control. It also is impossible to navigate using the keyboard with the data control.

You can use the DAO model to add this functionality to the data control form. The DAO model also can be used to add all the data functionality. Lastly, this model also gives you access to the querying capability of DAO.

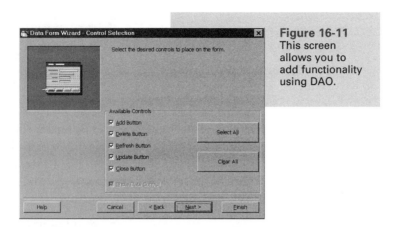

Figure 16-11
This screen allows you to add functionality using DAO.

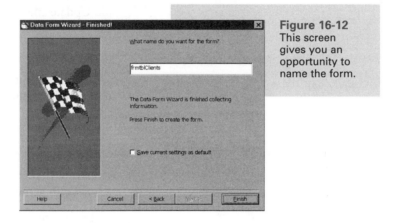

Figure 16-12
This screen gives you an opportunity to name the form.

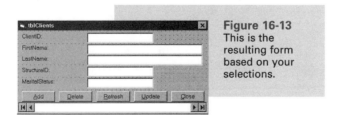

Figure 16-13
This is the resulting form based on your selections.

This section walks you through the steps necessary to enhance the form using the data control. It covers the steps necessary to create a form without the data control, and shows you several of the querying options.

Enhancing the Data Control's Performance

The Data Form Wizard adds functions by including new command buttons, but you can also add functionality by adding a menu. That's the approach used for this form.

You first need to consider which functions need to be added to the form. You might want to add a way to close the form. This can be accomplished by including a File menu containing an Exit command.

You also might want to provide navigation. This can be done through a Go To command added to an Edit menu. The same Edit menu can contain the capability to search for a record with a Find command.

You also might want a Record menu that can support the Add, Delete, and Update functions. If you're designing for a multi-user environment, a Refresh command can also be located on the Record menu.

Preparing the Form

To implement these actions for this form, you need to build a menu. You can use the Menu Editor to create the menu structure. Table 16-1 lists the menu items you need.

Table 16-1   Menu Items for `frmDataCtrl`

Caption	Name	Index	Enabled?	Indention
&File	mnuFile			0
E&xit	mnuExit			1
&Edit	mnuEdit			0
&Find ...	mnuFind			1
&Go To	mnuGoto			1
&First Record	mnuMove	0	No	2
&Next Record	mnuMove	1		2
&Previous Record	mnuMove	2	No	2
&Last Record	mnuMove	3		2
&Record	mnuRecord			0
&Add	mnuAdd			1
&Update	mnuUpdate			1
&Delete	mnuDelete			1
&Refresh	mnuRefresh			1

Once the menu is built, you're ready to begin adding functionality. The following sections consider each function separately.

Adding the Navigation

The first function to add is the Go To function. This allows navigation with the keyboard. The Go To menu item is implemented as a menu array to simplify the coding. You test the `Index` argument with a `Select Case` to determine which action has been chosen, and then you take the appropriate action. You need to move to the new record indicated, and also update the enabled state of this menu choice depending on the current record position.

A recordset has five move methods to allow you to navigate through it: `Move`, `MoveFirst`, `MoveNext`, `MovePrevious`, and `MoveLast`. `Move` moves a certain number of rows, and the other methods move to a specific record. The syntax for Move is:

```
RecordSet.Move??
```

For this project, you need to specify the data control's recordset, which requires the object name:

```
DatClients.RecordSet.Move??
```

For `MoveFirst` and `MoveLast`, the code is simple. You use the appropriate move method and then adjust the *Enabled* property so that users cannot go beyond the recordset's beginning or end.

For `MoveNext` and `MovePrevious`, the code is a little more complex. As you use these move methods, you do not know when you've hit the beginning or end of the recordset. This requires some checking. The `Recordset` object has *BOF* and *EOF* properties that can be tested to see if you're beyond one of the boundaries of the recordset. You test this with an `If` structure. If you are beyond a boundary, your code can issue the appropriate `MoveFirst` or `MoveLast` method to correct the situation. Here's the necessary code:

```
Private Sub mnuMove_Click(Index As Integer)
    Select Case Index
        Case 0   'First
            datClients.Recordset.MoveFirst
            mnuMove(0).Enabled = False
            mnuMove(1).Enabled = True
            mnuMove(2).Enabled = False
            mnuMove(3).Enabled = False
        Case 1   'Next
            datClients.Recordset.MoveNext
            If datClients.Recordset.EOF Then
                datClients.Recordset.MoveLast
                mnuMove(0).Enabled = True
                mnuMove(1).Enabled = False
                mnuMove(2).Enabled = True
                mnuMove(3).Enabled = False
            Else
```

```
                    mnuMove(0).Enabled = True
                    mnuMove(1).Enabled = True
                    mnuMove(2).Enabled = True
                    mnuMove(3).Enabled = True
                End If
            Case 2  'Previous
                datClients.Recordset.MovePrevious
                If datClients.Recordset.BOF Then
                    datClients.Recordset.MoveFirst
                    mnuMove(0).Enabled = False
                    mnuMove(1).Enabled = True
                    mnuMove(2).Enabled = False
                    mnuMove(3).Enabled = True
                Else
                    mnuMove(0).Enabled = True
                    mnuMove(1).Enabled = True
                    mnuMove(2).Enabled = True
                    mnuMove(3).Enabled = True
                End If
            Case 3  'Last
                datClients.Recordset.MoveLast
                mnuMove(0).Enabled = True
                mnuMove(1).Enabled = False
                mnuMove(2).Enabled = True
                mnuMove(3).Enabled = False
    End Select
End Sub
```

Adding the Add Function

The next function to code is the Add function. When you need to add a new
record, you can use the AddNew method for the recordset. Again, since you're
working with the recordset for the data control, you need to indicate this by
including the object reference. The mnuAdd_Click procedure is coded as follows:

```
Private Sub mnuAdd_Click()
    datClients.Recordset.AddNew
End Sub
```

Adding the Update Function

The Update function makes a feature that's built-in as part of the data control a
little easier for the user to visualize. The data control automatically begins to edit
as the user makes changes, and updates the record when the user moves to
another record or closes the recordset. If the user wants to force an update manually, this can be done using the UpdateRecord method of the data control.

For this application, the mnuUpdate_Click procedure is as follows:

```
Private Sub mnuUpdate_Click()
    datClients.UpdateRecord
End Sub
```

Adding the Delete Function

Deleting records is more complex than the procedures you've just seen. The process is to delete a record and then move to the next record, because deleting a record doesn't remove the space reserved for that record in the recordset. To delete a record, you need to use the Delete method.

You also might want to ask users to confirm that they want to delete the data. This can be done with a message box. The mnuDelete_Click procedure is coded as follows:

```
Private Sub mnuDelete_Click()
    'Verifies the user wants to delete a client and _
        repositions the pointer
    Dim strDelete As String, lngDeleteChk As Long
    strDelete = "Are you sure you want to delete this client?"
    lngDeleteChk = MsgBox(strDelete, vbYesNo + vbQuestion, _
        "Record Deletion")
    Select Case lngDeleteChk
        Case vbYes
            datClients.Recordset.Delete
            mnuMove_Click (1)
        Case vbNo
            MsgBox "Client wasn't deleted.", vbInformation, _
                "Deletion canceled"
    End Select
End Sub
```

 Note **Trying to delete a record that has related records in another table will create a data error. What to do about that error is discussed in greater detail in Chapter 17, "Testing the Client Management System."**

Adding the Find Function

Another feature you need to add to your application is the capability to search for a client. To locate a record, you have a choice. If you're using a Table record-set, you can use the Seek method; otherwise, you'll use the four find methods:

`FindFirst`, `FindNext`, `FindPrevious`, and `FindLast`. The syntax for the find methods is:

```
recordset.{FindFirst ¦ FindLast ¦ FindNext ¦ FindPrevious} criteria
```

These methods need the *criteria* argument to indicate what to search for. This argument is a string that's constructed using the same formatting as a SQL WHERE clause without the WHERE keyword.

The functionality of `mnuFind` is very limited. The user will be able to enter a last name and search for that name. The process is to store the current position in the recordset in case the find fails, and then use the `InputBox` function to get the last name. The last name is stored in a string variable that's used as part of the criteria string.

The `FindFirst` method is used to locate the first matching record. It is possible not to find a match. If so, the Recordset object's *NoMatch* property is set to `True`, and you use the stored position variable to reset the user to the record they were viewing prior to the find action. You can code the `mnuFind_Click` procedure as follows:

```
Private Sub mnuFind_Click()
    varBookmark = datClients.Recordset.Bookmark
    Dim strLookup As String, strFind As String
    strLookup = InputBox("Enter the client's last name.", "Find Client")
    If strLookup = "" Then Exit Sub
    strFind = "[LastName] = '" & strLookup & "'"
    datClients.Recordset.FindFirst strFind
    If datClients.Recordset.NoMatch Then
        MsgBox "Client not found.", vbInformation, "Find Failure"
        datClients.Recordset.Bookmark = varBookmark
    End If
End Sub
```

> **Note**
>
> **If you want to allow users to easily find the next record meeting the same criteria, you're better off creating a menu array to keep the code in one event, as well as creating a form-level variable to hold the search string to avoid asking for the name to be entered again.**

If you were using the `Seek` method with a Table recordset, the code would be different. The `Seek` method doesn't allow you to specify a string of criteria to use for the search; it relies instead on the table indexes. Here's its syntax:

```
table.Seek comparison, key1, key2, ...
```

Here you have to indicate what type of comparison you need to perform and what key(s) will be used. The rewritten `mnuFind_Click` procedure would look like this:

```
Private Sub mnuFind_Click()
    varBookmark = datClients.Recordset.Bookmark
    Dim strLookup As String
    strLookup = InputBox("Enter the client's last name.", "Find Client")
    If strLookup = "" Then Exit Sub
    datClients.Recordset.Index = "LastName"
    datClients.Recordset.Seek "=", strLookup
    If datClients.Recordset.NoMatch Then
        MsgBox "Client not found.", vbInformation, "Find Failure"
        datClients.Recordset.Bookmark = varBookmark
    End If
End Sub
```

Tip

Most users have used a find feature in another application, so you might want to design a form that resembles what they're used to. You also might want to allow them to select the fields to search.

Adding Refresh and Exit Capabilities

Two loose ends for this form are the capability for the user to refresh the record-set if working in a multi-user environment, and the capability for the user to exit the form. Allowing a user to refresh a dynaset to include any changes made by other users since the first user began working with the data is simple with the `Refresh` method:

```
Private Sub mnuRefresh_Click()
    datClients.RecordSet.Refresh
End Sub
```

Exiting the form can be accomplished with the `Unload` statement. It is easiest to use the `Me` keyword to identify what to unload:

```
Private Sub mnuExit_Click()
    Unload Me
End Sub
```

Accessing Data Directly

It's very easy to create a database form with the data control, and even easier to let the Data Form Wizard do as much of the setup as possible. Despite this easy method, you can (and might) want to access your data and populate a form directly without the data control. This approach is also useful if you need to work with data behind the scenes.

To illustrate the process of developing a form without the data control, you'll create an abbreviated version of the data control form. The number of fields are restricted to limit the amount of typing necessary for this portion of the project. The new form should look like the one shown in Figure 16-14.

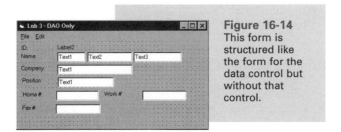

Figure 16-14
This form is structured like the form for the data control but without that control.

This form needs a menu system for the program functions, but for the sake of keeping the example short, the menu system is pared down. Table 16-2 lists all the necessary menu items.

Table 16-2 Menu Items for `frmDAO`

Caption	Name	Index	Enabled?	Indention
&File	mnuFile			0
&Open Database	mnuOpen			0
E&xit	mnuExit			1
&Edit	mnuEdit			0
&Go To	mnuGoto			1
&First Record	mnuMove	0	No	2
&Next Record	mnuMove	1		2
&Previous Record	mnuMove	2	No	2
&Last Record	mnuMove	3		2
&Record	mnuRecord			0
&Add	mnuAdd			1
&Delete	mnuDelete			1

Once the menu is built, name the form **frmDAO**, save the file as **dao.frm**, and you're ready to begin adding functionality. The following sections consider each function separately.

Establishing the Link to the Database

The first thing this form needs to do when it's displayed to the user is to connect with the data. This can be done with the Form_Load event or can be done manually as shown in this form.

When you want to work with a database using DAO, you need to establish data objects in your code. Since the database needs to be accessed from more than one procedure, it's best to declare the object variables in the General Declarations section.

A workspace is an area in memory that is taking advantage of specific security options for the database access.

When you're working with DAO, everything is controlled by the DBEngine object. You can work with the Workspace collection under this object. This allows you to maintain and interact with several databases with various levels of security. It's also how you implement transaction processing.

If you aren't using the security or you don't have more than one level of security to program, you can skip the workspace addressing. By default, VB looks at the default workspace. If you were using the workspace object, you would need to create an object variable for that object and use the CreateWorkspace method for the DBEngine object. The syntax is as follows:

```
Dim variable as Workspace
Set variable = CreateWorkspace(name, user, password)
```

In this case, no security has been used, so the default workspace is fine. To access a database, you then use the OpenDatabase method, which also requires an object variable. Since you need the database throughout this form, the variables need to be declared at the module level as follows:

```
Dim dbClients As Database, rsClients As Recordset
```

Once the variables are declared, you need to open the database. The syntax is:

```
Set database = [workspace.]OpenDatabase(dbname[,
    ➡exclusive[, read-only[, source]]])
```

This method can specify the workspace followed by the method. It has four possible arguments. The first is *dbname*, which is the full path and file name for the database. It must be enclosed in quotes to be recognized.

The Exclusive and ReadOnly arguments are Boolean to determine, respectively, whether or not you want others to be able to use the file while this user is working with it, and whether or not you want this user to be able to edit the file. You can enter True or False for these properties or use the built-in constants.

The last argument is *source*. It provides information about what type of database is being accessed. This is the same information that was needed for the *Connect* property for the data control.

In this form, the `mnuOpen_Click` procedure establishes error handling and then issues the `OpenDatabase` method without a workspace to take advantage of the default. It includes a *dbname* but relies on the defaults for the rest of the arguments.

You're now ready to access the recordset for this form. To access a recordset, you use the `OpenRecordset` method. The syntax is:

```
Set variable = database.OpenRecordset(source[, type[, options]])
```

An alternative syntax is:

```
Set variable = object.OpenRecordset([type[, options]])
```

There are two versions of this method because you may or may not already have an object variable on which to base the recordset. The first method is the one you'll use in the example form. It expects to get the *source* argument, which is the table name or stored query name enclosed in quotes. The *type* argument indicates the type of recordset that will be created; by default it's a dynaset.

The last argument is *options*. The `Exclusive` argument for the `database` object allows you to keep other users out of the database when a user is in, but you may not want to be that restrictive. The *options* argument lets you put restrictions on how this user and others can access the data in this recordset. The second syntax is to support recordset creation based on another object that has been defined in code—like a query.

The next line uses the recordset's *LockEdits* property to indicate what type of record locking will be used for the recordset. This is discussed in greater detail in Chapter 17.

The `mnuMove_Click` event is called to move to the first record in the recordset. Once that is accomplished, the *Enabled* property is adjusted for certain menu commands to prevent problems like trying to open the same database more than once.

Here's the necessary code:

```
Private Sub mnuOpen_Click()
    On Error GoTo OpenErr
    Set dbClients = OpenDatabase("c:\Lab 3\Client Management.MDB")
    Set rsClients = dbClients.OpenRecordset("tblClients", dbOpenDynaset)
    rsClients.LockEdits = True
    mnuMove_Click (0)
    mnuOpen.Enabled = False
    mnuGoto.Enabled = True
    mnuAdd.Enabled = True
    mnuDelete.Enabled = True
    Exit Sub
OpenErr:
```

```
        Dim strMsg As TextBox, strTitle As String
        strTitle = "Open Database Error"
        Select Case Err.Number
            Case 3044
                strMsg = "The path is not valid"
            Case 3024
                strMsg = "Could not locate database file."
            Case 3006
                strMsg = _
                    "Could not open the database because it is _
                    exclusively locked by another user."
            Case 3008
                strMsg = _
                    "Could not open the table because it is _
                    exclusively locked by another user."
            Case 3176
                strMsg = "Couldn't open the file."
            Case Else
                strMsg = _
                    "An unanticipated error has occurred. It is Error " & _
                    Err.Number & ", " & Error.Description
        End Select
        MsgBox strMsg, vbExclamation, strTitle
    End Sub
```

> **Note** The remainder of this procedure is error-handling code in case something fails. This is covered in detail in Chapter 17.

Navigating Records

The code for navigating records is very similar to what you used with the data control, but you now need a way to populate the fields after you move, because the data control isn't taking care of that for you. You also need to make sure that when you move to a new record, an edit isn't in progress.

The new mnuMove_Click procedure takes care of both these problems:

```
Private Sub mnuMove_Click(Index As Integer)
    If rsClients.EditMode = dbEditInProgress Or _
        rsClients.EditMode = dbEditAdd Then
        SaveData
    End If
    Select Case Index
        Case 0  'First
            rsClients.MoveFirst
```

```
                    mnuMove(0).Enabled = False
                    mnuMove(1).Enabled = True
                    mnuMove(2).Enabled = False
                    mnuMove(3).Enabled = False
                Case 1  'Next
                    rsClients.MoveNext
                    If datclients.Recordset.EOF Then
                        datclients.Recordset.MoveLast
                        mnuMove(0).Enabled = True
                        mnuMove(1).Enabled = False
                        mnuMove(2).Enabled = True
                        mnuMove(3).Enabled = False
                    Else
                        mnuMove(0).Enabled = True
                        mnuMove(1).Enabled = True
                        mnuMove(2).Enabled = True
                        mnuMove(3).Enabled = True
                    End If
                Case 2  'Previous
                    rsClients.MovePrevious
                    If datclients.Recordset.BOF Then
                        datclients.Recordset.MoveFirst
                        mnuMove(0).Enabled = False
                        mnuMove(1).Enabled = True
                        mnuMove(2).Enabled = False
                        mnuMove(3).Enabled = True
                    Else
                        mnuMove(0).Enabled = True
                        mnuMove(1).Enabled = True
                        mnuMove(2).Enabled = True
                        mnuMove(3).Enabled = True
                    End If
                Case 3  'Last
                    rsClients.MoveLast
                    mnuMove(0).Enabled = True
                    mnuMove(1).Enabled = False
                    mnuMove(2).Enabled = True
                    mnuMove(3).Enabled = False

        End Select
        PopulateData
        Exit Sub
    MoveError:
    EditErr:
        Select Case Err.Number
            Case 3167
                rsClients.Delete
                Resume
            Case Else
```

```
        MsgBox "An unanticipated error has occurred. It is Error " & _
        Err.Number & ", " & Error.Description, vbInformation, _
        "Unanticipated error"
    End Select
End Sub
```

The first line checks the *EditMode* property to determine if an edit is in progress. If one is, the procedure calls a routine named SaveData to update the data. The last line of mnuMove_Click calls a procedure to populate the fields (as explained in the next section).

Populating the Fields

Since the data control doesn't fill field values into the controls, you need to write code to take care of this. In this form, a separate procedure named PopulateData is written for this purpose.

To populate fields, you need to take the appropriate value property for a given control and assign it the field data. To access the field data, you need to specify the recordset followed by an exclamation point (!) and the field name. Access supports the use of spaces in names, but if you're working with table or field names with spaces in them, you need to surround the name with square brackets ([ ]). For the fields on this form, the PopulateData procedure is written as follows:

```
Private Sub PopulateData()
    lblClientID.Caption = rsClients!ClientID
    txtPrefix.Text = rsClients!Prefix
    txtFirstName.Text = rsClients!FirstName
    txtLastName.Text = rsClients!LastName
    txtCompany.Text = rsClients!Company
    txtPosition.Text = rsClients!Position
    mseHomePhone.Text = rsClients!HomePhone
    mseWorkPhone.Text = rsClients!WorkPhone
    mseFax.Text = rsClients!Fax
End Sub
```

If you're working with a check box, for instance, you need to set the check box's *Value* property to the field value. For a drop-down list, you need to set the *Text* property (the list must be created manually).

Editing Records

Another challenge when creating a form manually is tackling the issue of editing records. With the data control, editing was built into the control. You now need to manually begin the edit process. When the contents of a text box are changed, it kicks off the Change event, so this is the perfect place to begin the edit process.

Rather than code the edit routine into every `Change` event, you're better served by having another procedure that's called from each `Change` event. Give each `Change` event the following line of code:

```
x = EditData()
```

This calls the `EditData` procedure, which is where you do the real work of allowing the user to edit the data:

```
Private Function EditData()
    On Error GoTo EditErr
    If rsClients.EditMode <> dbEditAdd Or _
        rsClients.EditMode <> dbEditInProgress Then
        rsClients.Edit
    End If
    Exit Sub
EditErr:
    Select Case Err.Number
        Case 3260
            MsgBox "Record is currently locked by another user, _
                please try again later.", _
                vbInformation, "Locked"
        Case 3197
            MsgBox _
                "Data has been changed by another user, _
                the changes will be refreshed.", _
                vbInformation, "Changed Data"
            rsClients.Bookmark = rsClients.Bookmark
            PopulateData
        Case Else
            MsgBox "An unanticipated error has occurred. It is Error " & _
                Err.Number & ", " & Error.Description, vbInformation, _
                "Unanticipated error"
    End Select
End Function
```

The first line of this procedure starts error handling. The second line contains the `Edit` method, which is necessary to edit a record in the recordset. *How* you want to manage record locking and *when* you actually want to invoke the `Edit` method will have a direct impact on how you use this method. The remainder of the procedure is error handling that's discussed in Chapter 17.

Note Chapter 17 also discusses the important issues involved with deciding when to edit.

Saving Records

Once the Edit method (or AddNew method) is used, the record is locked so that no other user can make changes. Before the current user can move to a new record or proceed with a different action, the edited (or added) record needs to be saved. This was another task that the data control handled for you.

For this form, you'll handle saves of edited and added records with a procedure named SaveData that can be called from several places. This procedure essentially reverses the process of populating the data, by taking the value of each control and assigning it to the appropriate field:

```
Private Sub SaveData()
    rsClients!ClientID = lblClientID.Caption
    rsClients!Prefix = txtPrefix.Text
    rsClients!FirstName = txtFirstName.Text
    rsClients!LastName = txtLastName.Text
    rsClients!Company = txtCompany.Text
    rsClients!Position = txtPosition.Text
    rsClients!HomePhone = mseHomePhone.Text
    rsClients!WorkPhone = mseWorkPhone.Text
    rsClients!Fax = mseFax.Text
    rsClients.Update
    DBEngine.Idle dbFreeLocks
    rsClients.Bookmark = rsClients.LastModified
    PopulateData
End Sub
```

You need to be careful with this process and have a good understanding of all the relevant field properties. You can use the *Required* and *AllowZeroLength* properties to prevent the user from skipping fields.

AllowZeroLength is the one you need to be more careful with. If you have an empty string for a control value and *AllowZeroLength* is not set to True, an error is created. You might need to do some length testing for the string of information prior to placing the information in the field:

```
If Len(txtFirstName.Text) > 0 Then
    rsClients!FirstName = txtFirstName.Text
End If
```

Caution

> The same problem with empty strings can also wreak havoc with the **PopulateData** procedure.

Adding Records

The AddNew method is also used here to add records to the recordset, but again some checking needs to be done to prevent problems. If an edit is in progress and the user tries to add a new record, a runtime error results. The following code is used to avoid this problem:

```
Private Sub mnuAdd_Click()
    If rsClients.EditMode <> dbEditNone Then SaveData
    rsClients.AddNew
    ClearData
End Sub
```

The If structure tests the value of the *EditMode* property before invoking the AddNew method. This is followed by a call to the ClearData procedure to clean out the value properties and prepare all the fields for the user's data entry. Here's the code for the ClearData procedure:

```
Private Sub ClearData()
    lblClientID.Caption = ""
    txtPrefix.Text = ""
    txtFirstName.Text = ""
    txtLastName.Text = ""
    txtCompany.Text = ""
    txtPosition.Text = ""
    mseHomePhone.Text = ""
    mseWorkPhone.Text = ""
    mseFax.Text = ""
End Sub
```

Since the ClientID label cannot have data entered, you might want to consider placing another text entry in that field temporarily. An entry like Not Assigned Yet might make your user feel more comfortable.

Deleting Records

Deleting records in this form is similar to deleting them in the data control form, except that you need to handle the editing-in-progress issue. This can be done with the *EditMode* property as follows:

```
Private Sub mnuDelete_Click()
    On Error GoTo DeleteErr
    If rsClients.EditMode <> dbEditNone Then SaveData
    rsClients.Delete
    If rsClient.RecordCount < 1 Then
        ClearData
        Exit Sub
    End If
    mnuMove_Click(1)
```

```
DeleteErr:
    If Err.Number = 3200 Then
        MsgBox "Cannot delete a client that has existing Services.", _
            vbInformation, "Delete"
    Else
        MsgBox "Unanticipated Error " & Err.Number & _
            ": " & Err.Description, vbInformation, "Unexpected Error"
    End If
End Sub
```

The first line jumps to the error-handling code when necessary. The second line checks the *EditMode* property. The third line deletes the record. The next line checks the *RecordCount* property to determine if there are any records left. If there aren't, VB clears the fields and exits the procedure. Otherwise, the mnuMove_Click procedure is called with an index of 1 to initiate a move to the next record. The remainder of this procedure consists of error-handling steps that are explained in Chapter 17.

Exiting the Form

This form also needs an exit procedure. Use the following code:

```
Private Sub mnuExit_Click()
    If rsClients.EditMode = dbEditInProgress _
        Or rsClients.EditMode = dbEditAdd Then
        Dim lngResponse As Long
        lngResponse = MsgBox("Changes have been made to the current record, _
        do you wish to save these changes prior to exiting?", _
        vbQuestion + vbYesNo, "Changes?")
        If lngResponse = vbYes Then
            SaveData
        End If
    End If
    Unload Me
End Sub
```

This procedure is identical to that used for the data control form except that this one checks the *EditMode* property to make sure that an edit or add is not currently in progress.

Querying the Database

One of the most powerful aspects of DAO is that it lets you create Structured Query Language (SQL) statements to create a subset of the data. SQL is a language developed to retrieve and manipulate databases. There is an ANSI standard for SQL to create a common approach to these tasks.

SQL provides the capability to narrow the scope of a data set. If you're only interested in those clients who are incorporated, for example, why create a recordset based on the entire table? In VB, you can use SQL as a record source for the data control or to create a recordset using DAO.

If you are familiar with SQL, making the transition to the SQL provided with VB will be very simple. There's some specific formatting for different types of data, as explained in the following sections.

Understanding a SELECT Statement

The first place that SQL was used in this client management application was the population of the DB grid for the data control form. The DB grid's recordset needed to change based on which Client ID was displayed in the rest of the form. This was accomplished with the Reposition event:

```
Private Sub datClients_Reposition()
    Screen.MousePointer = vbDefault
    datClients.Caption = "Record: " & _
        datClients.Recordset.AbsolutePosition + 1
    Dim dbServices As Database, rsServices As Recordset
    Dim strSQL As String
    strSQL = "SELECT Service, ServiceDate From tblServices WHERE [ClientID] =
➥"& datClients.Recordset!ClientID
    Set dbServices = OpenDatabase("c:\Lab 3\Client Management.MDB")
    Set rsServices = dbServices.OpenRecordset(strSQL, dbOpenDynaset)
    Set datServices.Recordset = rsServices
End Sub
```

Rather than populate the recordset with the entire table, the SQL SELECT statement is used. When you create a SQL statement, you're creating a text string to be used. The syntax is:

```
SELECT [predicate] { * ¦ table.* ¦ [table.]field1 [AS alias1]
    ➥[, [table.]field2 [AS alias2] [, ...]]} FROM tableexpression [, ...]
    ➥[IN externaldatabase] [WHERE... ] [GROUP BY... ] [HAVING... ]
    ➥[ORDER BY... ] [WITH OWNERACCESS OPTION]
```

Tip

Although VB isn't case-sensitive in many contexts, it's recommended that you uppercase all SQL keywords to make them easy to recognize.

The first word is the keyword for the query type. The SELECT query creates a recordset. The first argument is *predicate*, which indicates how to return the records. It can be set to ALL (this is the default) to return all the records matching the conditions of the SQL statement.

You also can use DISTINCT or DISTINCTROW. DISTINCT returns all records matching the criteria, excluding duplicate records based on a particular field; DISTINCTROW returns all records matching the criteria, excluding complete duplicate records.

You can use the TOP *n* predicate where the number *n* indicates that you want the first *n* records of the matching records. If you add the PERCENT keyword after the number, you can get the first *n* percent of the records. (You could retrieve the top 10% of scores, sales, or whatever.)

Following *predicate* is the list of fields to return. You can use an asterisk (*) to indicate all the fields or enter individual field names if you want to narrow the number of fields returned. You can specify up to 255 fields.

 If your database supports spaces in field names, you need to surround any such field name with brackets ([ ]).

The FROM keyword followed by the table name indicates which table to retrieve the files from. If you need to pull information from more than one table at a time, that can be done with a single SELECT. You can combine up to 32 tables in a query. You just need to add the table indicator in front of your fields.

The WHERE keyword indicates that you intend to narrow the scope for the record-set. WHERE is followed by an expression, normally a field name with an operator and a value. In many cases, the value needs to be retrieved from a control on a form. This is the case with the Reposition event. You're using the ClientID field of the form to serve as the value.

If you are using controls to serve as the value in the expression, you need to know what type of data is stored in the field. In this case, ClientID is a long integer. When a control is representing a field of numeric data type, this structure will work. When you're working with a string field, however, you need to surround the value with single quotes (' '). If you construct a SQL statement to look at the State field, for instance, the code looks like this:

```
strSQL = "SELECT * From tblClients WHERE [State] = '" & _
    datClients.Recordset!State & "'"
```

VB also supports an IN clause and wild-card characters. If you want to get all the clients in Illinois and Georgia, for instance, you need to modify the SQL structure:

```
strSQL = "SELECT * From tblClients WHERE [State] IN ('IL', 'GA')
```

If you want to retrieve all the clients whose last name begins with M, you need the wild-card character as well as the LIKE keyword:

```
strSQL = "SELECT * From tblClients WHERE [LastName] LIKE 'M*'"
```

VB also supports the Date data type. If you do a select operation based on a date, the date value has to be surrounded by pound signs (# #). For instance, you can use the following statement to find only those clients born on April 12, 1964:

```
strSQL = "SELECT * From tblClients WHERE [Birthdate] = #4/12/64#"
```

Performing a select operation for one birthdate will most likely return a very small data set, so the Find method might be a better choice in that situation.

You can use the BETWEEN keyword if you want, for example, to find everyone who was born from 1955 through 1965:

```
strSQL = "SELECT * From tblClients WHERE [Birthdate] "
strSQL = strSQL & "BETWEEN #12/31/54# AND #1/1/66"
```

Notice that the dates are moved one day in each direction to get the desired results. To be user-friendly, you might want to ask the user for an age range, and then get the necessary dates for your SELECT statement by subtracting the input age from the current date and getting the first day of that year.

Note The WHERE clause can have more than one expression evaluated. It supports the use of the AND and OR keywords to combine expressions. You can have up to 40 expressions in a single clause if you do not exceed approximately 64,000 characters.

The last component is the ORDER BY keyword. By default a recordset displays the records in the order they were entered into the database. You can use ORDER BY to sort the recordset in a particular order. You can enter a field name alone to get the records sorted on that field in ascending order. If you want to sort in descending order, you need to include DESC at the end of the phrase. You can sort your query on as many as 10 fields.

Tack on a semicolon (;) to indicate the end of the SQL statement. Since you're working with a string, you need to surround the entire statement with quotation marks (" ").

Creating a Dynamic Select

The SELECT statement is used to get recordsets. Tying it to the data in a field is just a matter of constructing the statement and using it. Often, though, your users will make the request slightly more challenging.

Today they might need to see all clients in a particular city who have written wills, and tomorrow they might need to see everyone who has incorporated a business. You cannot build a SQL statement that will meet their changing needs every day. You need to give them an opportunity to establish their criteria at runtime, but the average user would take one look at the SELECT statement and run screaming from the room.

You can create a *dynamic select* form to give your users some selection options without forcing them to become database experts overnight. This form does not provide everything, but does give them a few choices. Figure 16-15 shows the Select form that's part of the client management application.

Even though there are many fields in your database, three fields have been isolated on this form for use in a selection. Seeing a list of clients by marital status could be beneficial. A DB combo control is combined with a data control to look at tblMaritalStatus and provide the choice.

The second field offered on the Select form is the field indicating whether or not the client has children, and the last field is the one tracking whether the client has a will. Users can work with any or all of these three fields to narrow the search for clients.

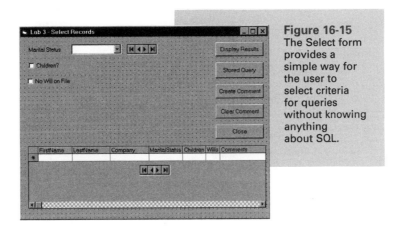

Figure 16-15
The Select form provides a simple way for the user to select criteria for queries without knowing anything about SQL.

The Display button activates the search. The process that needs to take place with a dynamic selection like this is to evaluate each component on the form and build an expression that reflects the user's input. Once all the expressions are built, they're combined and meshed in with the SELECT statement. Here's the code:

```
Private Sub cmdDisplay_Click()
' Test controls and build partial strings
    Dim strWill As String, strMaritalStatus As String
    Dim strChildren As String, strWhere As String, strSQL As String

    Select Case cboMaritalStatus
        Case "Single"
            strMaritalStatus = " MaritalStatus = 1 "
        Case "Married"
            strMaritalStatus = " MaritalStatus = 2 "
        Case "Widowed"
            strMaritalStatus = " MaritalStatus = 3 "
        Case "Divorced"
            strMaritalStatus = " MaritalStatus = 4 "
        Case "Single"
            strMaritalStatus = ""
    End Select

    If chkChildren = 1 Then
        strChildren = " Children > 0 "
    Else
        strChildren = ""
    End If
    Stop
    If chkWills = 1 Then
        strWill = " Wills = False"
    Else
        strWill = ""
    End If


    strWhere = ""
    If strMaritalStatus <> "" Then
        strWhere = " WHERE" & strMaritalStatus
    End If

    If strChildren <> "" Then
        If strWhere = "" Then
            strWhere = " WHERE" & strChildren
        Else
            strWhere = "AND" & strChildren
        End If
    End If
```

```
    If strWill <> "" Then
        If strWhere = "" Then
            strWhere = " WHERE" & strWill
        Else
            strWhere = "AND" & strWill
        End If
    End If

    strWhere = strWhere & ";"
    strSQL = "SELECT * From tblClients" & strWhere

' Create the recordset
    Dim dbClients As Database, rsClients As Recordset
    Set dbClients = OpenDatabase("c:\Lab 3\Client Management.MDB")
    Set rsClients = dbClients.OpenRecordset(strSQL, dbOpenDynaset)
    Set datclients.Recordset = rsClients
End Sub
```

The first evaluation is of the marital status combo box, which was populated with the relevant descriptions. The easiest tool for testing this is the Select Case statement. For each case, the string strMaritalStatus is assigned the field name, an equal sign, and the appropriate numeric value. This will end up serving as part of the test criteria in the WHERE clause of the SELECT statement. This has to be done manually because there isn't an underlying table to post the value to. Notice that you include a space on each side of the phrase assigned to the string.

The second evaluation is whether the client has children. On the form, you look at the appropriate check box, but in the SELECT statement you need to test another numeric field. Therefore, the string is set to Children > 0. In this case, the lawyer doesn't care how many children. This could be a selection to kick off some marketing about wills and estate planning.

The last evaluation is to determine if the client has a will. This is also represented by a check box, but the logic is reversed. If the value is 1, then you need to test for a false condition.

Once all three strings are built, they need to be combined. This is not a simple process of string concatenation. When you're building a WHERE clause, you need to combine the clauses with AND or OR. For this simple example, AND is used.

Since you might use multiple criteria (but might not), you need to add WHERE in some cases, but add AND if a WHERE already exists. This can be done by checking the string that holds the in-progress WHERE clause. This string, strWhere, is set to a zero-length string prior to evaluation. The first IF structure is for marital status. If strMaritalStatus isn't an empty string, then strWhere is evaluated to determine if it is empty. If it is, the appropriate marital status string is concatenated

using the WHERE keyword. Otherwise, the appropriate marital status string is concatenated using the AND keyword.

This process is repeated for each of the three component strings. The last step is to concatenate a semicolon to the string to end the SQL statement properly. This is then combined with the initial part of the SELECT string.

The last four lines are identical to the first SQL statement. The SQL statement is used to create a recordset, which is then assigned to the recordset for the data control for the DB grid.

When you're considering adding a dynamic select to an application, you need to determine which fields are most often needed for select operations. If your use is more sophisticated, you might want to look at the Microsoft Word mail-merge filter window. It's more flexible than the example just presented, and might give you a better idea of how to proceed.

This type of selection can be used to narrow down data records to be viewed on a form. It also can be used to print a report including only certain data.

Using a Stored Query

The opposite of the dynamic select is a *stored query*, which is a fixed query that's used frequently. Jet databases—and a few other databases—allow you to create a SQL statement and save it in a database.

You can access a stored query with DAO as easily as you access any table. A stored query has a performance advantage over a SQL statement in a Jet database. A stored query has already been assigned space in the file and has already been compiled. If you create a SQL statement to use with DAO, a temporary object is created for that query in the database. When you use it to create a recordset, it has to be compiled and run. The object then needs to be removed when the process is completed. This creates a larger file size. You periodically have to compact your Jet databases to remove this wasted space.

Whenever a stored query is used, however, it's executed without affecting the database file size. Moreover, it runs faster because it skips the compile step.

The Stored Query button is used in the client management application to access a stored query just like a table. The code linked to this button sets up the object variables, opens the database, opens the recordset using the query name, and then assigns the recordset to the data control for the DB grid. Here's the code:

```
Private Sub cmdStored_Click()
    ' Create the recordset
    Dim dbClients As Database, rsClients As Recordset
```

```
    Set dbClients = OpenDatabase("c:\Lab 3\Client Management.MDB")
    Set rsClients = dbClients.OpenRecordset("qryWills", dbOpenDynaset)
    Set datclients.Recordset = rsClients
End Sub
```

Using an Action Query

SELECT isn't the only SQL statement available through DAO. DAO also supports the SQL action queries. Often you aren't building a recordset to view data, but instead to make some global changes to the record. Rather than building a record-set and then using the move, edit, and update methods to navigate and edit each record, you may want to consider an action query. DAO supports the UPDATE, INSERT, and DELETE action queries.

An action query is a SQL statement that will alter the records of the recordset created with the criteria included in the statement.

The UPDATE query is designed to assist you with making global data changes to the recordset. For instance, in the client management application, you might want to indicate that a letter was mailed to certain clients. The syntax for the UPDATE statement is:

```
UPDATE predicate table SET newvalue1, newvalue2, ... WHERE criteria;
```

The UPDATE keyword is followed by a *predicate* just as SELECT is, but UPDATE does not allow for a field list, because this statement isn't used for viewing. The *table* argument is the name of the table containing the records to be updated.

The SET keyword indicates which fields are changing. This is followed by the new value expression(s) of whatever is changing. If there is more than one, you can separate them with commas.

The last clause is the WHERE clause that allows you to select a subset of the records in that table for updating, instead of updating every record in the table. For the client management application, the Create Comment and Clear Comment buttons were added to demonstrate how this works. Examine the following code:

```
Private Sub cmdCreate_Click()
    Dim dbClients As Database, rsClients As Recordset
    Set dbClients = OpenDatabase("c:\Lab 3\Client Management.MDB")
    Dim strSQL As String
    strSQL = "UPDATE DISTINCTROW tblClients SET _
        tblClients.Comments = 'Mailed Letter';"
    dbClients.Execute strSQL, dbFailOnError
    MsgBox dbClients.RecordsAffected & " records affected.", _
      vbInformation, "Update"
    Set rsClients = dbClients.OpenRecordset("tblClients")
    Set datclients.Recordset = rsClients
End Sub
```

```
Private Sub cmdClear_Click()
    Dim dbClients As Database, rsClients As Recordset
    Set dbClients = OpenDatabase("c:\Lab 3\Client Management.MDB")
    Dim strSQL As String
    strSQL = "UPDATE DISTINCTROW tblClients "
    strSQL = strSQL & SET tblClients.Comments = ' ';"
    dbClients.Execute strSQL, dbFailOnError
    MsgBox dbClients.RecordsAffected & " records affected.", _
      vbInformation, "Update"
    Set rsClients = dbClients.OpenRecordset("tblClients")
    Set datclients.Recordset = rsClients
End Sub
```

The `Mailed Letter` comment is added to all records, so there isn't a `WHERE` clause in this example. The first step is to declare the object variables. Then you need to establish the link to the database with `OpenDatabase`. The `strSQL` string is then assigned to the `UPDATE` statement.

When you did `SELECT` queries, the assignment of `strSQL` was followed by the `OpenRecordset` method. With an action query, however, you're not going to view the recordset.

The `database` object has an `Execute` method that runs the query and updates the records. The syntax is:

`database.Execute source[, options]`

source is the SQL statement and there are some *options* you can specify (for example, `dbFailOnError` rolls back the entire action if any record in the selected record-set cannot be updated successfully).

After the query is executed, you can use the *RecordsAffected* property to see how many records were changed. This property can only be viewed after the `Execute` method has been issued. If you want to preview the records that will be modified, you can use a `SELECT` query with the exact same `WHERE` clause you intend to use for the `UPDATE` statement, and actually open the recordset for viewing. The last part of the procedure is to refresh the recordset of the DB grid.

Two other action queries can be used with DAO. You can create an `INSERT` query to insert new records or a `DELETE` query to delete existing records.

The `INSERT` query takes an existing recordset and appends the records to another recordset provided that there are fields with matching data types. The syntax is:

```
INSERT INTO target [IN externaldatabase] [(field1[, field2[, ...]])]
   ➥SELECT [source.]field1[, field2[, ...] FROM tableexpression
```

`INSERT INTO` is followed by *target* (which is a table name). If you're inserting new records into a table in another database, you include the `IN` clause with an external database name. This is followed by a list of fields in the target table in which data should be inserted.

The SELECT keyword is used with a list of fields to be inserted; the FROM keyword is used with a table expression indicating the source table or query. The field lists must be placed in matching order—they do not have to have matching names, but the data types must match or else the insert operation will fail.

The DELETE query allows you to get rid of a block of records without using the Move and Delete methods for the recordset. The syntax is:

```
DELETE [table.*] FROM table WHERE criteria
```

The DELETE statement starts with the DELETE keyword followed by the table name. The table name has a period (.) and asterisk (*) after it if you want all fields. The FROM keyword and table name indicate which table you're deleting the records from. The WHERE clause lets you specify some criteria that records in the table must meet in order to be deleted.

If the database has any data relationships set up between tables, the capability to add and delete records may be impaired. If a record you are attempting to delete is providing information to another table, you will not be able to delete it. The subject of relationships and how they impact record deletion is addressed in Chapter 17.

Tying It All Together

The client management application has really grown throughout this chapter. You now need some type of management for all these different methods of working with your data. To accomplish this, the project needs a switchboard (see Figure 16-16).

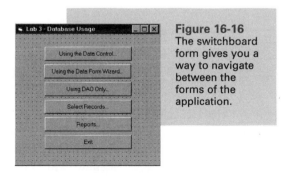

Figure 16-16
The switchboard form gives you a way to navigate between the forms of the application.

In most applications, you settle on one method for working with your data, and you do not require more than one method for viewing client information. If several methods are available, though, it helps to have a switchboard form. This is basically a series of buttons that can launch the appropriate forms. Here's the code for the switchboard form:

```
Private Sub cmdDataCtrl_Click()
    frmDataCtrl.Show
End Sub

Private Sub cmdDataOnly_Click()
    frmDAO.Show
End Sub

Private Sub cmdDataWizard_Click()
    frmDatawizard.Show
End Sub

Private Sub cmdReports_Click()
    frmReports.Show
End Sub

Private Sub cmdSelect_Click()
    frmSelect.Show
End Sub

Private Sub cmdExit_Click()
    Unload Me
End Sub
```

Notice that this code is very simple. When a given button is clicked, you display the corresponding form by issuing the Show method. When the Exit button is clicked, you use the Unload statement to close the application.

Summary

The client management application illustrates several methods for accessing data from your database. The data control provides the quickest method—it's as easy as setting the data properties for the control and then binding other controls to display the data.

The data control provides viewing, editing, and adding functionality. You may want to add the capability to delete records or navigate from a menu or button. The DAO model can enhance the functionality of the data control. DAO also can be used to provide your entire data access. It allows you to narrow the scope of your data by using SQL.

CHAPTER 17

Testing the Client Management System

Visual Basic doesn't have reporting built into its environment. It depends on a third-party package named Crystal Reports to provide the database reporting functions. This package gives you a visual design environment to construct reports as well as a control to access the reports easily from VB. This chapter will introduce you to the capabilities of Crystal Reports.

Another area that needs to be addressed for the client management application is support for data verification and multiple users. This is best provided using the standard error-handling process and a special event with the data control.

The last step to make this a working application is to create an executable. In the first project, you made a standard EXE. That type of executable relies on the VB runtime library to provide most of the functions. With Visual Basic, Enterprise Edition, you also have the ability to compile your code. This creates an executable that can be edited in C++, which may provide better performance for your application.

Using Crystal Reports

When you are creating a database application like the client management application, you might need to provide a mechanism for the user to generate printed output. Rather than use the Print statement (as you did in the first project) or use Automation to create a report through an external application (as you did in the second project), you can use Crystal Reports.

To add a report to your VB application, you create the layout for the report using the Crystal Reports application. This can be accessed from VB's Add-Ins menu. This application offers a selection of report types, along with a Report Expert to assist you (this is similar to the VB wizards).

Once a report is created and saved, you need to use the Crystal Reports control to add access to your application. This control is not part of the standard group of controls, so it needs to be added like the DB list and DB grid controls.

This application requires four reports: a standard phone list, a grouped list of services, mailing labels, and a report to show which clients do not have a will on file. The user will have the ability to preview the reports or send them directly to the printer. The first task is to design these reports.

Creating a Report

The first step toward creating a report is to launch the Crystal Reports application. You can select Crystal Reports from the Visual Basic group on the Start menu or from within VB. To launch it from the VB menu, select Add-Ins, Report Designer.

The first time you run Crystal Reports, you are asked to register the application. If you do not register the application, you'll be prompted to do so every time you log into Crystal Reports. Once you've completed the registration, you'll reach the Crystal Reports window (see Figure 17-1). This application doesn't assume that you're starting a report, so the window is empty when it first opens.

To begin a new report, select File, New or click the New tool on the toolbar. This opens the Create New Report dialog box (see Figure 17-2).

This dialog box offers you two approaches. You can choose one of the templates shown, to get the assistance of an Expert. If you do this, you can select from the following report styles: Standard, Listing, Cross Tab, Mailing Label, Summary, Graph, Top N, or Drill Down. Once you've selected a report style, dialog boxes prompt you through the creation of your report.

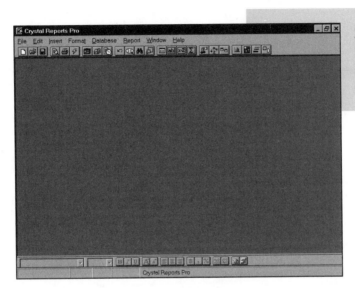

Figure 17-1
The Crystal Reports window opens to allow you to begin working.

Figure 17-2
The Create New Report dialog box allows you to select the type of report to create.

The second approach is to design your report without assistance. If you prefer to do this, select the Custom button. This opens the lower pane of the dialog box (see Figure 17-3) and allows you to design your own report using the Custom Report, Custom Cross-tab, or Custom Mail Label button. You also can select your data source. This pane of the dialog box is not needed if you choose to use an Expert.

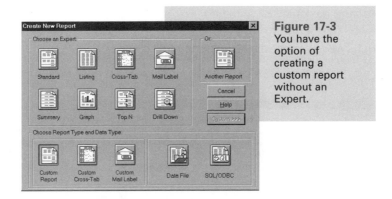

Figure 17-3
You have the option of creating a custom report without an Expert.

Creating a Basic Phone List

To begin your exploration of Crystal Reports, select Listing from the Expert choices. This opens the Create Report Expert dialog box to allow you to select a table (see Figure 17-4). The second tab is unavailable until a selection is made.

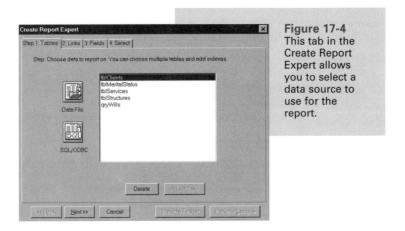

Figure 17-4
This tab in the Create Report Expert allows you to select a data source to use for the report.

You can select the Data File button to browse for the database file, or select the SQL/ODBC button to select a registered ODBC source. When you've selected the file, the tables are displayed and the Expert moves to the second tab. This tab displays the links in your database (see Figure 17-5).

Here you can view any existing links or create a new link if you are working with a database that puts each table in a separate file. After the relationships are established or changed, you can select the third tab to determine which fields to include (see Figure 17-6).

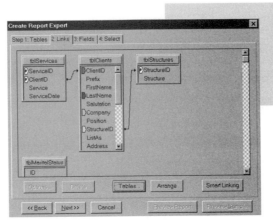

Figure 17-5
This tab allows you to view what relationships exist between the tables.

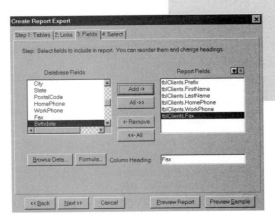

Figure 17-6
This tab allows you to select the fields and modify the order for the report.

The Fields tab allows you to select fields from a list to indicate which ones should be used to create the report. You can select directly from the list, click the Browse Data button to assist you with selecting the correct fields, or click the Formula button to create a custom formula.

The Formula button may prove to be more useful than the Browse Data button. For instance, assume that you're creating a telephone list. Do you want to list the first name and last name as separate fields or would it be better to display them as one? To create a formula named Fullname to concatenate the LastName and FirstName fields, follow these steps:

1. Click the Formula button to open the New Formula dialog box.

2. Enter a name for your formula and select OK.

    This opens the Edit Formula dialog box (see Figure 17-7).

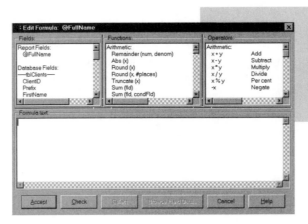

Figure 17-7
The Edit Formula dialog box allows you to create a custom field for your report.

3. Double-click the LastName field to place it in the Formula Text field.

4. Type a space, type + ", " +, and type another space.

5. Double-click the FirstName field to place it in the Formula Text field.

   The complete text should be the following:

   ```
   {LastName} + ", " + {FirstName}
   ```

6. Select Check to validate the resulting formula.

7. Select Accept when the formula is complete.

Once the formula is built, you can use it like any other field. For the phone list report, add the Fullname formula to the Report Fields list, along with the following fields: HomePhone, WorkPhone, and Fax. Select Preview Report. The application opens the report window with the Preview tab showing (see Figure 17-8).

The report has the fields arranged as columns and also places a date stamp at the top of the page to indicate when the report is printed. There's a page number at the bottom of the report. At this point, you might want to clean up a few problems. If you look at the column headings, you can see that they are just the field names with no spaces between the words.

Although the report is functional and is displaying the desired information, you should clean it up and then dress it up a little with some of the Crystal Reports tools. The following sections explain how to do this.

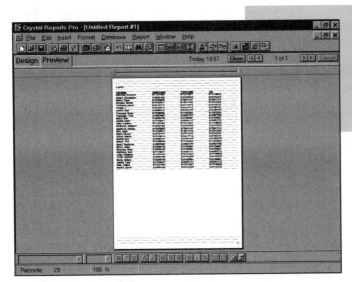

Figure 17-8
The Report Preview tab allows you to see what the report will look like when printed.

Making Modifications to the Report

To make any changes, the first step is to select the Design tab (see Figure 17-9). This allows you to view the field layout as well as any formatting objects like column headings.

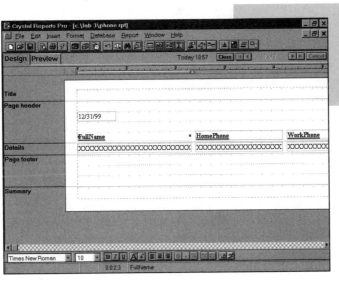

Figure 17-9
The Report Design tab allows you to make changes to your report.

To make a change to a label, simply right-click the label and select Edit Text Field from the pop-up menu. This opens the Edit Text Field dialog box (see Figure 17-10), where you can make your text changes and then select Accept.

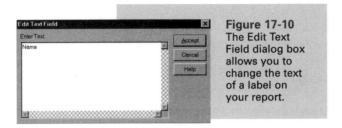

Figure 17-10
The Edit Text Field dialog box allows you to change the text of a label on your report.

You might also want to move a label or a column in one direction or another. For instance, the date is a very useful field, but you might want to have it at the right margin rather than directly above the left column. To move an object in Crystal Reports, you can drag and drop it from one location to another. Alternatively, you can select it and use the arrow keys to move it to a new location.

Changing the location of the label isn't the only change you can make. You also can change its attributes. With the control selected, you can use the Format menu or the buttons on the Formatting toolbar.

You might want to change the font and point size. You also might want to make it bold, italic, underline, or change its alignment. You can select any of these options by clicking the desired button on the toolbar.

If you're printing to a color printer, you might want to select Format, Borders and Colors and select a color or border style. You might want to experiment with these options to get the desired effect.

When you're looking at the report in design mode, notice that the report is organized into sections. The Title section is for information to be displayed on the first page only. The Page Header and Footer sections are for information that will be repeated on all pages. The Details section is for the fields, and the Summary section is for information that needs to appear at the end of the report.

You might want to include a title on the report. To do so, you need to add a new text field. The standard toolbar offers a choice of actions as well as a choice of objects to place on your report. One of these is a text field. To add a title to your report, complete these steps:

1. Select the Text tool to open the Edit Text Field dialog box.

2. Enter your text and select <u>A</u>ccept. This gives you a mouse pointer with a rectangle attached (the rectangle represents the new object).

3. Move the rectangle to the desired location and click. This releases the new object.

4. Using the Format toolbar, make any formatting changes you want, like using a larger point size or making the text bold.

If you prefer working with menus, you can insert a text field from the <u>I</u>nsert menu and make formatting choices from the F<u>o</u>rmat menu. To check your changes at any time, you can select the Preview tab.

 It is best not to have any object selected when you move to the Preview tab.

Once all the necessary changes are made to the report, you want to save it to your local or network drive. You can select the Save icon and enter a file name and path, but first you want to make sure that the Crystal Reports options are set correctly for your situation.

To view the Crystal Reports options, select <u>F</u>ile, <u>O</u>ptions. The Options dialog box that is displayed allows you to set up how you'll work with Crystal Reports. When saving reports, the most important option is on the Reporting tab. The second set of choices determines how the data and report are connected. If you want to create a dynamic link between your data and the report (and expect it to be updated every time the report is accessed), you might need to change these options.

The Refresh data on every print option needs to be selected so that the application retrieves the data each time it prints a report. The Save data with closed report option can be deselected to save space on your hard drive. This reduces the field size, especially with large data sets.

Once these options are selected, save this report as **Phone.rpt** in your c:\Lab 3\ directory. These steps create a simple list for your data, but the following sections explain how you can create different styles of reports.

Creating a Services Report

One of the other styles of report is a *Drill Down report*. This style of report allows you to create a report grouping records based on a field in your recordset. It also has an Expert to guide you through the process. For example, assume that you want to get a list of clients and the services they've had performed for them. To create an appropriate Drill Down report, use the following steps:

1. Select File, New.
2. Click the Drill Down button.
3. Select the client management database as the data file in Step 1 - Tables.
4. Delete the link from `tblServices` to `tblClients` and replace it with a link from `tblClients` to `tblServices` in Step 2 - Links.
5. Create a formula named Client identical to the Fullname formula used in the previous report, and add it. Also add LastName from `tblClients`, Service from `tblServices`, and ServiceDate from `tblServices` as report fields in Step 3 - Fields.
6. Indicate that you want to group by `tblClients.Lastname` in Step 4 - Sort.

   Step 5 of the Drill Down report (see Figure 17-11) lets you request a total for a group of records. In this report, there isn't any field for which a total would be of value, but totaling isn't the only type of calculation available in this step. It might be a nice idea to count how many services have been performed for each client.

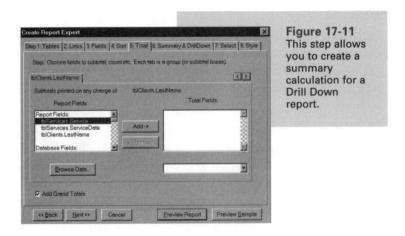

Figure 17-11
This step allows you to create a summary calculation for a Drill Down report.

7. Select `tblServices.Service` from the field list and select count from the drop-down list of calculations.
8. Make sure that the Add Grand Totals check box is not selected.

   Step 6 - Summary & Drill Down (see Figure 17-12) allows you to indicate which sections will be displayed in the report.

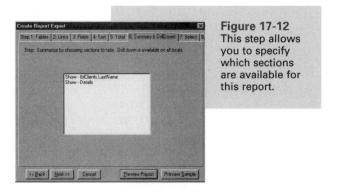

Figure 17-12
This step allows you to specify which sections are available for this report.

9. Make sure that both `tblClients.LastName` and `Details` have show to their left in the list. If not, click whichever one needs to change.

Step 7 - Select (see Figure 17-13) gives you an opportunity to select a field to create criteria to narrow the list of clients or services to work with for this report.

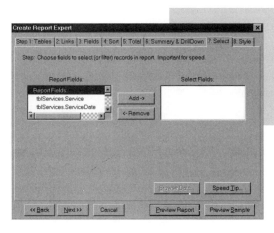

Figure 17-13
This step allows you to select a field and criteria to narrow the scope of your report.

10. Make sure that no fields are listed in the Select Fields list of Step 7 - Select.

The last tab for the Drill Down report (see Figure 17-14) allows you to select a style for your report. It gives you an opportunity to select a style and see a small sketch of what the report will look like. It also gives you an opportunity to add a title for the report.

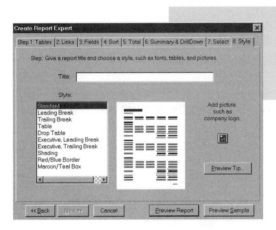

Figure 17-14
This step allows you to select a layout style for the report.

11. Enter **Client Services** as the Title.

12. Select Leading Break as the style.

13. Select <u>P</u>review Report.

When you preview this report, it will have some problems that detract from its effectiveness. The first item you'll notice is the duplication of the report name (see Figure 17-15). This is because the LastName field is in the wrong section. You need to make some changes.

To do so, you need to select the Design tab. When you move to the Design tab, the first thing you should notice is that the last name is repeated in the header and footer for the group, as well as in the detail section. You could just delete the extra occurrences by selecting them and pressing the Delete key, but in this case you don't need LastName at all. You can delete all the LastName information here.

Once that is removed, you want to move the client name over to the left margin of the report. You also want to move the FullName field up to the LastName Header section. If desired, you could save space by moving the label and line up, and then reducing the size of the section by dragging the dividing line up. This process is similar to what you do in Excel to resize rows or columns.

Figure 17-15
Here you can see the results of the Expert with the problems.

Now that Client is moved, you can move the remaining fields over. This gives you more room for the ServiceDate field which is currently being truncated at the right side of the page. To move all the fields at once, click the first one and Shift-click the remaining ones. You cannot use the selection tool in this case because some lines that are in-place are being used as formatting.

After this change, select the Service Date label and resize it to fit the contents. This is accomplished as it would be with any VB control, by dragging the handle to a new size. You might want to shrink the Count field, and also might want to add a label to identify the count for a client using the text field object.

Save Here ⮕ Once the formatting for the report is complete, save it as **Services.rpt** in your `c:\Lab 3\` directory. You do not need to set the options before saving this time, because once you've set the reporting options, they're used for all the new reports you create.

In addition to formatting the report and its text, you also might want to add graphics to your report. To practice adding a picture, follow these steps:

1. Select Insert, Picture.
2. Select a graphic such as `C:\Program Files\DevStudio\Visual Basic\Graphics\Assorted\notebook.bmp` from the file list.
3. Reposition and size the graphic using the handles.

It will accept the BMP, GIF, PCX, TIF, and TGA graphic formats.

◄EXERCISE

> ▼ **Tip** If you aren't printing in color, you might want to get a test print to make sure that the graphic meets your needs.

Creating Mailing Labels

Another report that can be very valuable is the Mailing Label report. It can be tailored to support many types of labels. Again, an Expert prompts you to make the necessary decisions regarding the report. To create mailing labels, follow this procedure:

1. Select File, New.

2. Select the Mail Label button.

3. Select your data file in Step 1 - Tables.

4. Select Next to skip Step 2 - Links.

5. Create the following formula named Name and add it to the field list:

   ```
   {tblClients.Prefix} + " " + {tblClients.FirstName} + " " {tblClients.Last
   ➥Name}
   ```

6. Add Company and Address to the field list.

7. Create the following formula named CityStateZip and add it to the field list:

   ```
   {tblClients.City} + ", " + {tblClients.State} + " " {tblClients.Postal
   ➥Code}
   ```

8. Select the correct Avery label number or set the custom dimensions for your labels in Step 4 - Label (see Figure 17-16).

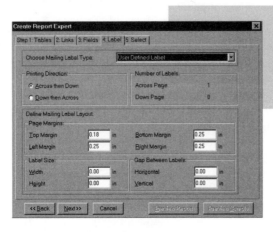

Figure 17-16
This step allows you to select a label from the list or specify custom settings.

9. Select Preview Report.

10. Save the report as **label.rpt** in your c:\Lab 3\ directory.

The hardest aspect of doing labels is the need to create the formulas to concatenate the fields for each line of the label. If you're used to Access, you've got a headstart — the wizard in Access is the same action, though it prompts for this concatenation a little differently.

Creating the Incorporated Report

Most of the Experts you've used so far have had a Select tab. This tab allows you to create the criteria for a report without using VB or a stored query. This gives you flexibility to change the criteria for a particular report.

To illustrate this process, you're going to create a listing of those clients who have incorporated businesses. This report will list the company and phone number for the business only. To create this report, use the following steps:

1. Select File, New.
2. Click the Listing button.
3. Select your data file in Step 1 - Tables.
4. Select Next to skip Step 2 - Links.
5. Select {tblClients.Company} and {tblClients.WorkPhone} as the fields in Step 3 - Fields.
6. Select Next to get to Step 4 - Select.
7. Select Incorporated as a Select field.
8. Select True from the drop-down list to indicate a value.
9. Select Preview Report.
10. Save the report as **Inc.rpt** in your c:\Lab 3\ directory.

The resulting report displays the records for clients who have incorporated a business. This has been done without creating a stored query in Access or creating a SQL statement in VB. At this point, you can do whatever formatting is desired.

Accessing the Report from the Client Management Application

Once the reports are built, you need to build an interface for VB to access them. One common approach is to build a separate form, providing a frame with option buttons to select a report and a frame with option buttons to indicate whether you want to print or preview the report. The user makes their choices and clicks the OK button to activate their choices. This form might resemble the Report form in this project (see Figure 17-17).

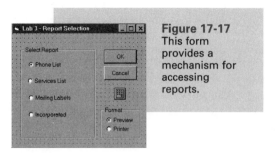

Figure 17-17
This form provides a mechanism for accessing reports.

To access the reports from your VB application, you need to add the Crystal Reports control to a VB form. This control isn't part of the standard toolbox, so it needs to be added to the toolbox before it can be added to the form.

When you add this control to your form, it doesn't matter where you place the control, because it's an invisible control like the common dialog control. You can place it in any out-of-the-way spot on your form.

Like the common dialog control, you do not write code for an event of this control. To access your reports, you need to set properties for the control and then issue the PrintReport method for the control.

The first property to set is *ReportFileName*. This property lets you set the path and file name for the report created in Crystal Reports' Report Designer. For frmReports, this needs to be done when the form is loaded and when the user clicks one of the option buttons to make a choice. In the Form_Load event procedure, this is a straight assignment using the first report in the list. In the optReport_Click event, this is assigned using a Select Case structure to allow the button selected to determine the report name. Here's the code:

```
Private Sub Form_Load()
    cryReport.ReportFileName = "c:\Lab 3\Phone.RPT"
    cryReport.Destination = Index
End Sub

Private Sub optReport_Click(Index As Integer)
    Select Case Index
```

```
        Case 0
            cryReport.ReportFileName = "c:\Lab 3\Phone.RPT"
        Case 1
            cryReport.ReportFileName = "c:\Lab 3\Services.RPT"
        Case 2
            cryReport.ReportFileName = "c:\Lab 3\Label.RPT"
        Case 3
            cryReport.ReportFileName = "c:\Lab 3\Inc.RPT"
    End Select
End Sub
```

The second property to set is *Destination*. It can be assigned to print to the printer, a window, a print file, or a text file. For this project, the destination defaults to the window in the Form_Load event and is a selection between window and printer in the optFormat_Click event. Here's the necessary code:

```
Private Sub Form_Load()
    cryReport.ReportFileName = "c:\Lab 3\Phone.RPT"
    cryReport.Destination = Index
End Sub

Private Sub optFormat_Click(Index As Integer)
    cryReport.Destination = Index
End Sub
```

> **If you're going to support a system that allows printing to a file, you need to provide a way for the user to indicate a file name and assign it to the *DataFiles* property.**

Once these properties are set, you can use the PrintReport method to display or print the report. For frmReports, this is done with the cmdOK button. When you invoke the PrintReport method, it needs to be set up in an expression because the control indicates whether it successfully displayed or printed a report by sending a code.

To handle a failure situation, you need to include some error-handling code. In this case, you can use an If structure after invoking the method to test the variable. If it isn't 0, then display the error and message returned by the control. Here's the code:

```
Private Sub cmdOK_Click()
    Dim iPrint As Integer
    iPrint = cryReport.PrintReport
    If iPrint <> 0 Then
```

```
        MsgBox cryReport.Last & " " & cryReport.LastErrorString,
➥vbExclamation, "Report Error"
        End If
End Sub
```

Tip

Your error-handling code could be more specific. You could trap the errors and create your own error handler, to pinpoint a missing file or a printer that's offline. To view the possible errors, open the help file for Crystal Reports and look at a list of the possible return codes.

The final bit of code is for the `cmdCancel_Click` procedure. It just unloads the report selection form to return to the switchboard form:

```
Private Sub cmdCancel_Click()
    Unload Me
End Sub
```

The last report created was one with criteria selected through the Expert. You can change the criteria of a report as needed through VB if desired. You can set the *SelectionFormula* property to change the criteria or the *GroupSelectionFormula* property to change the grouping arrangement for a report. Here you construct a text string like you do when building a SQL statement for use with DAO. You have to remember to surround fields with curly brackets ({ }) rather than square brackets ([ ]).

You also can adjust report sorting if needed. You can set the *SortFields* property with the field you want used to sort the report.

Adding Error Handling

As explained in the last section, the Crystal Reports control sends back a return code to indicate the success or failure of a print operation. You have to add some mechanism for dealing with any problem that's returned. Error handling is critical for the rest of the application as well.

You have to tackle error handling on several levels for a database application. The first concern is successfully accessing the database. You need to make sure that the connection to the database is successful.

The next area of concern is data entry. You need to make sure that information entered into a field is valid. Has the user entered a number if a number is needed, and does the value entered fall within an appropriate range?

You also need to protect the integrity of the data in the database. Make sure that the user cannot assign a value to a field depending on values from another table that doesn't exist. Likewise, don't allow the user to delete a record if there are other tables with records depending on it.

You also need special protection if your system allows more than one user to access the data simultaneously. You need to make sure that two people do not edit the same record at the same time, and that if a record is deleted by one user, it is not accidentally shown to another user.

Handling some of these errors requires including additional code in your application. The process for tackling errors is different depending on which approach you take for your database development.

Error Handling with the Data Control

The first and second forms developed for the client management application used the data control to establish data access. This control has many built-in data functions. It allows you to edit data into bound controls, add new records to the recordset, and navigate between records without outside intervention. It also has a built-in mechanism for dealing with errors. The Error event is designed to deal with any error that crops up.

The Error event has two arguments, DataErr and Response. DataErr is the number of the error generated. Response is what you want to do with the resulting error. If you don't do anything, the error is displayed to the user and the action that caused the problem is canceled. This leaves the user exactly where they were prior to the problematic action. For instance, if the user is trying to move to the next record, and an error occurs during the automatic update of some data they've changed on the current record, the error is displayed and they're left viewing the current record, where they can make further changes.

You can add your own error handling to the Error event and take a more active approach to error handling with data management. The remaining discussion focuses on solving particular error problems. The code has been added to the DAO.frm for the sample project, but it could easily be adapted to add to the Error event for the data control.

Caution

> The `Error` event will not protect against a failure to connect to the database, because that action takes place before the control is in operation. That problem needs to handled separately as explained in the following section.

Opening the Database

One of the first challenges when creating a database application is the access to the database. Whether you're using the data control or DAO to make the connection, it must be completed before anything else can take place.

The data control in `frmDataCtrl` and `frmDataWizard` establishes the connection without code. *DatabaseName* was set at design time, so if the database has moved or a needed network drive isn't currently available, the application crashes!

If the location of the database may change or it's on a network, you're better off establishing the connection with code. The DAO form has an Open menu item. In the `mnuOpen_Click` event, the object variables are set up and the *Enabled* properties are set correctly. Here's the code:

```
OpenErr:
    Dim strMsg As TextBox, strTitle As String
    strTitle = "Open Database Error"
    Select Case Err.Number
        Case 3044
            strMsg = "The path is not valid"
        Case 3024
            strMsg = "Could not locate database file."
        Case 3006
            strMsg = "Could not open the database because it is exclusively "
            strMsg = strMsg & "locked by another user."
        Case 3008
            strMsg = "Could not open the table because it is exclusively "
            strMsg = strMsg & "locked by another user."
        Case 3176
            strMsg = "Couldn't open the file."
        Case Else
            strMsg = "An unanticipated error has occurred. It is Error " & _
                Err.Number & ", " & Error.Description
    End Select
    MsgBox strMsg, vbExclamation, strTitle
    Unload Me
End Sub
```

The key to this procedure is that error handling is activated before the code attempts to connect with the database. If it fails, it jumps to the `OpenErr` line label. Here the `Select Case` structure builds a message for display with the message box function. It then displays the message and unloads the form.

There are error cases for an invalid path, a missing file, a locking problem, and a file access problem, as well as a generic error line. The error handler displays the appropriate message and then closes the form. This is the minimum that needs to be done to protect against a connection problem. For the path and missing file problems, you might want to use the common dialog control to allow the user to browse for the file on their system. For the file being locked, there isn't much you can do to prevent someone else from locking the entire database or table. You might want to make sure that your code doesn't lock the database or recordset exclusively when you call those methods.

You might want to generalize this error handler to include the possibility of losing your connection to the network during the operation of your application. The client management application wasn't developed with a network in mind, so the error handler doesn't cover that.

Once the database is open, you need to worry about protecting the data. You want to make sure that any data entered by the user is accurate for the field in which it's entered.

Validating User Entries

Validating user input entries can be very easy with a little attention to detail when the interface is created. The first step to creating an interface that protects the data as much as possible is to use the correct forms.

If you take a look at the design of the DAO form, you'll see that a label is used for the client ID. The client ID is a number assigned by Access that cannot be edited by your users. By displaying it as a label, you ensure that the user can view it but has no way of making changes to it.

If you allowed them to change the client ID, you would have to write code to protect against Error 3022. This error occurs when a user attempts to create a record with a duplicate field in the field that serves as the primary key or unique identifier for the record.

Another design tool that can protect against data errors is the use of the *MaxLength* property. The text box and masked edit controls have this property. If you set it to the same length as the field, your users cannot overrun the field.

On frmDataCtrl, the user is further protected from making mistakes. Since the StructureID and MaritalStatus fields rely on other tables for their lists, the combo boxes were set up as drop-down lists. The users can select valid values from the list, but cannot enter any values of their own.

The use of the masked edit control also provides some protection against invalid data. It restricts the number of characters that can be entered.

For example, if a user enters a value for the Birthdate field on the data control form that doesn't meet the specifications for a date, the form returns a Data conversion error.

If the same thing happens on the DAO form, you have to test the value manually before saving the data to the form. If you add a text box for the date to the DAO form, you need to modify the SaveData procedure to test the value before saving it to the field:

```
Private Sub SaveData()
    rsClients!ClientID = lblClientID.Caption
    rsClients!Prefix = txtPrefix.Text
    rsClients!Firstname = txtFirstname.Text
    rsClients!Lastname = txtLastname.Text
    rsClients!Company = txtCompany.Text
    rsClients!Position = txtPosition.Text
    If IsDate(txtBirthDate.Text) Then rsClients.Birthdate = txtBirthDate.Text
    rsClients!HomePhone = mseHomePhone.Text
    rsClients!WorkPhone = mseWorkPhone.Text
    rsClients!Fax = mseFax.Text
    rsClients.Update
    DBEngine.Idle dbFreeLocks
    rsClients.Bookmark = rsClients.LastModified
    PopulateData
End Sub
```

You also can check the contents of a text box. If you can guarantee, for example, that all clients live within the United States, you can test using a Select Case statement to make sure that they've entered a valid two-character state abbreviation.

EXERCISE

If you're using a native Jet database, the fields have two built-in properties to assist with validation. You can set *ValidationRule* as an expression to be tested and *ValidationText* to indicate the message that should be displayed when a value is incorrect. This cuts down on the testing of data you must do in code.

Protecting the Access to the Database

When you're developing a system that may be used by more than one person, you need to take some extra care to prevent problems. The first issue that needs to be addressed is what type of record locking will be used.

DAO supports two types of record locking. The first type is *pessimistic locking*. If two users are viewing the same record, they can both make changes. When one of the users attempts to update the record with the Update method, this locks the record. Once the update is completed, the record is released. The basic concept of pessimistic locking is that the users are both making changes to the record without any knowledge of the other.

The second type is *optimistic locking*. This method locks the record as the Edit method is invoked. This indicates to the second user that the first one is making changes. This is a more-informed approach. The second user won't waste time entering data only to end up unable to update the record.

To set the locking for your recordset, you can use the *LockEdits* property. In the mnuOpen_Click event, *LockEdits* is set to True as soon as the recordset is opened. A False value indicates pessimistic locking.

This also changes the EditData function that is called from each field's Change event. The EditData function is designed to get the user into edit mode if needed. It also has error handling to tackle locking conflicts, as shown in the following code:

```
Private Function EditData()
    On Error GoTo EditErr
    If rsClients.EditMode <> dbEditAdd or _
            rsClients.EditMode <> dbEditInProgress Then
        rsClients.Edit
    End If
    Exit Sub
```

```
EditErr:
    Select Case Err.Number
        Case 3260
            MsgBox "Record is currently locked by another user, please try
➥again later.", vbInformation, "Locked"
            PopulateData
        Case 3197
            MsgBox "Data has been changed by another user, the changes will be
➥refreshed.", vbInformation, "Changed Data"
            rsClients.Bookmark = rsClients.Bookmark
            PopulateData
        Case Else
            MsgBox "An unanticipated error has occurred. It is Error " &
➥Err.Number & ", " & Error.Description,
➥vbInformation, "Unanticipated error"
    End Select
End Function
```

The first line enables error handling. The second line finds out what action is in progress. As discussed earlier, you can use AddNew or Edit but you do not need both. Here the *EditMode* property is checked to see if AddNew or Edit has already been invoked; if not, this procedure invokes edit mode. With *LockEdits* set to True, this is where an error can occur with more than one user.

If another user has this record locked or the data has been changed, it jumps to the error-handling routine. Here a Select Case structure tests for Error 3260 to see if the record has been locked and Error 3197 to see if the data has been changed.

For Error 3260, a message is given to the user to indicate that the record is locked, and the data is repopulated with PopulateData.

For Error 3197, the message is different, but the process is the same to recover from the editing changes. It rolls back the changes by resetting the *Bookmark* property to refresh the record from the database, and repopulates the data with PopulateData.

Another issue when supporting multiple users is what happens when one user deletes a record from a recordset. If you're using the dynaset type, then as each person creates the recordset for their instance of the application, it creates a list of records that are a part of the set. If one user deletes a record, it still shows up in the recordset of other users who have created recordsets prior to the delete operation. This requires error handling like the following in the navigation code:

The way Error 3197 is handled here might be more brutal than you desire. You're rejecting any changes made by this user in favor of the changes made by the other user. You might instead want to give this user a chance to preview both sets of changes to the fields and then offer the option of using the other user's changes or their own. This requires some swapping of information, and might or might not be a worthwhile process in your applications. In most cases, it's more protection than you really need, because the Change event for the control is kicked off the first time the user types a character. If a record has been changed by someone else, the loss of one character by the current user is probably insignificant.

```
Private Sub mnuMove_Click(Index As Integer)
    On Error GoTo MoveError
    If rsClients.EditMode = dbEditInProgress Or rsClients.EditMode = dbEditAdd
➥Then
        SaveData
    End If
    Select Case Index
        Case 0   'First
            rsClients.MoveFirst
            mnuMove(0).Enabled = False
            mnuMove(1).Enabled = True
            mnuMove(2).Enabled = False
            mnuMove(3).Enabled = False
        Case 1   'Next
            rsClients.MoveNext
            If datclients.Recordset.EOF Then
                datclients.Recordset.MoveLast
                mnuMove(0).Enabled = True
                mnuMove(1).Enabled = False
                mnuMove(2).Enabled = True
                mnuMove(3).Enabled = False
            Else
                mnuMove(0).Enabled = True
                mnuMove(1).Enabled = True
                mnuMove(2).Enabled = True
                mnuMove(3).Enabled = True
            End If
        Case 2   'Previous
```

```
                    rsClients.MovePrevious
                    If datclients.Recordset.BOF Then
                        datclients.Recordset.MoveFirst
                        mnuMove(0).Enabled = False
                        mnuMove(1).Enabled = True
                        mnuMove(2).Enabled = False
                        mnuMove(3).Enabled = True
                    Else
                        mnuMove(0).Enabled = True
                        mnuMove(1).Enabled = True
                        mnuMove(2).Enabled = True
                        mnuMove(3).Enabled = True
                    End If
                Case 3  'Last
                    rsClients.MoveLast
                    mnuMove(0).Enabled = True
                    mnuMove(1).Enabled = False
                    mnuMove(2).Enabled = True
                    mnuMove(3).Enabled = False
            End Select
            PopulateData
            Exit Sub
    MoveError:
        Select Case Err.Number
            Case 3167
                rsClients.Delete
                Resume
            Case Else
                MsgBox "An unanticipated error has occurred. It is Error " & _
                Err.Number & ", " & Error.Description, _
                vbInformation, "Unanticipated error"
        End Select
    End Sub
```

Dealing with record locks and deleted records aren't the last of the error handling requirements for most database applications. You also need to protect against data errors as explained in the next section.

Protecting Against Data Errors

As your users manipulate the data, they may try to take an action without completing the last action. They may also try to take an action that cannot occur. These situations require error handling.

The first problem is if a user attempts to start a new action without completing an action that's already in progress. For instance, the user might decide to add a new record when he has made changes to the current record that haven't yet been saved.

As changes are made to a record, the *EditMode* property for the recordset changes. It can detect if an add or edit operation is in progress. For mnuAdd and mnuMove, a simple If structure tests the value of *EditMode* and saves the changes if necessary. For mnuDelete, which doesn't call on the SaveData procedure, you use the CancelUpdate method to cancel the update in progress.

Another problem is if a user tries to delete records that have dependent records in other tables. In tblServices, you must specify a client ID for each service. If you attempt to delete a client that has services outstanding, you get Error 3200. This requires some error handling, as shown in the following code:

```
Private Sub mnuDelete_Click()
    On Error GoTo DeleteErr
    If rsClients.EditMode <> dbEditNone Then rsClients.CancelUpdate
    rsClients.Delete
    If rsClients.RecordCount < 1 Then
        ClearData
        Exit Sub
    End If
    mnuMove_Click (1)
DeleteErr:
    If Err.Number = 3200 Then
        MsgBox "Cannot delete a client that has existing Services.",
➥vbInformation, "Delete"
    Else
        MsgBox "Unanticipated Error " & Err.Number & ": " & Err.Description,
➥vbInformation, "Unexpected Error"
    End If
End Sub
```

Here the error handler displays a message box indicating that the record cannot be deleted. No further action is taken because the record is still current and displayed. Notice the test after the Delete method to protect against trying to work with an empty database. It checks the *RecordCount* property to make sure that there are records remaining in the database before invoking the move procedure.

If you hadn't used the combo boxes in frmDataCtrl, you would have to add code to the Error event for Error 3201. If you try to add a value that isn't part of a supporting table (as happens when you add a service for a non-existent client), it generates Error 3201.

With careful consideration of the issues that are likely to arise as users use your system, you can protect the users from many of the database problems that can occur.

Compiling Your Application

After you have completed all your programming, you want to ship your application to your users. In Project 1, you used the Make EXE command to create an executable. That executable relied on the VB runtime library to provide many necessary functions, which required you to ship at least one more file with your application.

You have another choice with the Professional and Enterprise Editions of Visual Basic 5. You can compile your application's code into the native code for C++. This might increase your application's performance.

Compiling versus Making

When you made an executable with the Make EXE command, it created an interpreted executable. The VB runtime library was required to translate the code in the executable into commands for the machine running the application.

When you compile (as opposed to making) an executable, you create a *native code executable* storing as much of your code as possible in the native C++. This does not require the VB runtime library to function, and it can increase the performance of your application because it cuts out the interpretation.

Note

Creating a native code executable will not always improve your application's performance. You need to evaluate the particular type of application you're working with.

If you have an application that has many calculations or string manipulations, the native code often gives you a performance gain. If you're using VBA or the Windows API, however, your performance savings might not be greater with the native code. If you're using many subroutines, you also might fail to see a performance gain with a native code executable.

Tip

When in doubt, make an executable and also compile a native code executable. Then do some speed tests to determine which is better for that particular application.

Compiling the Client Management Application

The process to create a native code executable is similar to the process of making an executable. You still need to open the Make EXE dialog box. Follow these steps to compile the client management application:

1. Select File, Make Lab3 EXE.
2. Indicate a file name and path for the executable.
3. Select Options.
4. Make any necessary changes to the Make tab.
5. Select the Compile tab (see Figure 17-18).

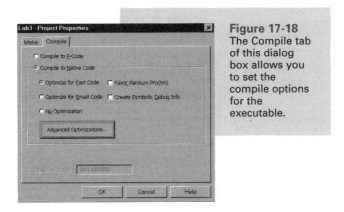

Figure 17-18
The Compile tab of this dialog box allows you to set the compile options for the executable.

6. Select Compile Native Code.
7. Set any desired compile options.
8. Select Advanced Optimizations.
9. Select any desired advanced optimization choices.
10. Select OK to accept the advanced settings.
11. Select OK to accept the compile options.
12. Select OK to begin compiling.

The two areas that need the most consideration are the compile options and the advanced optimization choices. When you choose to compile to native code, you can choose what you want to optimize for.

You can compile for a faster application, but this might increase the size of the file. If you compile for smaller code, this attempts to give you a smaller field size rather than speed. You can also choose no optimization.

If you want, you can favor the Pentium Pro. This does not prevent your executable from running on other systems, but it won't run as well on those systems. You can also create Symbolic Debug information—this allows you to work on the file with Visual C++.

The advanced optimization options allow you to turn off specific compile features that normally are included with a VB compile. These are selected by clicking the Advanced Optimizations button on the Compile tab to open the Advanced Optimizations dialog box (see Figure 17-19).

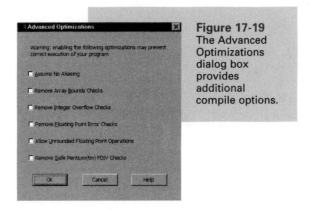

Figure 17-19
The Advanced Optimizations dialog box provides additional compile options.

The following list describes the available options:

- You can prevent the program from using aliases with Assume No Aliasing. This is beneficial if you're not using aliases to reference specific memory locations.

- You also can select Remove Array Bounds Checks. VB by default checks the index of an array against the bounds every time the array is accessed, to prevent your program from going out of bounds. If you have protected the user from going out of bounds with your code, you can shut off this option.

- Selecting Remove Integer Overflow Checks removes the validation of calculations to determine if they're within the bounds of the data type. This only applies to Byte, Integer, and Long.

- Selecting Remove <u>F</u>loating Point Error Checks accomplishes the same thing for Single and Double calculations. You can also select Allow Unrounding Floating Point Numbers. This might increase efficiency because your application can use the registers more effectively, but you might have some problems when comparing numbers.
- Selecting Remove <u>S</u>afe Pentium FDIV Checks turns off the test for the bug in some Pentium machines that causes certain calculations to be incorrect when completing floating point division.

All these choices can create a faster compile for your executable, but they introduce a higher risk of failure at runtime. You need to be very selective about which options you take advantage of when compiling your executable.

Summary

This chapter helped you to add some elements to the client management system to finish it. The first part of the chapter added reporting to the project, because most database applications need some form of printed output for users to share with people who don't have access to the system online. This was accomplished with the Crystal Reports application and the Crystal Reports tool.

The second part of the chapter focused on some specific error-handling needs of a database application. You have to protect against two things when adding error-handling code to a database application: invalid actions with the data and multiple users working with the same record.

The final part of the chapter explained how to compile your application. You can increase the performance of many VB applications by compiling them in native code format. You should determine on a project-by-project basis if this will be beneficial.

Project 3 Summary

This project gave you an opportunity to experiment with some of the data access features available in VB. You can take an assisted approach with the data control or can manage data entirely on your own with the Data Access Object model (DAO).

You created a database viewer and editor, and provided a way for your application's user to navigate through data records. You then added functionality for editing, adding, and deleting records. You learned how you can use DAO to provide a mechanism for viewing a subset of your data.

This project also showed you how to get printed output with Crystal Reports. You learned to create a formatted report and then call it from VB in a manner that's very similar to using the common dialog control to access the File Open and Save As dialog boxes.

You also saw how important error handling is in a database application. You learned how to protect your users from invalid entry, from data errors that might prevent deletion or addition of records, and from the danger of multiple users accessing the same database and table simultaneously.

Last but not least, you were introduced to some options that you can use to compile a faster or more compact executable. The opportunity to compile your applications is only available in the Professional and Enterprise Editions of VB.

CHAPTER 18

Connecting to the Internet

Visual Basic 5 provides a wide range of Internet controls and objects that you can incorporate into your projects. Many of these controls and objects are surprisingly easy to use. This chapter provides you with hands-on exercises to learn to use several of them.

Overview of VB's Internet Capabilities

The Internet is everywhere and Microsoft has responded to this fact by adding Internet development tools to Visual Basic 5. Using the tools provided with VB, you can easily add a Web browser to your application, launch Internet Explorer from a toolbar button, or design an ActiveX document to include on your Web page. The following list describes some of the Internet development features that VB provides:

- **ActiveX Documents**—By using ActiveX documents, you can create forms that appear within Internet browser windows. ActiveX documents support scrolling, menu negotiation, and hyperlinks.

- **ActiveX Control Creation**—Because VB has Internet features, ActiveX controls that you create using VB can also have Internet features, including hyperlinking, FTP support, and asynchronous data downloads.

- **Internet Transfer Control**—This control provides support for FTP and HTTP.

- **WinSock Control**—The WinSock control provides the capability for your applications to connect to a remote machine and exchange data with that computer using either UDP (User Datagram Program) or TCP (Transport Control Protocol).

- **Hyperlink Navigation**—The Hyperlink object is used in conjunction with a control to give that control access to ActiveX hyperlinking functionality.

- **WebBrowser**—The WebBrowser control is an ActiveX control that, when added to a form, makes that form act as a Web browser. This Web browser can be used to browse the Internet or an intranet.

- **InternetExplorer Object**—The InternetExplorer object allows your application to create an instance of Microsoft Internet Explorer (IE). Once the instance has been created, you can control it with the properties and methods of the InternetExplorer object.

Hyperlinking is the process of jumping to an URL or navigating through the history list. Hyperlink text is often included on Web pages; by clicking hyperlink text, the user is taken to another Web page.

An intranet is an internal network. An intranet's directory and file structure is typically navigated using a browser in much the same fashion as you navigate the Internet.

> **Tip**
>
> The Internet features listed here are only available in the Professional and Enterprise Editions of VB.

In this chapter you're going to work with three of these features: ActiveX documents, the WebBrowser control, and the InternetExplorer object.

Working with ActiveX Documents

How would you like to be able to design an object using VB that could be activated within Internet Explorer? Well, you can—it's known as an *ActiveX document*. ActiveX documents are ActiveX objects that can be placed and activated within ActiveX document containers such as IE. ActiveX documents are designed the same way as VB forms—you place controls on them.

Creating an ActiveX document is like working with any other project; it requires a series of steps:

1. Start a new project and select ActiveX Document EXE as the type of project.
2. Instead of getting Form1 to work with, you get UserDocument1. Add any necessary controls to UserDocument1.
3. Add any necessary code.
4. Add more ActiveX documents or forms if you want them.
5. Run and test your application.
6. Compile the document. The file created has a VBD extension.

> **You must have IE 3.0 or higher installed on your system to be able to complete this section. IE 3.0 ships with VB and is found in the Tools folder of your Visual Basic CD.**

Creating an ActiveX Document

Because the word "document" is in its name, you might think that creating an ActiveX document would be radically different from creating a standard EXE application. It's not... in fact, it's a very similar process.

To create an ActiveX document, use the following steps:

1. Start Visual Basic.
2. Select ActiveX Document EXE from the New Project dialog box and click OK.
3. Open the User Documents folder from the Project Explorer. Open UserDocument1.
4. UserDocument1 is displayed (see Figure 18-1). A user document looks like a form without a border or title bar.
5. Place a frame on the user document.
6. Create three option buttons within the frame.
7. Add a command button to the form just outside the lower-right corner of the frame.
8. Set the *Name* and *Caption* properties as listed for the controls in Table 18-1, and adjust the size and location of these controls so that the user document resembles the one shown in Figure 18-2.

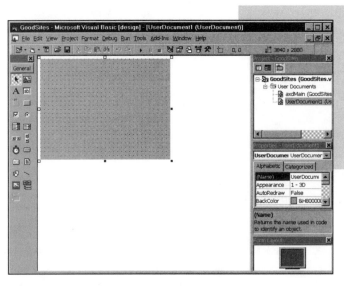

Figure 18-1
A user document must reside inside a container application such as IE, so a user document does not have a border or title bar.

Table 18-1   Property Settings for the User Document

Object	Name	Caption
Project1	GoodSites	
UserDocument1	axdMain	
Frame1	fraSites	Good Sites
Option1	optPrima	Prima Publishing's Home Page
Option2	optMSVB	Microsoft Visual Basic Site
Option3	optYahoo	Search the Internet with Yahoo
Command1	cmdTakeMeThere	Take Me There

9. Double-click optPrima to open the Code window.

10. Go to the General Declarations section; you need to create a variable here to hold the text representing an URL. Type the following line:

    ```
    Dim sURL As String
    ```

11. Select cmdTakeMeThere from the Object box to display the cmdTakeMeThere_Click procedure. Enter the following statement:

    ```
    Hyperlink.NavigateTo sURL
    ```

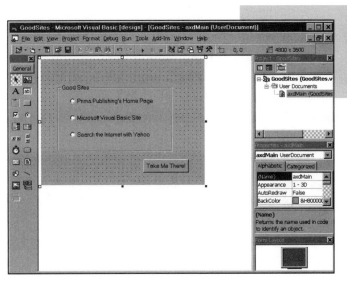

Figure 18-2
The completed user document looks similar to a form.

12. The Hyperlink object gives your user document access to ActiveX hyperlinking functionality. The NavigateTo method executes a hyperlink jump to a specified target, which in this case is a Web site. That's all the code you need to jump to an URL. The only thing left to do is to assign values to the sURL variable. Select optPrima from the Object box to display the optPrima_Click procedure. Type the following statement:

    ```
    sURL = http://www.primapublishing.com/series/series.html
    ```

13. Select optMSVB from the Object box to display the optMSVB_Click procedure. Type the following statement:

    ```
    sURL = http://www.microsoft.com/vbasic
    ```

14. Select optYahoo from the Object box to display the optYahoo_Click procedure. Type the following statement:

    ```
    sURL = http://www.yahoo.com/
    ```

15. Select File, Save Project. The Save File As dialog box is displayed. Enter **GoodSites** as the file name for the form, and press Enter.

16. Enter **GoodSites** for the project name as well, and press Enter.

17. Press F5 to run the application. Unlike running a Standard EXE project, no forms are displayed when you run an ActiveX document.

18. Minimize VB.

19. Start Internet Explorer. Enter a username and password if prompted.

20. In the Address box, type **c:\program files\devstudio\vb\axdMain.vbd** and press Enter.

Tip

If you did not save your project to the VB directory, substitute the correct path.

21. The ActiveX document loads (see Figure 18-3). Click the Take Me There button.

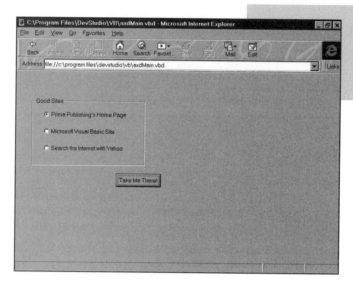

Figure 18-3
The ActiveX document is contained and displayed in IE.

22. The Prima Publishing page is displayed. To return to the ActiveX document, select `file://c:\program files\devstudio\vb\axdMain.vbd` from the Address drop-down list.

23. Select `Microsoft Visual Basic Site` and click the Take Me There button to go to the Microsoft Visual Basic page.

24. Select File, Close to exit IE.

25. Select Run, End from the VB menu.

Note

These steps take you through the process of creating an ActiveX document, but do not explain how to integrate the created document with your Web site. You need to do that using HTML.

This gives you an idea of how to use an ActiveX document. You can get more information on using ActiveX documents by referring to your HTML documentation or to a Web development environment such as FrontPage.

 Tip If you'd like more details about FrontPage, pick up a copy of *Create FrontPage Web Pages in a Weekend* (Prima Publishing, 1997).

Using the Application Wizard To Create an Internet-Enabled Application

The Application Wizard is a great tool designed to create a foundation from which you can build your project. You can create a project with either an SDI or MDI interface. By the time you finish using the Application Wizard, you have an application that contains a menu system, toolbar, and status bar. You only need to add controls and code.

Using the Application Wizard basically involves responding to several prompts. To create an Internet-enabled application using the Application Wizard, follow these steps:

1. Select File, New Project to display the New Project dialog box.
2. Select VB Application Wizard and click OK.
3. The first window that appears is the Introduction window (see Figure 18-4). Click Next.
4. The Interface Type window is displayed (see Figure 18-5). You can select from three types of interfaces. Select Single Document Interface (SDI) but do not click Next. Notice that the hint and the preview window change. Select Multiple Document Interface (MDI) and click Next.

EXERCISE

Note You've worked with MDI and SDI applications earlier in this book. The third type, Explorer Style, is similar to SDI. It has tree view and list view controls.

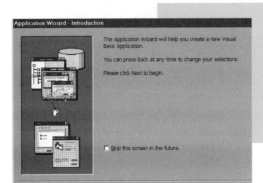

Figure 18-4
The Introduction window gives you some background information about the Application Wizard.

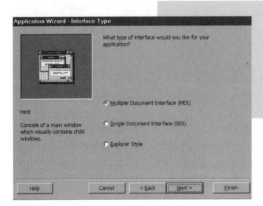

Figure 18-5
The Interface Type window prompts you to select the type of interface for the application.

*A resource file **is a file that contains bitmaps, text, and other data. This information can be used, for example, to customize an application for different languages without having to change any code. Resource files have an RES extension.***

5. The Menus window is displayed (see Figure 18-6). The Application Wizard creates the structure of the application's menu system for you (of course, you can pick the exact menus you want). In this case, you just want to accept the default menus, so click Next.

6. The Resources window (see Figure 18-7) wants to know if you want to use a resource file with this project. You do not, so click Next.

7. The next window is the Internet Connectivity window (see Figure 18-8). This window lets you indicate whether or not to provide a Web browser as part of the application. Select Yes and click Next.

8. The Standard Forms window (see Figure 18-9) allows you to select additional forms for the project.

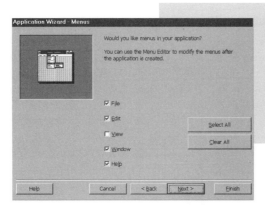

Figure 18-6
The Menus window allows you to select which of the standard menus you want to include in your application.

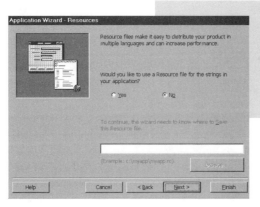

Figure 18-7
If you choose to use a resource file, you must also specify where you want to save it.

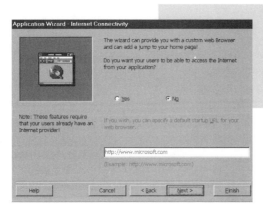

Figure 18-8
The Application Wizard uses **http://www.microsoft.com** (surprise!) as the default URL for the browser.

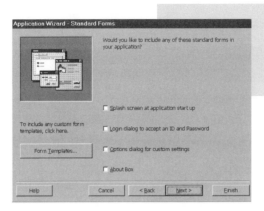

Figure 18-9
You can add standard or custom forms to your application.

9. The Data Access Forms window is displayed (see Figure 18-10). If you select the Yes ... option, child forms are created for your application based on the selected local database. You do not want to create forms from a database, so make sure that the No ... option is selected, and click Next.

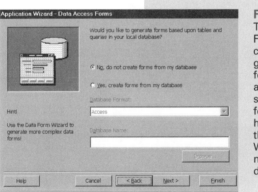

Figure 18-10
The Data Access Forms window can be used to generate simple forms based on a local data source. This form provides a hint about using the Data Form Wizard to create more complex data forms.

10. The final window is the Finished! window (see Figure 18-11). Type **BrowseMe** for the name of the project and click Finish.

11. Quite a bit of action takes place for the next few moments. When the Application Wizard is finished creating the application, the Application Created message box is displayed (see Figure 18-12). Click OK. Click Close when the Summary Report window is displayed.

Figure 18-11
The last thing you need to do is name the project.

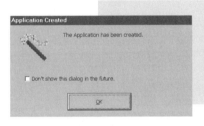

Figure 18-12
This message box is displayed when the application is complete.

Examine the Project Explorer. Your new project has three forms and one module.

Follow these steps to explore what the Application Wizard has done for you:

1. Press F5 to run the application (see Figure 18-13).

2. The child form that's displayed is a text box. You can type in this box if you want to.

3. Navigate the menu system. You can see that a standard set of menus has been created. Some menus (such as <u>N</u>ew and <u>O</u>pen) are fully functional, while others (such as <u>S</u>ave) display message boxes.

4. Notice that there's a standard Office-style toolbar. Position your pointer over various buttons to view the ToolTips.

5. Select View, Web Browser to display the Web browser form, as shown in Figure 18-14. If you're prompted for a username and password, enter them.

6. Type an URL into the <u>A</u>ddress box (for example, **http://www.primapublishing.com/series/series.html**—yes, the author is shameless!) and press Enter to go to that site. The site is displayed in the browser's window.

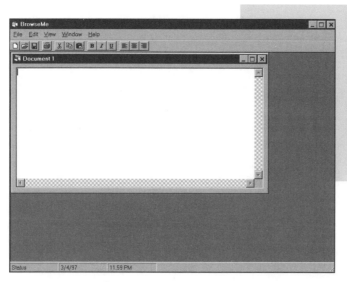

Figure 18-13
This is the application that was created using Application Wizard. No changes have been made to the objects created by the Wizard.

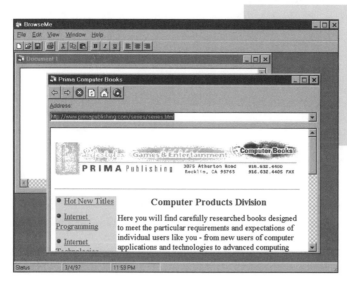

Figure 18-14
The Web browser form provides you with standard browser buttons such as Stop, Back, Forward, and Reload.

7. Select File, Exit to end the application.

8. Open frmBrowser from the Project Explorer.

9. Select the text box. Notice that it has been named for you.

10. Select the Address label. It also has been named. You'll find this is true of all the controls.

11. Open the Code window and examine the code that has been written by the Application Wizard.

12. To locate the code you need to add, select Edit, Find. The Find dialog box is displayed. Type **To Do** in the Find What text box.

13. Select Current Project and click Find Next to locate the first procedure that needs code. All procedures that need code contain To Do as a comment. Continue to click Find Next to locate all the relevant procedures.

14. Save the project if you want to.

Adding a Web Browser to Your Application

You may think that the Application Wizard did all the work to set up the Web browser in the last section. This is not true. The WebBrowser control did all the work. You can easily add a Web browser to any of your projects and not have to do one bit of programming!

To experiment with the WebBrowser control, complete these steps:

1. Select File, New Project to display the New Project dialog box.

2. Select Standard EXE for the project type and click OK.

3. Select Project, Add Form to display the Add Form dialog box.

4. Select BROWSER as the form type and click Open. The new form is added to the project (see Figure 18-15).

5. Double-click the form to open the Code window. This is the same code you saw earlier when you used the Application Wizard.

6. Select Project, Add MDI Form to add an MDI parent form. Browser forms are MDI child forms and require a parent.

7. Double-click the form to open the Code window and display the MDIForm1_Load procedure.

8. Enter the following statement:

```
frmBrowser.Show
```

9. Right-click Form1 in the Project Explorer. Select Remove Form1.

10. Select Project, Project1 Properties to display the Project Properties dialog box.

11. Select MDIForm1 from the Startup Object drop-down list and click OK.

12. Press F5 to run the application. The browser is displayed.

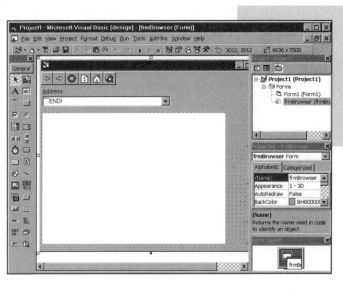

Figure 18-15
The newly added browser form is identical to the one in the project created with the Application Wizard.

13. Enter an URL in the <u>A</u>ddress text box.

14. Click the Close button on MDIForm1 to end the application.

That's all there is to it! If you want additional documentation about the WebBrowser control, its help file is located on the Visual Basic CD in the \Tools\Unsupprt\Webbrwsr folder.

Accessing Internet Explorer from Your Application

You might want to add the capability for the user to access IE from your application with a click of a button. This is almost as easy as adding a Web browser to your application. You simply use the InternetExplorer object.

To access IE from your project, complete these steps:

1. Select <u>F</u>ile, <u>N</u>ew Project to display the New Project dialog box.

2. Select Standard EXE and click OK.

3. Right-click the toolbox and select <u>C</u>omponents. The Components dialog box is displayed.

4. Select Microsoft Internet Controls and click OK.

5. Add a command button to the form.

6. Double-click the command button to open the Code window.

7. Enter the following statements:

```
Dim oIE As InternetExplorer
Set oIE = New InternetExplorer
oIE.Visible = True
```

Tip

To see IE, you must make the object visible; the last code statement does this.

8. Press F5 to run the application.

9. Click the command button. IE is displayed.

10. Enter an URL. After it is accessed, select File, Close to exit IE.

11. End the application by clicking its Close button.

As you can see, it took only three lines of code to create an instance of IE. If you want additional documentation about the InternetExplorer object, its help file is located on the Visual Basic CD in the \Tools\Unsupprt\Webbrwsr folder.

Summary

In this chapter, you got to experiment with several of the Internet controls and objects provided by VB. You created an ActiveX document and used IE as your container application. You got further exposure to ActiveX objects and controls by working with the Application Wizard. The Wizard is a wonderful tool for generating the basic forms, menu system, and toolbar needed by your application. You also got to work with the WebBrowser control, and learned how easy it is to add a Web browser to your application. You also easily accessed IE from a VB project. This chapter provided the fundamental knowledge you need to add Internet access to any of your VB projects.

CHAPTER 19

Creating a Help System

You'll find that a system without good documentation is basically useless, and that few of its features are used. You probably know what it's like to use an application with a bad help system. You press F1 looking for guidance on what you're currently doing, but the screen that's displayed tells you little-to-nothing of any relevance. Your experience with an application's help system often colors your opinion of the application as a whole.

Designing a Help System

The hallmark of a great help system is planning. With a little effort in the planning stage, you can provide your user with a system that provides documentation, guidance, and clarification on all of your application's functions and features. The help system can be as important as the application itself.

After designing, writing, and testing your application, your first thought upon completion is probably not "Goody, I get to do the help system now!" In fact, it's probably safe to say that most programmers consider creating a help system to be about as much fun as having a root canal. But this needn't be true. Think of the help system as an area where you can freely brag about your application. You're designing something to provide users with information about everything your application can do. Although your coworkers, boss, and significant other are tired of hearing you extol the virtues of your application, you suddenly have a chance to tell an entire new audience everything about the system. Not only that, the members of this new audience (the application's users) are particularly begging you to tell you them about your program by pressing the F1 key or selecting the Help menu!

The first step to designing a help system is to define your audience. Your audience determines the style of your help system. If you feel you have a relatively sophisticated audience, you can design your system to be procedural with little (or no) discussion of terms and concepts. If you decide that your audience needs something more friendly, you can take a more tutorial approach to the help system. Or you can include some aspects of each approach. Just be sure you've considered what's best for your particular audience.

After determining the audience, you need to develop a list of the topics for your help system. This should be a hierarchical listing starting with general topics and building to more detailed topics. For example, your application saves files but also provides save options such as password-protecting the file and allowing the user to select from a variety of file formats. In this case, the topic "Saving a File" should appear toward the top of your list of help topics, and below that in the hierarchy might be "File Save Options," "Saving your File with a Password," and "Supported File Formats."

A good starting point for any help system is a map of the menu system and a listing of each control on each form in the application. You try to fit this information into an outline format to create your hierarchy.

Once you have your hierarchy identified, you're ready to write the text for each topic. Type this text directly into a word processor. The word processor you select needs to be able to save files to Rich Text Format (RTF). This means that you can use just about any high-end word processor, including Word, WordPerfect, and Ami Pro. The RTF file you create is compiled into a help file with an HLP extension.

To make a file usable as a help file, you must include codes to identify items as help topics, keywords, definitions, and so on. These codes are formatted in the document as footnotes. You can do this with your word processor or use one of the many third-party tools that are designed to assist you with help file creation. Table 19-1 lists all the codes you need to know.

Table 19-1	Help Compiler Codes	
Code	**Name**	**Description**
#	Context string	The context string uniquely identifies a help topic.
$	Title	Titles appear in the list box that is used during Search mode. Titles are optional but highly recommended.
K	Keyword	Keywords are used in standard keyword searches. Keywords are optional but highly recommended. You can have more than one keyword per topic.
+	Browse sequence	The browse sequence is a number used to determine the user browse order if you've included browse buttons in your help system. The browse sequences is optional.
<u>Underline</u>	Definition	Definitions are areas for which a pop-up window appears when the user right-clicks.
~~Strikethrough~~	Jump text	Jump text is used to jump to another topic. (<u>Double underline</u> may be used instead of strikethrough.)

You are going to create a partial help file for the invoice system you created in Project 2. This help system will document the items on the File menu. To create it, follow these steps:

1. Start Word.

2. Select Insert, Footnote to display the Footnote and Endnote dialog box shown in Figure 19-1.

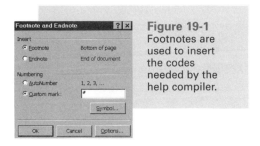

Figure 19-1
Footnotes are used to insert the codes needed by the help compiler.

3. Click the Custom Mark option button and type # in its text box. Click OK to insert the footnote mark.

4. Type **New_Menu**. This is the item's *context string*. All help items must have context strings.

5. Select Insert, Footnote to display the Footnote and Endnote dialog box. Click the Custom Mark option button and type **$** in its text box. Click OK to insert the footnote mark.

6. Type **New Menu**. This is the *title* for this topic.

7. Select Insert, Footnote to display the Footnote and Endnote dialog box. Click the Custom Mark option button and type **K** in its text box. Click OK to insert the footnote mark.

8. Type **New Menu;Entering New Billing Information;New Billing Information** (do not end this string with a period). These are the keywords for this topic.

9. Type the following help text for this topic:

   The New menu, located under File, when selected opens a new Billing Information form. You can open multiple Billing Information Forms if you wish.

10. Press Enter to start a new line.

11. Select Insert, Break and press Enter to insert a page break.

12. Using the procedures you used in Steps 2 through 8, create the following footnotes:

Custom Mark	Context String
#	Save_Menu
$	Save Menu
K	Save Menu;Saving Billing Information

13. Type the following help text for this topic:

   When you select the File, Save menu the current information on the Billing Information form is saved.

14. Press Enter to start a new line.

15. Select Insert, Break and press Enter to insert a page break.

16. Using the procedures you used in Steps 2 through 8, create the following footnotes:

Custom Mark	Context String
#	Print_Menu
$	Print Menu
K	Print Menu;Printing an Invoice

17. Type the following help text for this topic:

    The Print menu allows you to print an invoice based on the billing information in the active window.

18. Press Enter to start a new line.

19. Select Insert, Break and press Enter to insert a page break.

20. Using the procedures you used in Steps 2 through 8, create the following footnotes:

Custom Mark	Context String
#	Exit_Menu
$	Exit Menu
K	Exit Menu;Exiting the Application;Leaving the Invoice System

21. Type the following help text for this topic:

    This command closes the Invoice system.

22. Press Enter to start a new line.

23. Select File, Close. The Save dialog box is displayed.

24. Select the directory where you saved your invoice project files.

25. Enter **Invoice** for the file name.

26. Select Rich Text Format for the type.

27. Click Save to save and close the document.

As you can imagine, this process can become tedious when creating a large help file. Most programmers invest in a third-party help-generation tool such as Robo-HELP by Blue Sky Software or Doc-To-Help by WexTech.

Setting the *HelpContextID* Property

EXERCISE ▲

The *HelpContextID* property is used to set a context number for an object.

In your help file you have four help topics, so you'll have four *HelpContextID* values. To make the appropriate property settings, complete these steps:

1. Open frmMDIMain from the Project Explorer.

2. Select mnuFileNew from the Object box of the Properties window.

3. Set the *HelpContextID* property for mnuFileNew to **1**.

4. Select mnuFileSave from the Object box of the Properties window.

5. Set the *HelpContextID* property for `mnuFileSave` to **2**.
6. Select `mnuFilePrint` from the Object box of the Properties window.
7. Set the *HelpContextID* property for `mnuFilePrint` to **3**.
8. Select `mnuFileExit` from the Object box of the Properties window.
9. Set the *HelpContextID* property for `mnuFileExit` to **4**.

Installing Help Workshop

The context number is used in a file called the help project file to create a map linking particular objects to particular context strings in the file you just created.

After you create the RTF file that contains the help information, you need to compile it into an HLP file. This is done using a tool named Help Workshop. Help Workshop helps you create the *help project (HPJ) file* that the help compiler needs. The help project file has instructions for the help compiler regarding which options you want to use and how the help topics map to the *HelpContextID* property values.

Help Workshop is not installed as part of VB's standard installation, so you need to use the following steps to install Help Workshop on your system:

1. Open the `Tools` folder on your Visual Basic CD-ROM. Open the `Hcw` folder.

2. Start Setup. The Welcome window is displayed (see Figure 19-2).

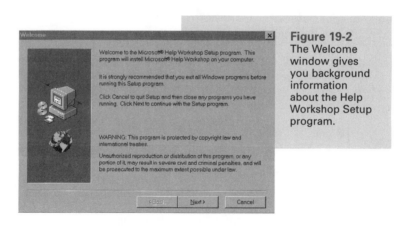

Figure 19-2
The Welcome window gives you background information about the Help Workshop Setup program.

3. Click <u>N</u>ext. The Choose Destination Location window is displayed as shown in Figure 19-3. Either accept the default destination or click B<u>r</u>owse and select a different location. Click <u>N</u>ext.

EXERCISE

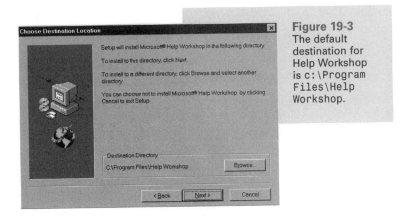

Figure 19-3
The default destination for Help Workshop is c:\Program Files\Help Workshop.

4. The Setup Type window (see Figure 19-4) is displayed. Click Next to perform a typical installation.

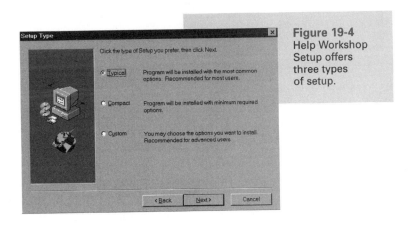

Figure 19-4
Help Workshop Setup offers three types of setup.

5. The program files are copied to your system. When the installation is complete, a message box is displayed. Click OK. Help Workbook has been installed.

Creating the Help Project File

Now that you've installed Help Workbook, you can use it to create the help project file.

To use Help Workbook to create the help project file, follow these steps:

1. Click the Start button from the Windows desktop.

2. Select Programs, Microsoft Help Workshop, Help Workshop to start Help Workshop (see Figure 19-5).

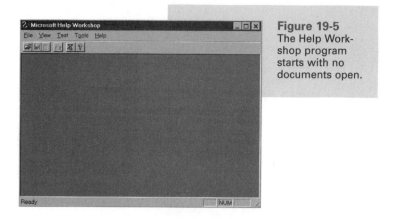

Figure 19-5
The Help Workshop program starts with no documents open.

3. Select File, New to display the New dialog box. Select Help Project and click OK.

4. The Project File Name dialog box is displayed. Type **Invoice** and click Save to display the basic project file contents shown in Figure 19-6.

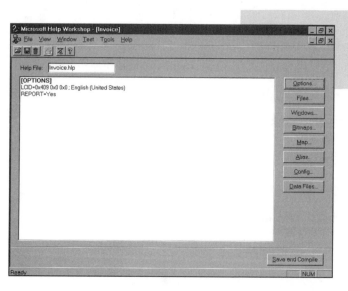

Figure 19-6
The basic project initially has only two settings.

5. Click the F<u>i</u>les button to display the Topic Files window (see Figure 19-7).

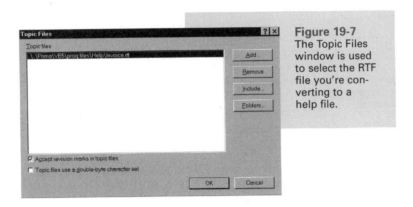

Figure 19-7
The Topic Files window is used to select the RTF file you're converting to a help file.

6. Click <u>A</u>dd to display the Open dialog box. Locate and select the `Invoice.rtf` file and click <u>O</u>pen.

7. Click OK to add the information to the project file.

8. Click <u>M</u>ap to display the Map dialog box as shown in Figure 19-8.

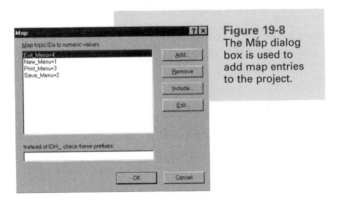

Figure 19-8
The Máp dialog box is used to add map entries to the project.

9. Click <u>A</u>dd to display the Add Map Entry dialog box (see Figure 19-9).

10. Enter **New_Menu** for the Topic ID and **1** for the Mapped Numeric Value. Click OK to add the entry.

11. Click <u>A</u>dd to display the Add Map Entry dialog box. Enter **Save_Menu** for the Topic ID and **2** for the Mapped Numeric Value. Click OK to add the entry.

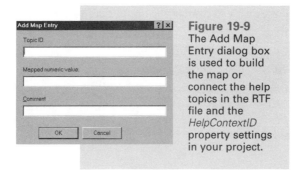

Figure 19-9
The Add Map Entry dialog box is used to build the map or connect the help topics in the RTF file and the *HelpContextID* property settings in your project.

12. Click Add to display the Add Map Entry dialog box. Enter **Print_Menu** for the Topic ID and **3** for the Mapped Numeric Value. Click OK to add the entry.

13. Click Add to display the Add Map Entry dialog box. Enter **Exit_Menu** for the Topic ID and **4** for the Mapped Numeric Value. Click OK to add the entry. The complete mapped entries are displayed in Figure 19-10.

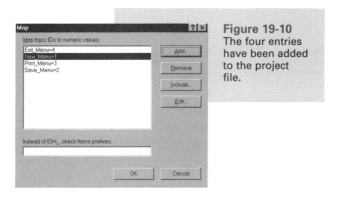

Figure 19-10
The four entries have been added to the project file.

14. You have entered the information that the help compiler needs (see Figure 19-11). Click Save and Compile to create the help file.

15. The Help Workshop disappears for a few moments and then returns with the results of the help file compile (see Figure 19-12).

16. Close Help Workshop.

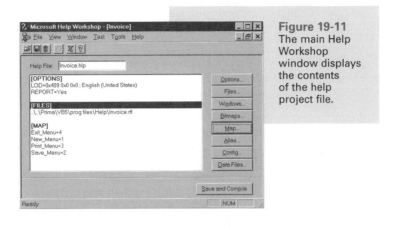

Figure 19-11
The main Help
Workshop
window displays
the contents
of the help
project file.

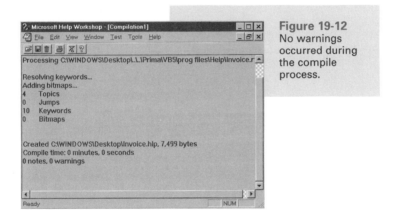

Figure 19-12
No warnings
occurred during
the compile
process.

The help file, which is named Invoice.hlp, is saved to the same directory where Invoice.rtf is located. Now there's only one more step to get context-sensitive help in the invoice system; the next section discusses this step.

Assigning the Help File to Your Project

Associating the help file with the project is done through a project's help file name property, which is accessed through the Project Properties dialog box.

To associate the invoice project with the `Invoice.hlp` file, complete these steps:

1. Return to your invoice project in VB.

2. Select <u>P</u>roject, `Invoice` Prop<u>e</u>rties to display the Project Properties dialog box (see Figure 19-13).

Figure 19-13
The General tab of the Project Properties dialog box is used to enter the help file for this project.

3. Click the selection button next to the <u>H</u>elp File Name text box. Locate and select your help file. Click <u>O</u>pen.

4. Click OK to save the changes.

You're now ready to test your help system. Notice that you have not had to write any VB code.

Testing Help

Testing help is the process of going to different objects and pressing F1 to verify that you're taken to the correct help topic. It's a good idea to thoroughly test your help system before releasing your product. You don't want to accidentally take application users to the wrong place when they press F1!

In this chapter's example help system you don't have much functionality to test, but you can get the general idea by completing these steps:

1. Press F5 to run the application.

2. Click the frame of the splash screen to display the input box.

3. Type your name and press Enter to display the application's main form.

4. Select the <u>F</u>ile menu. The <u>N</u>ew menu item is automatically highlighted. Press F1 to view help on this object (see Figure 19-14).

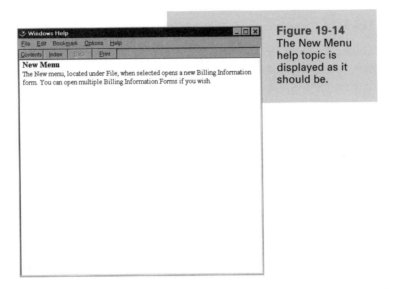

Figure 19-14
The New Menu
help topic is
displayed as it
should be.

5. Select Index to display the Index tab of the Help Topics dialog box
   (see Figure 19-15).

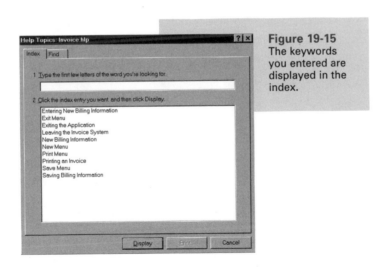

Figure 19-15
The keywords
you entered are
displayed in the
index.

6. Double-click Printing an Invoice. The Print Menu help topic is
   displayed.
7. Close Help.
8. Select File, Exit to end the application.

Summary

You have successfully completed your first help system. Though small, this help system illustrated some of the basics of help system design and creation. As you can see from this chapter, creating a help system is a team effort with several applications coming into play. Word is used to create the RTF file that eventually gets converted to an HLP file. Help Workshop helps you create the help project and compile the help file. Finally, you set control and project properties in VB.

An earlier chapter mentioned that the developer of an application is not the best person to test it; likewise, someone other than the developer should write the help system. Having someone else do this usually results in a help system that's more detailed and in-depth. As the developer, you've been working with the application for quite some time, and might mistakenly make assumptions about what your users know. Another person has less risk of making these assumptions.

CHAPTER 20

ActiveX Controls

ActiveX controls provide a way for you to extend the capabilities of the Visual Basic environment. ActiveX controls are broken into two categories. One category includes the desktop ActiveX controls, formerly called OLE controls. This type of ActiveX control provides standard user interface elements that allow you to create forms and dialog boxes. The other category includes Internet ActiveX controls that are optimized for Internet download.

In the past, if you wanted a specialized control such as a full-featured text editor, you typically purchased a third-party control. These controls were developed using a language other than VB (such as C++). With VB 5 this is no longer the case, because VB 5 allows you to create your own controls. Using skills you already have, you can create your own ActiveX controls without leaving the VB environment. You can create new controls from scratch or combine existing controls to create a new control. These controls have properties, events, and methods just like any other controls.

Once you create your ActiveX control, you compile it either directly into your application's executable or into an OCX file that can be used with development tools including VB, Microsoft Visual C++, and Borland Delphi. You also can use your compiled ActiveX control in end-user development environments such as Microsoft Office 97 that support the use of ActiveX controls.

Using the ActiveX Control Interface Wizard

Have you noticed that controls like the option button and check box come with their own labels? Have you ever wondered why other controls—such as the list box—do not come with labels? More often than not, you include a label whenever you add a list box to a form. Wouldn't it be nice if, whenever you drew a list box on a form, it included its own label? You're now going to create this type of control using the ActiveX Control Interface Wizard.

The ActiveX Control Interface Wizard helps you create the public interface for a VB-generated ActiveX control after you've created your user interface. The user interface is the control itself. The public interface consists of the properties, events, and methods that a programmer can use to manipulate the control. You can create the public interface without using the ActiveX Control Interface Wizard, but why would you want to abuse yourself that way? The ActiveX Control Interface Wizard makes the entire process extremely easy and lets you complete the needed work in a fraction of the time it would take you to code it yourself. In particular, the Wizard allows you to do the following:

- Add standard properties, events, and methods for your ActiveX control. These are the same ones—such as *Caption, Enabled,* Click, Changed, AddItem, and SetFocus—that you've already used with other controls.

The user interface of an ActiveX control is the control as it appears when a developer places the control on a form. It's the visual portion of the control.

- Add custom properties, events, and methods to the ActiveX control. This allows you to further tailor the control to suit your needs.

- Map the functionality of properties, events, and methods to individual controls that make up the new ActiveX control.

- Define attributes for the properties, events, and methods used by the ActiveX control.

Creating the User Interface

The first thing you have to do is create your ActiveX control's user interface. This has to be done before you can use the Wizard. In this exercise you're going to create a control that combines a label with a list box.

Use the following steps to create this control's user interface:

1. Select File, New Project to display the New Project dialog box.
2. Select ActiveX Control and click OK.
3. The new project is displayed with the user control active, as shown in Figure 20-1.

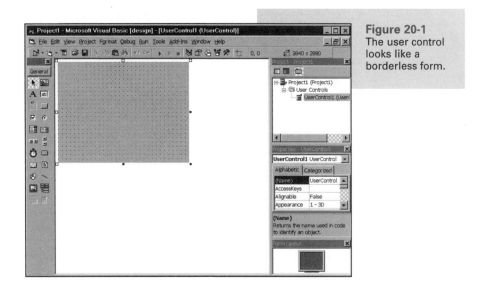

Figure 20-1
The user control looks like a borderless form.

4. Use the values in Table 20-1 to set the properties of the user control.

Table 20-1 Property Settings for `UserControl1`

Property	Value
Name	ListWithLabel
Height	2000
Width	1700

5. Place a label on the user control. Use the values in Table 20-2 to set the properties of this label.

Table 20-2 Property Settings for `lblCaption`

Property	Value
Name	lblCaption
Caption	Caption:
Height	252
Left	120
Top	120
Width	1452

6. Place a list box on the user control. Use the values in Table 20-3 to set the properties of this list box.

Table 20-3 Property Settings for lstListBox	
Property	**Value**
Name	lstListBox
Height	1200
Left	120
Top	480
Width	1452

The public interface consists of all the properties, events, and methods a programmer can use to manipulate the ActiveX control.

You've completed the necessary work on the new control's user interface. It now should look like Figure 20-2. You're ready to add the control's public interface as described in the following sections.

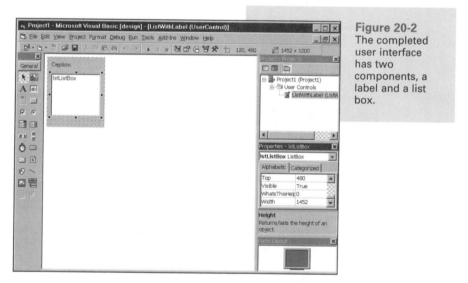

Figure 20-2
The completed user interface has two components, a label and a list box.

Adding the Application Control Interface Wizard to VB

The ActiveX Control Interface Wizard is an add-in that you need to include in the VB development environment.

EXERCISE

Include the Wizard as an add-in by completing these steps:

1. Select Add-Ins, Add-In Manager to display the Add-In Manager dialog box (see Figure 20-3).

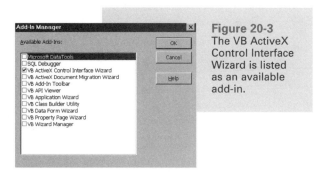

Figure 20-3
The VB ActiveX Control Interface Wizard is listed as an available add-in.

2. Select VB ActiveX Control Interface Wizard from the Available Add-Ins list box.

3. Click OK to add the Wizard to your VB development environment.

The ActiveX Control Interface Wizard is now available for your use via the Add-Ins menu.

Creating the ActiveX Control's Public Interface

To create the new ActiveX control's public interface, you're going to use the ActiveX Control Interface Wizard.

Use the following steps to build the public interface:

1. Select Add-Ins, ActiveX Control Interface Wizard to start the Wizard.

2. The Introduction window is displayed (see Figure 20-4). This window provides you with background information about the Wizard. Review the text and click Next.

3. The Select Interface Members window is displayed (see Figure 20-5). The Wizard has already selected some properties, events, and methods frequently used by controls—these are listed in the Selected Names list box. You need to add to these names. Because your control is a list box, you want to be able to use the AddItem method. Select AddItem from the Available Names list box and click the right arrow (>) button to add this method.

EXERCISE

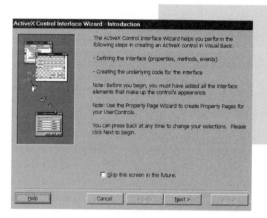

Figure 20-4
The Introduction window reminds you that you must have your user interface created before beginning this process.

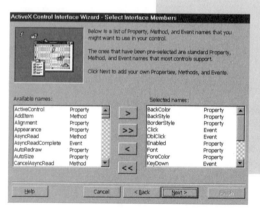

Figure 20-5
The Select Interface Members window allows you to select properties, methods, and event names that you want to use with your new control.

4. You also need the *Caption* property of the label. Select Caption from the Available Names list box and click the right arrow (>) button to add this property.

5. Click Next to display the Create Custom Interface Members window (see Figure 20-6). You would use this window if you wanted to add your own unique properties, events, and methods. This control doesn't require any, so click Next.

6. The Set Mapping window is displayed (see Figure 20-7). Select AddItem from the Public Name list box. Select lstListBox from the Control drop-down list box. This maps the AddItem method to the lstListBox component of the user control.

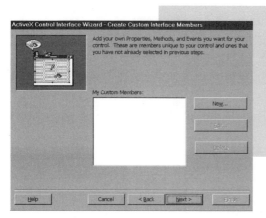

Figure 20-6
The Create Custom Interface Members window allows you to define new properties, methods, and events for your ActiveX control.

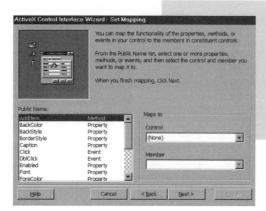

Figure 20-7
The Set Mapping window lets you connect each component of the user control to a specific property, event, or method.

7. Select Caption from the Public Name list box, and select lblCaption from the Control drop-down list box. Click Next.

8. The Set Attributes window is displayed (see Figure 20-8). Use this window if you want to set attributes for the unmapped properties, events, and methods of the user control. You won't do so for this user control, so click Next.

9. The Finished! window is displayed (see Figure 20-9). At this point, the Wizard has all the information it needs to build the user control's public interface. Click Finish.

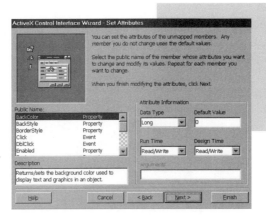

Figure 20-8
This window lets you set attributes for any unmapped properties, events, and methods.

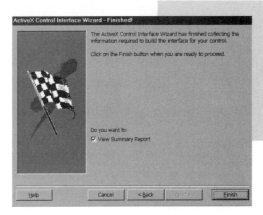

Figure 20-9
When you click the Finish button, the Wizard creates the public interface for your new ActiveX user control.

10. The ActiveX Control Interface Wizard Summary report is displayed (see Figure 20-10). Review this text and click Close.

Note

If you want to save the summary report to a file so that you can review it later, click Save.

11. Double-click the user control (the grid area) to view the generated code. Press Page Up and Page Down to move through the code.

12. Select File, Save Project to display the Save Project dialog box.

13. Click Save to save the user control file with the name `ListWithLabel.ctl`.

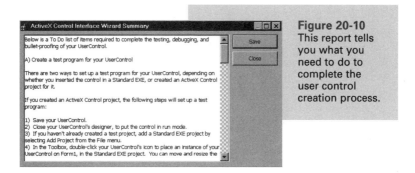

Figure 20-10
This report tells you what you need to do to complete the user control creation process.

14. The Save Project As dialog box is displayed. Type **AXDemo** in the File Name text box and press Enter.

Creating a Test Program for the User Control

The summary report told you to create a test form in order to test and possibly debug your new ActiveX user control. To do so, you need to add a project.

Tip You're adding a project rather than starting a new project so that both projects reside in the same workspace.

To add a project for the test form, complete these steps:

1. Select File, Add Project to display the Add Project dialog box.

2. Select Standard EXE and click Open to add the project.

3. Open ListWithLabel from the Project Explorer. When an ActiveX user control is open, it's in design mode and cannot be used to test; to start an ActiveX control in run mode, you must close it. Click the Close button in the upper-right corner of the menu bar to close the user control.

4. A new tool is added to the toolbox (see Figure 20-11). This represents the currently running ActiveX control. Double-click the ActiveX user control's toolbox button to place the control on the form.

5. Select the user control. Set the *Name* property to **lwlClients**. The lwl in this name represents ListWithLabel.

6. Set the *Caption* property to **Clients:**.

7. Double-click the form to open the Code window. The Form_Load procedure is displayed.

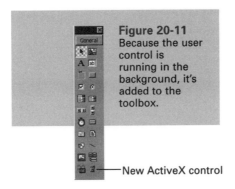

Figure 20-11
Because the user control is running in the background, it's added to the toolbox.

New ActiveX control

8. Enter the following code for this procedure:

```
With lwlClients
        .AddItem "ABC Corp."
        .AddItem "XYZ Inc."
        .AddItem "My Company"
        .AddItem "User Controls R Us"
        .AddItem "Acme Widgets"
End With
```

9. Press F5 to run the application. The items are added to the list box (see Figure 20-12).

10. End the application.

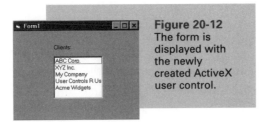

Figure 20-12
The form is displayed with the newly created ActiveX user control.

Summary

You now know the basics of creating an ActiveX user control using the ActiveX Control Interface Wizard. The Wizard is easy to use and offers quite a bit of functionality. You can use the techniques presented in this chapter to combine existing controls into new ActiveX desktop controls, or you can use the ActiveX Control Interface Wizard to create a foundation on which you build custom properties, methods, and events.

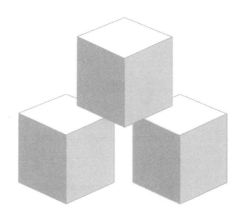

APPENDIX A

Recommended Naming and Programming Conventions

Naming and programming conventions are important to the development effort. Standards are useful not only to the programmer who develops an application originally, but to any programmer who supports the application in the future. Standards provide a mechanism for bringing greater structure to an application's code. Naming conventions serve as an additional form of documentation because objects are named with a prefix that easily identifies them in code. This appendix provides recommendations for naming and programming conventions.

Environment Options

The settings for *environment options* are available by selecting <u>T</u>ools, <u>O</u>ptions. It is recommended, at the very minimum, that you have Auto Syntax Checking and

Require Variable Declaration selected. When Require Variable Declaration is selected, `Option Explicit` is placed in the General Declarations section of forms and modules.

Naming Prefixes

Naming prefixes make your code easier to read and help you organize your variables and controls. Table A-1 lists recommended naming prefixes for use with controls.

Table A-1 Naming Prefixes for Controls

Object Type	Prefix
Animated push button	ani
Application	app
Check box	chk
Combo box	cbo
Command button	cmd
Common dialog	dlg
Data	dat
Directory list box	dir
Drive list box	drv
File list box	fil
Form	frm
Frame	fra
Gauge	gau
Graph	gph
Grid	grd
Horizontal scroll bar	hsb
Image	img
Label	lbl
Line	lin
List box	lst
MAPI message	mpm
MAPI session	mps
Masked edit	msk
Menu	mnu
OLE object	ole
Option button	opt

Object Type	Prefix
Outline	out
Panel	pnl
Picture box	pic
Progress bar	prb
Rich text box	rtf
Shape	shp
Slider	sld
Spin button	spn
Status bar	sbr
Tab	tab
Text box	txt
Timer	tmr
Toolbar button	btn
Toolbar	tbr
Vertical scroll bar	vsb

Table A-2 lists recommended naming prefixes for use with variables.

Table A-2	Naming Prefixes for Variables	
Data Type	**Short Prefix**	**Long Prefix**
Array	a	ary
Boolean	f	bln
Byte	b	byt
Currency	c	cur
Date/Time	dt	dtm or dat
Double	d	dbl
Integer	i	int
Long	l	lng
Object	o	obj
Single		sng
String	s	str
Variant	v	var

Use the qualifiers listed in Table A-3 when naming certain variables and procedures. Here are some examples: iFirstValue, sGetLastItem, and sSaveName.

Table A-3 Qualifiers for Variable and Procedure Names

Qualifier	Description
First	First item in set
Last	Last item in set
Next	Next item in set
Prev	Previous item in set
Cur	Current item in set
Min	Smallest value in set
Max	Largest value in set
Save	A variable to preserve that must be reset later
Tmp	Temporary variable
Src	Source
Dst	Destination

Table A-4 lists recommended prefixes to indicate the scope of a variable.

Table A-4 Naming Prefixes That Indicate Variable Scope

Scope	Prefix
Form	f
Local (procedure)	*none*
Module	m
Public (global)	g

Table A-5 lists recommended prefixes for naming DAO objects.

Table A-5 Naming Prefixes for DAO Objects

Object Type	Prefix
Container	cnt
Containers	cnts
Database	db
Databases	dbs
DBEngine	dbe
Document	doc
Documents	docs
Error	err
Errors	errs
Field	fld
Fields	flds

Object Type	Prefix
Group	grp
Groups	grps
Index	idx
Indexes	idxs
Parameter	prm
Parameters	prms
PrivDBEngine	pdbe
Property	prp
Properties	prps
Query	qry or qdf or qd
Queries	qrys or qdfs
Recordset	rst or rs
Recordsets	rsts
TableDef	tbl or tdf
TableDefs	tbls or tdfs
User	usr
Users	usrs
Workspace	wrk
Workspaces	wrks

Table A-6 lists recommended prefixes for naming database objects.

Table A-6	Naming Prefixes for Database Objects
Object Type	**Prefix**
ODBC database	db
ODBC dynaset	ds
Field collection	fdc
Field object	fd
Index object	ix
Index collection	ixc
QueryDef	qd
Snapshot	ss
Table	tb
TableDef	td

Constant Names

Constants should be named using only uppercase letters. Use the underscore character (_) to represent a space. Here are some examples of constant names:

```
SALESTAX
SALES_TAX
MINIMUM_WAGE
```

If you want to, you can use the naming prefixes presented in Table A-4 to indicate scope with constants. For example, if SALESTAX is a public constant, you can name it gSALESTAX.

Commenting Code

You should begin each procedure with a brief comment describing the purpose of that procedure. Follow the purpose with a description of any arguments used by the procedure. If the procedure is a function and returns values, also describe the return values. You might also want to include the developer's name and the date the procedure was created (or last modified) in this section.

Comments should appear immediately before the lines they're documenting. The rationale for this is that someone reviewing the code should read a comment and then be ready to read the next program statement with an understanding of what's going on in that statement.

APPENDIX B

Visual Basic 5 Quick Reference

This appendix is designed to provide you with basic reference information that is frequently used by Visual Basic programmers. This includes an explanation of Visual Basic data types, the values for the Button argument of the MsgBox function, and a list of comparison operators.

Table B-1 lists the Visual Basic data types. Use these data types when declaring variables with the Dim statement.

Table B-1	Visual Basic Data Types		
Data Type	**Naming Prefix**	**Size**	**Range**
Boolean	bol	2 bytes	True/False
Byte	byt	1 byte	0 through 255
Currency	c or cur	8 bytes	-922337203685477.5808 through 922337203685477.5807

continues

Table B-1	Continued		
Data Type	**Naming Prefix**	**Size**	**Range**
Date	dtm	8 bytes	January 1, 100 through December 31, 9999
Double	dbl	8 bytes	-1.79769313486232D308 through 1.79769313486232D308
Integer	i or int	2 bytes	-32,768 through 32,767
Long	l or lng	4 bytes	-2,147,483,648 through 2,147,483,647
Single	sng	4 bytes	-3.042823E38 through 3.402823E38
String	s or str	1 byte per character	0 through 65,535 characters
Variant (numbers)	v or var	16 bytes	Any numeric value up to the range of a Double
Variant (text)	v or var	22 bytes+string length	Same range as String

Table B-2 shows the values used by the `Button` argument of the `MsgBox` function. You can combine these values by selecting one value from the button group, one value from the icon group, one value from the default group, and one value from the modal group. If you do not select a value from a particular group, default values—designated by the value 0—are used by the `MsgBox` function. An example of an acceptable value is the following:

```
VbYesNo + VbQuestion
```

Table B-2	Values for the `Button` Argument of the `MsgBox` Function	
Value	**Constant**	**Description**
Button Group		
0	VbOKOnly	OK button only
1	VbOKCancel	OK and Cancel buttons
2	VbAbortRetryIgnore	Abort, Retry, and Ignore buttons
3	VbYesNoCancel	Yes, No, and Cancel buttons
4	VbYesNo	Yes and No buttons
5	VbRetryCancel	Retry and Cancel buttons
Icon Group		
16	VbCritical	Critical Message icon
32	VbQuestion	Warning Query icon
48	VbExclamation	Warning Message icon
64	VbInformation	Information Message icon

Value	Constant	Description
Default Group		
0	VbDefaultButton1	First button is default
256	VbDefaultButton2	Second button is default
512	VbDefaultButton3	Third button is default
768	VbDefaultButton4	Fourth button is default
Modal Group		
0	VbApplicationModal	Application modal
4096	VbSystemModal	System modal

The values shown in Table B-3 are the return values that are generated when a user responds to a message box.

Table B-3   MsgBox Return Values

Value	Constant	Description
1	VbOK	OK
2	VbCancel	Cancel
3	VbAbort	Abort
4	VbRetry	Retry
5	VbIgnore	Ignore
6	VbYes	Yes
7	VbNo	No

Table B-4 contains a list of comparison operators used by a variety of statements, including the If and Select Case statements.

Table B-4   Comparison Operators

Comparison Operator	Meaning
=	Equal to
<>	Not equal to
>	Greater than
<	Less than
>=	Greater than or equal to
<=	Less than or equal to

Table B-5 lists the logical operators; these are frequently used in expressions along with the comparison operators.

Table B-5   Logical Operators

Logical Operator	Meaning
And	If both conditions are True, then the result is True.
Or	If either condition is True, then the result is True.
Not	If the conditional expression is False, then the result is True. If the conditional expression is True, then the result is False.
Xor	If one and only one of the conditions is True, then the result is True. If both are True or both are False, then the result is False.

APPENDIX C

What's on the CD?

The CD that accompanies this book contains the three example projects from the book, as well as the Control Creation Edition of Microsoft Visual Basic, Version 5.0, which enables you to create your own ActiveX controls quickly and easily. You also will find the latest versions of WinZip and Drag And View to assist you in managing and viewing your files.

Running the CD

To make the CD more user-friendly and take up less of your disk space, no installation is required. The only files transferred to your hard disk will be the ones that you choose to copy or install.

Caution

> **This CD has been designed to run under Windows 95 and Windows NT. Please be advised that, while the CD will run under Windows 3.1, you might encounter unexpected problems.**

Windows 3.x

To run the CD, complete these steps:

1. Insert the CD in the CD-ROM drive.
2. From File Manager, select <u>F</u>ile, <u>R</u>un to open the Run window.
3. In the Command Line text box, type **D:\primacd.exe** (where D: is the drive letter of your CD-ROM drive).
4. Select OK.

Windows 95

Since there is no installation routine, running the CD in Windows 95 is a breeze, especially if you have autorun enabled. Simply insert the CD in the CD-ROM drive, close the tray, and wait for the CD to load.

If you have autorun disabled, insert the CD in the CD-ROM drive and then complete these steps:

1. Select Run from the Start menu.
2. Type **D:\primacd.exe** (where D: is the drive letter of your CD-ROM drive).
3. Select OK.

The Prima User Interface

Prima's user interface is designed to make viewing and using the CD contents quick and easy. It contains four category/title buttons and four option buttons. Select a category/title button to display the available selections. Choose a title to see a description and the associated URL. Once you've selected a title, click an option button to perform the desired action upon that title.

Category/Title Buttons

- **Book Examples**—Example projects from *Hands On Visual Basic 5*
- **VB5 CCE**—The Control Creation Edition of Microsoft Visual Basic, Version 5.0 (for creating ActiveX controls)
- **Drag And View**—OLEISAPI.ZIP for Windows NT and OLEISAPI.W95 for Windows 95; these are ISAPI extension DLLs for Internet Information Server that enable programmers to access the HTTP server as an Automation object

- **WinZip**—One of the leading file compression utilities for Windows 3.x, 95, and NT

Option Buttons

- **Explore**—Click this option in Windows 95 or NT to view (using the Windows Explorer) the folder containing the program files. Right-click this option in Windows 3.x, 95, or NT to bring up the Windows File Manager from which you can easily explore the CD.

- **Install**—If the selected title contains an installation routine, click this option to begin the installation process. (If no installation routine is available, an appropriate message is displayed.)

- **Information**—Click this option to open the Readme file associated with the highlighted title. If no Readme file is present, the help file is opened.

- **Exit**—Click this option when you're finished and ready to move on.

- **Prev**—Click this option to return to the previous screen.

 Prev doesn't necessarily take you to the last screen you viewed; it takes you to the screen that actually precedes the current one.

- **Next**—Takes you to the next screen.

APPENDIX D

Glossary

Action query: SQL statement that will alter the records of the created recordset with the criteria included in the statement.

ActiveX Control Interface Wizard: Helps you create the public interface for a VB- generated ActiveX control after you've created your user interface. The user interface is the control itself. The public interface consists of the properties, events, and methods that a programmer can use to manipulate the control.

ActiveX control user interface: ActiveX control as it appears when a developer places the control on a form. It's the visual portion of the control.

ActiveX control: ActiveX controls provide a way for you to extend the capabilities of the Visual Basic environment. ActiveX controls are broken into two categories. One category includes the desktop ActiveX controls, formerly called *OLE controls*. This type of ActiveX control provides standard user interface elements that allow you to create forms and dialog boxes. The other category includes Internet ActiveX controls that are optimized for Internet download.

ActiveX Document EXE form: Form that can appear within Internet browser windows using a browser such as Internet Explorer.

ActiveX document: ActiveX object that can be placed and activated within ActiveX document containers such as Internet Explorer.

ActiveX public interface: Consists of all the properties, events, and methods a programmer can use to manipulate the ActiveX control.

Add-in: Tool you create to customize the Visual Basic environment.

Advanced filter: Allows you to filter based on more sophisticated criteria that can include multiple conditions for a single column, multiple criteria for multiple columns, and conditions that incorporate the use of a formula. See also *Filters*.

Application Wizard: Tool designed to create a foundation from which you can build your project. You can create a project with either an SDI or MDI interface. By the time you finish using the Application Wizard, you have an application that contains a menu system, toolbar, and status bar. You only need to add controls and code.

Argument: A value that is passed to a procedure that is used by that procedure in the task it performs.

Automation (formerly called *OLE Automation*): The process of controlling one application's functionality from another application. Automation is a technology that allows you to incorporate the functionality of Windows applications into your VB code. To use Automation you must own a copy of the application whose functionality you want to incorporate into your application, and that application must support Automation. Windows-based applications that fully support Automation are said to *expose* (make available) their objects, properties, methods, and events. By using these exposed objects, you can use the application's features.

Basic (Beginner's All-purpose Symbolic Instruction Code): Programming language that forms the foundation of Visual Basic.

Binding: 1) Process of resolving the reference to the object library made by some type of object variable declaration. 2) Process of tying other controls in a VB application to the data control to display the data.

Bookmark: Named location within a Word document that is used for reference purposes. When you define a bookmark, you specify its location and name.

Break Mode: Temporarily suspends the execution of the application.

Breakpoint: Stops execution of the application before executing the line that contains the breakpoint.

Bug: Defect in an application.

Cell reference: Used by Excel and given in row/column format (for example, A2). An example of a formula using this type of reference is =B1*A2. See also *Named cell*.

Centralized error handler: A separate function that processes each error that's generated and then, based on the error number, initiates an action.

Check box: There are two uses for a check box, which is created with the check box control. One is as a toggle selection. If there is a checkmark in the check box at runtime, then the user has set something to True. If there is no checkmark in the check box, then the user has set the item to False. The check box is sometimes used to present a user with multiple options from which they may select one or more.

Child form: Any form contained within an *MDI parent form* when the application is running.

Code window: Used to enter, view, and edit VB code.

Combo box: Functionally a cross between a list box and a text box, it allows a user to either type a value or select one from a list.

Command button: Used to prompt a user to select an action. For example, you might have a form with the following command buttons on it: Yes, No, and Cancel. A user clicks the desired button and the associated action is initiated. A command button ordinarily appears as a gray rectangle with rounded corners.

Common dialog control: Provides a standard set of dialog boxes: file open and save, print options, and colors and fonts. This is not an intrinsic control, so it has to be added to the toolbox if you want to use it.

Constant: Named value. The use of constants adds readability and maintainability to your application. In a given code line, you may use either an actual value like .05 or a constant like SALESTAX.

Context number: Used in the *help project file* to create a map linking particular objects to particular context strings in the help file you just created.

Controller application: Controls a server application during *Automation*. See also *Server application.*

Control: Provides a tool your application's users need in order to interact with your program. VB provides a variety of controls you can use as part of your application's interface.

Crystal Reports: A tool used to create custom reports, lists, and form letters using data from an existing database.

DAO: See *Data Access Objects.*

Data Access Objects: A collection of objects allowing you to create and manipulate a database.

Data control: Allows you to provide access to databases through bound controls, such as text boxes, on your form. The data control is used to move from record to record and to display the resulting data. This allows you to design front-end interfaces to back-end database engines such as Microsoft Access and Microsoft SQL Server. The data control provides buttons for the following operations: move to first record, move to next record, move to previous record, and move to last record. See also *Binding (2)*.

Data validation: Involves verifying the data entered by a user to make sure that it meets the information needs of the system.

Design time: The mode in which you build the application; the time when you add forms to your application and place controls on those forms.

Directory list box: Control used to display directories and paths in a list box format. Typically used with the drive list box control. See also *Drive list box*.

DLL: See *Dynamic Link Library*.

Drive list box: Control used to display valid disk drives in a list box format.

Dynamic Link Library: File containing a collection of functions designed to perform a specific class of operations. DLLs must by declared to your application using the `Declare` statement to make them available for use by your application.

Encapsulation: The concept that objects contain both their code and their data.

Enterprise Edition: The edition of Visual Basic geared at developers who need to create distributed applications in a team environment. It includes all the features of the Professional Edition as well as advanced tools including the Automation Manager, Component Manager, database management tools, and the Microsoft Visual SourceSafe project-oriented version control system. Documentation provided with the Enterprise Edition includes all the documentation found in the Professional Edition, as well as *Building Client/Server Applications with Visual Basic and the SourceSafe User's Guide*.

Error handler: A routine for trapping and dealing with errors in your application.

Event procedure: A procedure that is executed when an event such as `Click` or `Load` occurs.

Event: A specific runtime action such as the user selecting a menu or clicking a button.

File list box: Control that displays a list of files.

File Transfer Protocol: An Internet communication protocol used for performing file transfer operations.

Filters: Used to display rows that meet certain criteria that you select or enter.

Focus: Determines which object has the attention of the system. The object with focus is the object with which the user can currently interact through the keyboard.

Form: Usually translates into a window when your application runs, but can be hidden at runtime if you want.

Frame: Used to visually and functionally group controls. Allows you to create a graphical or functional grouping for controls. To create a group of controls, you must draw the frame first and then place the controls inside the frame.

FTP: See *File Transfer Protocol.*

Function: A procedure that computes a value and returns the value through its name.

GUI: Graphical user interface.

Help project file: Has instructions for the help compiler regarding which options you want to use and how the help topics map to the *HelpContextID* property values.

Hyperlink: Text that users click to jump to another location. See also *Hyperlinking.*

Hyperlinking: The process of jumping to an URL or navigating through the history list by clicking a *hyperlink.*

Image list control: Contains a collection of *list image* objects. A unique index or key refers to each list image object in the collection. The image list control is only displayed on the form in design mode. This type of control is not meant to be used alone; it acts as a holding place for images that are to be used by another control (such as a toolbar).

Image: Control used to display a graphical image. It can be used in place of a *picture box control* and has the advantage of using fewer resources than a picture box. It can display the following file types: bitmap, icon, or metafile.

Immediate window: This window allows you to enter programming statements, execute them, and view the results immediately in the same window.

Index: A specified order for viewing the records of a table. This usually speeds up data access.

Interface: The forms and the objects contained on those forms that the user can use to interact with your application.

Intranet: An internal network. An intranet's directory and file structure is typically navigated using a browser in much the same fashion as you navigate the Internet.

Jet engine: Visual Basic's native database engine used to store, retrieve, and update data. The Jet engine provides the programmer with the DAO programming interface.

Keyword: A word that has specific meaning to the compiler.

Label: Static area of text on your forms. This text might be helpful information, a graphic's caption, a description for a control, and so on.

Learning Edition: The edition of VB that's designed to allow programmers to easily create powerful applications for Windows 95 and Windows NT. This edition includes all intrinsic controls, such as command buttons, list boxes, and option buttons. It also has grid, tab, and data-bound controls.

Line label: Descriptive text used to create a branching point within a procedure. Line labels must end with a colon.

List box: Control used to display a list of items from which the user can choose one item.

Local: Level of scope where a variable or constant is only defined within the procedure in which it was declared.

Locals window: Displays all the declared variables in the current procedure and their current values.

Logic error: The result of a programmer mistake. Logic errors typically have to do with your approach to a situation. More often than not, these errors occur when you set up conditional tests, and a mistake somewhere in the test produces an incorrect result at runtime. Sometimes logic errors result from mistakes in calculations. If unexpected results occur during your application, but the application continues to run, you have a logic error.

MDI parent form: Provides a workspace for all the *child forms* in your application.

MDI: See *Multiple document interface*.

Menu Editor: A tool used to create new menus and menu bars, add new commands to existing menus, replace existing menu commands with your own commands, and change and delete existing menus and menu bars.

Method: Tells an object to do something; can be thought of as an object-specific function.

Module: Block of code stored as a file that contains one or more procedures, variable declarations, and constant declarations.

Multiple document interface: Windowing environment in which one main window contains as many other windows as the program requires. An *MDI parent form* contains the *child forms*.

Named cell: Replaces the cell reference in formulas in Excel. For example, consider the formula =B1*A2. This is not the friendliest-looking formula. If you named A2 something like TaxRate and named B1 something like SalesPrice, you could create the same formula as =SalesPrice*TaxRate, which is much easier to read and understand.

Object Browser: Displays classes, properties, methods, events, and constants available from object libraries and from procedures in your project.

Object library: File that provides information to a *controller application* about available objects in a *server application*; has an OLB file extension.

ODBC Direct: Allows you to access an *ODBC* database without the *Jet engine*.

ODBC: See *Open Database Connectivity*.

OLE Automation: See *Automation*.

OLE control: Allows you to link and embed objects from other applications in your forms.

Open Database Connectivity: A method of communicating with client/server databases such as Microsoft SQL Server.

Option button: Control that displays one of the available choices for an item that has multiple choices. A user is allowed to select only one option from a group of options. Contrast this with the *check box*, which can be used to provide a group of options from which the user may select more than one option.

Picture box: Control used to display a graphical image on a form. The image can be either decorative or active.

Pointer: Tool used to resize or move a control that you have already drawn on a form.

Primary key: A single field that identifies a database record; it is unique by nature.

Predefined value: One of several values from which the user may select one value in a user input situation. Typically the user must select one of the predefined values for that input item, rather than having the option of entering another value. This is a way to force a user to enter valid input. An example of predefined values is the font list for your system. If you want to select a font for use with your word processor, you must select from the ones listed on your system.

Procedure: Unit of code that's called from other parts of the application's code. This code may be called from another procedure or function, or may be initiated because of an event.

Professional Edition: This edition of VB gives developers a full-featured set of tools for application development. It includes all features of the *Learning Edition* and has several additional ActiveX controls. The most notable additional controls are the Crystal Reports control and a set of Internet controls. This edition includes online help, the *Programmer's Guide*, the *Component Tools Guide*, and the *Crystal Reports for Visual Basic User's Manual.*

Project Explorer: Window in design mode that lists the forms and modules in your current project.

Project: 1) Set of procedures, functions, and forms. Once you are finished designing and creating a project, you compile it into an application. 2) The set of files that combine to create the particular application you are developing.

Properties window: Window in design mode that lists the property settings for the selected user interface object.

Property: A characteristic of an object.

Recordset: Set of records returned from a definition like a table or query.

Referential integrity: Set of rules developed to protect the integrity of data. This prevents a user from altering table relationships by adding data to one table in a relationship without adding matching information to the related table. It also prevents the user from deleting data involved in a relationship.

Replication: Process of making a copy of a database and later synchronizing the copy with the original database. This allows for independent accessing of the copied database with the benefits of a single data source.

Resource file: File used during help file creation that contains bitmaps, text, and other data. This information can be used, for example, to customize an application for different languages without having to change any code. Resource files have an RES extension.

Runtime: The period when an application is running; also known as *run mode.*

Runtime error: A runtime error is any error that makes a program stop running. Sometimes this is the fault of the programmer (for example, if you mistype the name of a procedure when calling it from another procedure). Other times it's the result of a user action that you cannot control or even predict (for example, if you have a program that needs to save something to a floppy drive and the user forgets to insert a diskette).

Scope: In VB, the location and way in which you define your variables, constants, and procedures will determine where you can use them.

SDI: See *Single document interface*.

Security: A system for a database to establish user access requirements to restrict undesirable actions.

Separator bar: Horizontal line displayed between items on a menu to present the menu items in logical groups.

Server application: Application that provides its objects, events, properties, and methods by exposing them to a *controller application* during Automation.

Single document interface: Windowing environment in which only one document can be open at a time. In this environment, one window flows to another window in a linear progression.

SQL: See *Structured Query Language*.

Status bar: Window that an application uses to display status information, such as current page position or date and time; typically anchored to the bottom of an MDI parent form.

Structured Query Language: Adopted standard for getting answers to particular questions about your data.

Syntax error: Type of error that occurs when you incorrectly use the VB language.

Syntax: Rules of a language.

Tab order: Order in which controls receive focus on a form as a user presses the Tab key.

Testing: Process of anticipating and trying out everything users might do to your application.

Text box: Control used to provide an area in which a user can type information; can hold either new or changed text.

Timer: Used by a programmer to generate timer events at set intervals. This control is visible at design time as a small clock, but is invisible at runtime, which means that a user never sees a timer control.

Toolbox: Provides a set of controls and other tools that you use at design time to place controls on a form and build your application's interface.

Transaction: The ability to group more than one database action and treat the group as a single unit. If any individual action fails to perform correctly, the entire group fails and the database can be rolled back (returned to the state before the transaction was executed).

Transact-SQL: A superset of the SQL language used by Microsoft SQL Server and Sybase SQL Server.

Twip: 1/20 of a point or 1/1440 of an inch.

Variable: Place for holding data that can change each time your application runs, or even within one running of the application. For example, if you ask a user to type her name, and plan to use that name later in the application, you need a variable to hold the name that she enters.

VBCCE: See *Visual Basic, Control Creation Edition.*

Visual Basic, Control Creation Edition: This edition is designed to be used to easily and quickly create ActiveX controls. This edition is different from the other three editions of Visual Basic in that it cannot be purchased in retail outlets. The only way to get it is by downloading it through the Internet. Other than any download and connection costs, the Control Creation Edition is free. Unlike its cousins, the Control Creation Edition cannot be used to create a stand-alone application. It can be used only to create ActiveX controls for use in other development environments.

Visual SourceSafe: Version control tool that is integrated with the Visual Basic environment and monitors a variety of project-related items, including visual differences and project history. Not available in all editions of VB.

Watch expression: Expression created during testing or debugging that lets you observe the behavior of a variable or an expression as your application runs.

Windows API (Application Programming Interface): Interface of calls used by programmers to access and interact directly with the operating system.

Workspace: Object representing an area in memory that is taking advantage of specific security options for the database access.

Index

Send Us
Your COMMENTS

Dear Reader:

Thank you for buying this book. In order to offer you more quality books on the topics *you* would like to see, we need your input. At Prima Publishing, we pride ourselves on timely responsiveness to our readers' needs. If you'll complete and return this brief questionnaire, *we will listen!*

Name: (first) _____ (M.I.) _____ (last) _____

Company: _____ Type of business: _____

Address: _____ City: _____ State: _____ Zip: _____

Phone: _____ Fax: _____ E-mail address: _____

May we contact you for research purposes? ❏ Yes ❏ No

(If you participate in a research project, we will supply you with your choice of a book from Prima CPD)

❶ How would you rate this book, overall?

❏ Excellent ❏ Fair
❏ Very Good ❏ Below Average
❏ Good ❏ Poor

❷ Why did you buy this book?

❏ Price of book ❏ Content
❏ Author's reputation ❏ Prima's reputation
❏ CD-ROM/disk included with book
❏ Information highlighted on cover
❏ Other (Please specify): _____

❸ How did you discover this book?

❏ Found it on bookstore shelf
❏ Saw it in Prima Publishing catalog
❏ Recommended by store personnel
❏ Recommended by friend or colleague
❏ Saw an advertisement in: _____
❏ Read book review in: _____
❏ Saw it on Web site: _____
❏ Other (Please specify): _____

❹ Where did you buy this book?

❏ Bookstore (name) _____
❏ Computer Store (name) _____
❏ Electronics Store (name) _____
❏ Wholesale Club (name) _____
❏ Mail Order (name) _____
❏ Direct from Prima Publishing
❏ Other (please specify): _____

❺ Which computer periodicals do you read regularly? _____
_____
_____
_____

❻ Would you like to see your name in print?

May we use your name and quote you in future Prima Publishing books or promotional materials?

❏ Yes ❏ No

❼ Comments & Suggestions: _____
_____
_____

PLEASE
PLACE
STAMP
HERE

---

8 **Where do you use your computer?**

Work	❏ 100%	❏ 75%	❏ 50%	❏ 25%
Home	❏ 100%	❏ 75%	❏ 50%	❏ 25%
School	❏ 100%	❏ 75%	❏ 50%	❏ 25%

Other _____

9 **How do you rate your level of computer skills?**

❏ Beginner
❏ Advanced
❏ Intermediate

10 **What is your age?**

❏ Under 18
❏ 18-24   ❏ 40-49
❏ 25-29   ❏ 50-59
❏ 30-39   ❏ 60-over

11 **I would be interested in computer books on these topics**

❏ Word Processing   ❏ Database
❏ Networking   ❏ Spreadsheets
❏ Desktop Publishing   ❏ Web site design
Other _____

SAVE A STAMP

Visit our Web Site at: **http://www.primapublishing.com**
and simply fill in one of our online Response Forms

To Order Books

Please send me the following items:

Quantity	Title	Unit Price	Total
_____	_____	$ _____	$ _____
_____	_____	$ _____	$ _____
_____	_____	$ _____	$ _____
_____	_____	$ _____	$ _____
_____	_____	$ _____	$ _____

Subtotal $ _____

Deduct 10% when ordering 3-5 books $ _____

7.25% Sales Tax (CA only) $ _____

8.25% Sales Tax (TN only) $ _____

5.0% Sales Tax (MD and IN only) $ _____

Shipping and Handling* $ _____

Total Order $ _____

Shipping and Handling depend on Subtotal.

Subtotal	Shipping/Handling
$0.00–$14.99	$3.00
$15.00–$29.99	$4.00
$30.00–$49.99	$6.00
$50.00–$99.99	$10.00
$100.00–$199.99	$13.50
$200.00+	Call for Quote

Foreign and all Priority Request orders:
Call Order Entry department
for price quote at 916/632-4400

This chart represents the total retail price of books only
(before applicable discounts are taken).

By Telephone: With MC or Visa, call 800-632-8676, 916-632-4400. Mon-Fri, 8:30-4:30.
WWW {http://www.primapublishing.com}

Orders Placed Via Internet E-mail {sales@primapub.com}
By Mail: Just fill out the information below and send with your remittance to:

Prima Publishing
P.O. Box 1260BK
Rocklin, CA 95677

My name is _____

I live at _____

City _____ State _____ Zip _____

MC/Visa# _____ Exp. _____

Check/Money Order enclosed for $ _____ Payable to Prima Publishing

Daytime Telephone _____

Signature _____

Other books from Prima Publishing, Computer Products Division

ISBN	Title	Price	Release Date
0-7615-0801-5	ActiveX	$40.00	Available Now
0-7615-0680-2	America Online Complete Handbook and Membership Kit	$24.99	Available Now
0-7615-0915-1	Building Intranets with Internet Information Server and FrontPage	$45.00	Available Now
0-7615-0417-6	CompuServe Complete Handbook and Membership Kit	$24.95	Available Now
0-7615-0849-X	Corporate Intranet Development	$45.00	Available Now
0-7615-0743-4	Create FrontPage Web Pages in a Weekend	$29.99	Available Now
0-7615-0692-6	Create Your First Web Page in a Weekend	$29.99	Available Now
0-7615-0428-1	The Essential Excel 97 Book	$24.99	Available Now
0-7615-0969-0	The Essential Office 97 Book	$27.99	Available Now
0-7615-0695-0	The Essential Photoshop Book	$35.00	Available Now
0-7615-0752-3	The Essential Windows NT Book	$27.99	Available Now
0-7615-0427-3	The Essential Word 97 Book	$24.99	Available Now
0-7615-1008-7	Excel 97 Visual Learning Guide	$16.99	Available Now
0-7615-1013-3	Hands-On Java	$40.00	Spring '97
0-7615-0955-0	Hands-On Visual Basic 5 for Web Development	$40.00	Spring '97
0-7615-1005-2	Internet Information Server 3 Administrator' Guide	$40.00	Available Now
0-7615-0815-5	Introduction to ABAP/4 Programming for SAP	$45.00	Available Now
0-7615-0901-1	Leveraging Visual Basic with ActiveX Controls	$45.00	Available Now
0-7615-0690-X	Netscape Enterprise Server	$40.00	Available Now
0-7615-0691-8	Netscape FastTrack Server	$40.00	Available Now
0-7615-0852-X	Netscape Navigator 3 Complete Handbook	$24.99	Available Now
0-7615-1162-8	Office 97 Visual Learning Guide	$16.99	Spring '97
0-7615-0759-0	Professional Web Design	$40.00	Available Now
0-7615-0773-6	Programming Internet Controls	$45.00	Available Now
0-7615-0780-9	Programming Web Server Applications	$40.00	Available Now
0-7615-0063-4	Researching on the Internet	$29.95	Available Now
0-7615-0686-1	Researching on the World Wide Web	$24.99	Available Now
0-7615-0769-8	VBScript Master's Handbook	$45.00	Available Now
0-7615-0684-5	VBScript Web Page Interactivity	$40.00	Available Now
0-7615-0903-8	Visual FoxPro 5 Enterprise Development	$45.00	Available Now
0-7615-0814-7	Visual J++	$35.00	Available Now
0-7615-0726-4	Webmaster's Handbook	$40.00	Available Now
0-7615-0751-5	Windows NT Server 4 Administrator's Guide	$50.00	Available Now
0-7615-1007-9	Word 97 Visual Learning Guide	$16.99	Available Now
0-7615-1083-4	WordPerfect 8 Visual Learning Guide	$16.99	Spring '97

License Agreement/Notice of Limited Warranty

By opening the sealed disk container in this book, you agree to the following terms and conditions. If, upon reading the following license agreement and notice of limited warranty, you cannot agree to the terms and conditions set forth, return the unused book with unopened disk to the place where you purchased it for a refund.

License:

The enclosed software is copyrighted by the copyright holder(s) indicated on the software disk. You are licensed to copy the software onto a single computer for use by a single concurrent user and to a backup disk. You may not reproduce, make copies, or distribute copies or rent or lease the software in whole or in part, except with written permission of the copyright holder(s). You may transfer the enclosed disk only together with this license, and only if you destroy all other copies of the software and the transferee agrees to the terms of the license. You may not decompile, reverse assemble, or reverse engineer the software.

Notice of Limited Warranty:

The enclosed disk is warranted by Prima Publishing to be free of physical defects in materials and workmanship for a period of sixty (60) days from end user's purchase of the book/disk combination. During the sixty-day term of the limited warranty, Prima will provide a replacement disk upon the return of a defective disk.

Limited Liability:

THE SOLE REMEDY FOR BREACH OF THIS LIMITED WARRANTY SHALL CONSIST ENTIRELY OF REPLACEMENT OF THE DEFECTIVE DISK. IN NO EVENT SHALL PRIMA OR THE AUTHORS BE LIABLE FOR ANY OTHER DAMAGES, INCLUDING LOSS OR CORRUPTION OF DATA, CHANGES IN THE FUNCTIONAL CHARACTERISTICS OF THE HARDWARE OR OPERATING SYSTEM, DELETERIOUS INTERACTION WITH OTHER SOFTWARE, OR ANY OTHER SPECIAL, INCIDENTAL, OR CONSEQUENTIAL DAMAGES THAT MAY ARISE, EVEN IF PRIMA AND/OR THE AUTHORS HAVE PREVIOUSLY BEEN NOTIFIED THAT THE POSSIBILITY OF SUCH DAMAGES EXISTS.

Disclaimer of Warranties:

PRIMA AND THE AUTHORS SPECIFICALLY DISCLAIM ANY AND ALL OTHER WARRANTIES, EITHER EXPRESS OR IMPLIED, INCLUDING WARRANTIES OF MERCHANTABILITY, SUITABILITY TO A PARTICULAR TASK OR PURPOSE, OR FREEDOM FROM ERRORS. SOME STATES DO NOT ALLOW FOR EXCLUSION OF IMPLIED WARRANTIES OR LIMITATION OF INCIDENTAL OR CONSEQUENTIAL DAMAGES, SO THESE LIMITATIONS MAY NOT APPLY TO YOU.

Other:

This Agreement is governed by the laws of the State of California without regard to choice of law principles. The United Convention of Contracts for the International Sale of Goods is specifically disclaimed. This Agreement constitutes the entire agreement between you and Prima Publishing regarding use of the software.